This item has to be renewed or returned on or before
the last date below

| TWO WEEK LOAN | LRC 1 |

5/2/18
19/2/18
21/6/18
17/10/18
5/11/18

SERVICE-ABILITY

SERVICE-ABILITY

CREATE A CUSTOMER CENTRIC CULTURE AND

GAIN COMPETITIVE ADVANTAGE

KEVIN ROBSON
DIPM MBA FCIM

A John Wiley & Sons, Ltd., Publication

This edition first published 2013

© 2013 Herbert Kevin Robson

Registered office

John Wiley & Sons Ltd, The Atrium, Southern Gate, Chichester, West Sussex, PO19 8SQ, United Kingdom

For details of our global editorial offices, for customer services and for information about how to apply for permission to reuse the copyright material in this book please see our website at www.wiley.com.

The right of the author to be identified as the author of this work has been asserted in accordance with the Copyright, Designs and Patents Act 1988.

All rights reserved. No part of this publication may be reproduced, stored in a retrieval system, or transmitted, in any form or by any means, electronic, mechanical, photocopying, recording or otherwise, except as permitted by the UK Copyright, Designs and Patents Act 1988, without the prior permission of the publisher.

Wiley publishes in a variety of print and electronic formats and by print-on-demand. Some material included with standard print versions of this book may not be included in e-books or in print-on-demand. If this book refers to media such as a CD or DVD that is not included in the version you purchased, you may download this material at http:// booksupport.wiley.com. For more information about Wiley products, visit www.wiley. com.

Designations used by companies to distinguish their products are often claimed as trademarks. All brand names and product names used in this book are trade names, service marks, trademarks or registered trademarks of their respective owners. The publisher is not associated with any product or vendor mentioned in this book. This publication is designed to provide accurate and authoritative information in regard to the subject matter covered. It is sold on the understanding that the publisher is not engaged in rendering professional services. If professional advice or other expert assistance is required, the services of a competent professional should be sought.

Library of Congress Cataloging-in-Publication Data
9781118345566

A catalogue record for this book is available from the British Library.

ISBN 9781118345566 (hardback) ISBN 9781118457856 (epub)
ISBN 9781118457863 (emobi) ISBN 9781118457870 (epdf)

Set in 10/14.5 pt Palatino by Toppan Best-set Premedia Limited

Printed in Great Britain by TJ International Ltd, Padstow, Cornwall, UK

CONTENTS

Chuang-tzu

(4th century BC)

'I have heard my teacher say that whoever uses machines does all his work like a machine. He who does his work like a machine grows a heart like a machine, and he who carries the heart of a machine in his breast loses his simplicity. He who has lost his simplicity becomes unsure in the strivings of his soul.'

(Morgan G. (1993) Images of Organization. Sage. London, p.19)

PREFACE

We live in a much changed world from that which prevailed in the post-Second World War era. Britain (and to broadly the same extent, the countries of the EU and the USA) is now regarded as a service economy. At least in terms of employment, our manufacturing base has been progressively eroded. Coal mining no longer exists and heavy engineering such as ship building and steel making has gone abroad where labour is cheaper.

The term 'service' embraces a wide definition, including the provision of a 'pure service' such as knowledge, expertise and experience as, for example, in the financial services provided by the City of London, and hybrid services, such as restaurants, that provide a tangible product but with a heavy element of personal attention as part of the overall package. However, falling within this definition is a vast array of organizations of all kinds, commercial, public and third sector (including social enterprises as well as charities) in which the relationship with the consumer now, more than ever before, has to be an integral part of the 'product' offering.

In this fundamental shift in economic stance, however, with a few notable exceptions, the practice of organizations of all types has failed to keep up with the actuality. Britain is now suffering from a widespread lack of truly customer-satisfying service. We lack the very thing that we need to make this new paradigm work efficiently: service ability.

Today, customers are becoming increasingly discerning: demanding even; and the need for absolute customer focus is paramount. Organizations of all types are facing high customer churn, serious customer antagonism, loss of consumer confidence and plummeting customer satisfaction. Research is showing us that whatever the type of organization, only totally satisfying the customer is the thing that will secure loyalty and offer significant competitive advantage by differentiation in this new kaleidoscope world, and yet poor or indifferent treatment of customers is widespread.

The rapid emergence of new technology is undoubtedly bringing incalculable benefit to organizations of all types (this is emphatically not a Luddite book), but the argument is that, in our gold-rush fervour to apply computerization willy-nilly, people and processes have become conformed to systems thinking and this is depersonalizing both the employee and the customer to such a degree that it is preventing truly customer-satisfying interactions. The design of customer interaction processes has become standardized and characterized by indifference. Machines are increasingly being used to mediate the customer relationship and organizations of all kinds have lost sight of the basic principle that people do business with people. Today, through efficient technology, our organizations may be serviceable but they are not service able.

Increasingly, organizations, whether private, public or third sector, are facing the reality that their poor customer service is being mediated through social media. (Many firms are now monitoring Twitter and Facebook for negative chatter and pouncing on it to mitigate damage.) The case of 'United Breaks Guitars', the YouTube video that since 2009 has spread that damning message to over 10 million people worldwide about United Airlines' appalling treatment of their customer and his property, is a classic example of this phenomenon.

As this trend continues, however, a major opportunity for sustainable competitive advantage is opening up. Organizations that challenge this emerging paradigm and refocus on the need to treat customers in a way that satisfies them, not the technology, will have better customer retention, lower costs of replacement and will build their brand value through better reputations. We must put the technology behind us as a support, not between us as a barrier to the customer.

Customer satisfaction is about a depth of relationship that extends from the very centre of the organization to the loyal satisfied customer, through the loyal satisfied employee and this book is about the skill of the organization as a whole to deliver strategic customer-satisfying service capability through 'Service-Ability'. It is of little use simply to improve the skills of customer-facing employees: training people in customer service is only part of the answer. You cannot bolt-on service skill to an organization that is unable to nurture and sustain it without ensuring an organization-wide, dedicated culture of service.

The term 'marketing mix' was first used in 1953 when Neil Borden coined it in his presidential address to the American Marketing Association. Later, in 1960 E. Jerome McCarthy proposed a 4 P classification (product, price, place, promotion), which has become deeply embedded in the study of marketing ever since. It appears in every textbook and teaching paper, and is the framework of choice of marketing practitioners the world over. No doubt in response to the inexorable shift from a manufacturing base to a service base in the economies of the developed World, the last ten years has seen the incorporation of another 3 Ps: people, process and physical evidence.

The adoption of these additional elements, in particular the P of People, signalled the point at which marketing spilled over into the much broader world of management and organizational theory. Process, for example, is informed by organizational design and physical evidence (essentially the 'packaging' of the intangible service-product) is intended to enhance the customer's experience and to enhance service quality, which is a production operations strategy.

The definition of Marketing is also subject to change. The current definition officially adopted by the Chartered Institute of Marketing of the UK in 1976 is: 'The management process responsible for identifying, anticipating and satisfying customer requirements profitably'. This puts emphasis on marketing as a management process with, as its ultimate end (and appropriately) the aim of satisfying customer requirements profitably.

However, a debate underway in the Chartered Institute seeking a new definition to reflect the modern era resonates even more with the message

Seven Ps marketing mix

of this book. The draft definition under consideration at the time of writing is:

> The strategic business function that creates value by stimulating, facilitating and fulfilling customer needs: It does this by building brands, nurturing innovation, developing relationships, creating good customer service and communicating benefits. With a customer-centric view, marketing brings positive return on investment, satisfies shareholders and stakeholders from business and the community, and contributes to positive behavioural change and a sustainable business future.

It is more wordy and, no doubt, will be honed to a more concise form, but herein lies the central thesis of what is being put forward here: the need to structure, manage, lead and organize in order to be able, holistically, to develop relationships with customers and to be totally customer-centric; all with the aim of return on investment both financial and, in the broader senses we know today, societal. That is why this book has been written.

This is not a book about how to do customer service, neither is it a book about marketing *per se*. It is a book about people and process in organizations, and how to get them aligned to deliver effectively what the customer needs, wants and expects, and that makes it as much about management as about marketing. It seeks to explore the reasons for the lack of Service-Ability that seems to be widespread in all our organizations, and to provide a framework for thinking, intervening, training, and organizing, so that this inherent disability can be better understood and rectified.

Service-Ability is a structured idea, underpinned by an understanding of morale (*esprit de corps* or team spirit). High organizational morale is necessary for success, it sustains purpose and it is a matter of strategic intervention, but it needs four key elements:

- trust in leadership;
- trust in, and meaningful relationship with, colleagues;
- being well-fitted to your job and having pride in doing it; and
- knowing, believing in, and espousing the aims of the organization.

These respectively result in initiative, involvement, professionalism and engagement in the individual employee, and I argue that these attributes are needed in every employee, at all levels, not just those in customer-facing roles.

These attributes are inferred back into the organization and classified into four core values: 'Effective Leadership', 'Getting the People Right', 'Appropriate Organization' and 'Clarity of Purpose'.

Drawing on latest thinking on leadership, management, organizational design and strategy, the argument is that effective leadership derives from the emerging understanding of the servant leader; that getting the people right comes from a management approach that draws on modern thinking about reward and motivation; that an appropriate organization is one whose form follows function, and that facilitates people to work well together, not militates against it; that clarity of purpose is achieved by having a purposeful strategy and ethical values, and communicating these effectively so that the people, who are the organization, become imbued with its aims, objectives and values, and a clear sense of direction.

The whole idea is illustrated by a quadrant model that is useful for analyzing, thinking, intervening, training and organizing for Service-Ability, and this forms the framework for the book's four main chapters in which implementation issues are discussed and remedies offered.

FOREWORD

As technology and customer knowledge and expectations have changed, the demands on business to go beyond merely meeting needs and create a transaction based on requirements have changed – and continue to change. Customers make choices using the internet, see what is available across the world, and gain feedback from other commentators and customers, sometimes live,real time.

These go beyond the product or immediate service and establish a new realm of the interface between customers and businesses – one that will be about exceeding expectations. This can very rarely be about solely product, physical or service – it sees and expands the less quantifiable aspects of the emotional bond formed from always 'being there' for the customer, and anticipating what will please.

These behaviours by your business, or more accurately the people in your business, are becoming the most significant element in creating a lasting customer relationship of value in world where the internet and immediate 24hr order capabilities tend to promote grazing and 'promiscuity' in customers.

A few exceptional businesses have already recognised this and built levels of loyalty, belief and reputation that others can only envy. The success of Apple in anticipating customer desires,and the relationships built by a number of Japanese brands with consumers are matched by the customer loyalties being developed by FreshDirect in New York. In contrast, regular car manufacturers and food supermarkets in Europe are seeing customers not differentiating between them and treating them as 'all the same' – disposable suppliers of a product or undifferentiated service.Given the costs of customer acquisition and the growth of social media encouraging experimentation by customers , businesses that do not adopt change in their view of service will be commoditised, where the only factor affecting choice is price on the web on the day.

Kevin Robson has captured, explained and codified this trend so that management can understand what their businesses need to do to survive and succeed in a new and more demanding service environment. He shows us how to look differently and more comprehensively at what it is that businesses must do to build the loyalties with customers.

He correctly identifies that this is not solely about product or service design and provision, but needs the whole organisation to see their role differently, and to realise that marketing/service disciplines are neither the only location for a structural solution, nor an adequate engagement of the organisation as a whole.

This book provides not just the rationale for and explanation of the changes, but goes beyond to lay out for executives the changes in corporate behaviour and structure that are the underlying enablers of new forms of anticipation and response to customers. For managers it shows the tools they need to identify what's missing, and how to develop their organisations and people to create a customer interface that wins, rewards, and brings loyalty.

Kevin has described what I think is one of the most significant changes of the next 10 years and gives those that follow the guidance in his book the chance to be not a survivor but a 'thrive –r'. It is timely, thoughtful and important.

Sir Ian Gibson
Chairman of Morrison plc

1

In July 2009, a musician, Dave Carroll, released 'United Breaks Guitars', a music video he had produced with his band, Sons of Maxwell, in which he stars. He did this in response to an all-too-common experience for many air travellers: irresponsible baggage handling followed by an almost unbelievable arrogance by the company concerned. The video rapidly became one of YouTube's greatest hits and caused a media frenzy across the internet, which was picked up by major global networks including CNN, the *Los Angeles Times*, the *Chicago Tribune*, *Rolling Stone* Magazine and even the BBC on the opposite side of the Atlantic. Here is Carroll's story, slightly edited for simplicity:[1]

> 'On March 31, 2008 Sons of Maxwell began our week-long-tour of Nebraska by flying United Airlines from Halifax to Omaha, by way of Chicago. On that first leg of the flight we were seated at the rear of the aircraft and upon landing and waiting to deplane in order to make our connection a woman sitting behind me, not aware that we were musicians cried out: "My God they're throwing guitars out there." Our bass player Mike looked out the window in time to see his bass being heaved without regard by the United baggage handlers. My $3500 710 Taylor [guitar] had been thrown before his. I immediately tried to communicate this to the flight attendant who

[1]For the full story and to view the video, go to http://www.davecarrollmusic.com/ubg/

cut me off saying: "Don't talk to me. Talk to the lead agent outside." I found the person she pointed to and that lady was an 'acting' lead agent but refused to talk to me and disappeared into the crowd saying "I'm not the lead agent." I spoke to a third employee at the gate and when I told her the baggage handlers were throwing expensive instruments outside she dismissed me saying "but hun, that's why we make you sign the waiver." I explained that I didn't sign a waiver and that no waiver would excuse what was happening outside. She said to take it up with the ground crew in Omaha. When I got to Omaha it was around 12:30 am. The plane was late arriving and there were no employees visible... Air Canada gave me a phone number to start my claim with United. When I called the number United said I had to return to the Halifax airport with the guitar to show the damage to someone and open a claim. When I returned to the Halifax airport I met with an Air Canada employee, because United has no presence there, and that person acknowledged the damage, opened a claim number but "denied" the claim because Air Canada would not be responsible for damage caused by United employees in Chicago (which still makes sense to me). I took the claim number and called United back. They never seemed to be able find the claim number on several subsequent phone calls but at the last minute it would always surface. I spoke several times to what I believe were agents in India who, ironically were the most pleasant, and seemed genuinely sorry for what had happened. Three or four months later I got directed to the Chicago baggage offices of United and after several attempts to speak with someone was told to simply bring in the guitar for inspection... to Chicago... from Halifax, Canada. When I explained that Halifax is far from Chicago someone then said my claim needed to go through Central Baggage in New York and they gave me a toll free phone number. I phoned that number and spoke to someone. She couldn't understand why someone in Chicago thought she would be able to help me but she seemed to feel for me and asked me to fax her all the information. I did and a few weeks passed with no reply. I called back and the lady said she'd never received the fax. Then I asked her to look for it and surprisingly, there it was. When she found it she asked me to give her a couple of days and to call back. I did, and by the time I phoned again two days later, the number had been discontinued. I had to start all over again with the same 1-800 # to India, where they were as sorry as ever for what happened, couldn't find my claim at first, and told me I needed to bring the guitar into Chicago's O'Hare for inspection. Six months had gone by and the guitar had now been repaired for $1200 to a state that it plays well but has lost much of what made it special. I spoke to a customer service manager in India who promised to forward a note to have someone in Chicago contact me. I received a letter about month later from Chicago with no name or contact info, saying someone would be contacting me about this. Another month went by and I received an email from a Ms Irlweg in Chicago I believe. It basically said she was sorry this happened and denied my claim. Some of her reasons were: I didn't report it to the United employees who weren't present when we landed in Omaha; I didn't report to the Omaha airport within 24 hours while I was driving to places that weren't Omaha; It was an Air Canada issue; Air Canada already denied the claim (as I mentioned because Air Canada would not pay for United's damages), but I'm still unsure as to why I needed to report it in Omaha within 24 hours if it was clearly Halifax's responsibility; someone from United would need to see the damage to a guitar that was repaired. So after nine months it came down to a series of emails with Ms. Irlweg and, despite asking to speak to her supervisor, our conversations ended with her saying United would not be taking any responsibility for what had happened and that that would be the last email on the matter. My final offer of a settlement of $1200 in flight vouchers, to cover my salvage costs repairing the Taylor, was rejected. At that moment it occurred to me that I had been fighting a losing battle all this time and that fighting over this at all was a waste of time. The system is designed to frustrate affected customers into giving up their claims and United is very good at it but I realized then that as a songwriter and traveling musician I wasn't without options. In my final reply to Ms. Irlweg

I told her that I would be writing three songs about United Airlines and my experience in the whole matter. I would then make videos for these songs and offer them for free download on YouTube and my own website, inviting viewers to vote on their favourite United song. My goal: to get one million hits in one year. To date I have written "United: Song 1" and "United: Song 2" and I'm proud to now release the first video in the trilogy. The response has been incredible so far. Everyone involved in the recording of the track and filming/editing of the video has volunteered their time and pre-production work is underway for the filming of "United: Song 2" (hopefully to be released later this summer). United has demonstrated they know how to keep their airline in the forefront of their customers' minds and I wanted this project to expand upon that satirically. I've done being angry for quite some time and, if anything, I should thank United. They've given me a creative outlet that has brought people together from around the world. We had a pile of laughs making the recording and the video while the images are spinning on how to make "United: Song 2" even better than the first. So, thanks United! If my guitar had to be smashed due to extreme negligence I'm glad it was you that did it. Now sit back and enjoy the show.'[2]

Song 1 was posted on 6th July 2009. Within 24 hours it had drawn 461 comments on YouTube, most of them maligning the airline. However, it went viral after that with *The Consumerist* website reporting more than 24,000 views by the following night. When the YouTube count exceeded 150,000 hits, the international news media picked up the story and ran it around the world. Today, it has received over 9.2 million views on YouTube alone.[3] Let no one be in any doubt that we live in an age where information technology is empowering consumers and massively lever-

[2]For the full story and to view the video, go to http://www.davecarrollmusic.com/ubg/

[3]For a spoof response by United, visit this YouTube link: http://www.youtube.com/watch?v=xDoSFqqL4WI&feature=related

aging inherent social networking capability. Bad news can spread easily. As with United Airlines, with the leverage of social networking, it can spread like wildfire, and so an organization that fails to satisfy its customers, whether it is big or small, courts disaster.

Migram and six degrees of separation

Even if we discount the power of the internet, society is amazingly connected. We do not live in discrete cells in which information is contained. Our personal real-life, life-built social networks are extraordinarily connected and have always been effective in the transmission of information.

> *'Word of mouth' has always been the most effective way of disseminating social information for the good of the whole of society, and it can make or break those whose behaviour is socially unacceptable. It was ever thus.*

As long ago as the late 1960s, the American social psychologist Professor Stanley Milgram of Yale University carried out what became known as: 'The Small World Experiment'. Milgram[4] sought to examine the average path length of social networks in the population at large. He had collaborated with other academics in the University of Paris in the 1950s who had been working on mathematical models of social contacts and influences, and whose ideas had probably been triggered by a

---

[4]Milgram was also influenced by the events of the Holocaust and sought to prove the relationship between obedience and authority. He is famous for his highly controversial experiments in the early 1970s in which he demonstrated that human beings were able to dissociate themselves from the consequences of their actions. He devised a method whereby he was able to get people to administer apparently lethal but pseudo electric shocks to actors posing as human guinea pigs; all under the orders of his researchers who wore white coats and carried clipboards, thereby appearing to be expert and authoritative.

Hungarian, Frigyes Karinthy (around 1910) who laid down a challenge for anyone to find another person through at most five other people.

Milgram's team of researchers ran an experiment in parallel, with two targets: one a stockbroker who lived in Boston, and the other the wife of a divinity graduate student who lived in Sharon, Massachusetts. The names of 160 people in Omaha, Nebraska were randomly obtained, and a similar number living in Wichita, Kansas. Both of these cities are more than 2300 kilometres away from Boston. Milgram wrote to each person enclosing a packet that contained the name and address of the chosen target in Boston, a photograph of that person, and a letter asking them to take part in a social contact study in American society.

The respondents were specifically asked to send the packet directly to the target only if they knew him or her on a personal basis. Otherwise, they were asked to send it to a personal acquaintance whom they thought more likely to know that person. In each case, they were asked to put their name on a card that was to accompany the packet throughout, and to send a pre-paid card to Harvard University as they handed the packet on. Sixty-four packets arrived at the target destinations and the tracking mechanism revealed that whilst some had take nine or ten referrals to complete the journey, many had done so in only two hops. The average path length (a measure of how easy it is to negotiate a network is) was 5.5.

Despite the size and complexity of society, in theory we are only separated from any other person by five or six others.

This famous experiment, with its astonishing results, led to the term 'Six Degrees of Separation' which has fired the imagination of writers and filmmakers as well as sociologists and marketers ever since.

Dunbar's number

How many Christmas cards do you send? If you're unenthusiastic about Christmas, the chances are it will be 15 or so. If you are more into it, maybe you have around 50 people on your list. If Christmas is a major event in your year, the chances are it could be up to 150 although it is highly unlikely to be more than that. Robin Dunbar, Professor of Evolutionary Anthropology at Oxford University has concluded that in common with all primates, humans have a natural limit to the number of relationships they can reasonably handle. This, he argues, is based on the size of the neocortex,[5] that highly developed part of the brain in higher mammals where social awareness is present. In the case of humans this is about 150 and it is called 'Dunbar's Number', more popularly known as 'The Magic Number'.

One hundred and fifty appears to be the optimum size for human social groups. Beyond that level, relationships are not easy to make and maintain, and in support of his theory, Dunbar points to communalistic fundamental Christian sects such as the Amish and Hutterites of America whose communities are about this size. He also cites the average village size as recorded in the Domesday Book, which is 150 there or thereabouts, and the size of the smallest standalone unit in modern armies, the Company. Interestingly, he points out that around 150 is also the level at which businesses start to need formal management structures, hierarchies and rules if they are not to fall apart as they grow.

There is an optimum size of social group beyond which people cannot easily relate, therefore. Peer pressure and personal loyalties, together with the ability to know a leader personally and a sense of belonging to a whole entity, disintegrate beyond this point but, crucially, Dunbar also demonstrates that a person's social network expands in layers, and that is governed by multiples of three.

We tend to have about five or six close friends, 15 or so not-so-close ones, then around 45 wider acquaintances until we reach the neocortex manageable limit, the magic number, of around 150.

Dunbar's work suggests that social networks in our modern societies ripple out from the individual in a series of layers, or circles, tripling in

[5]Dunbar, R. (1992) Neocortex size as a constraint on groups size in primates. *Journal of Human Evolution* **20**, 469–93.

size as each layer is added. He also suggests that these layered networks become fragmented with time and social movement:

> 'The trends towards urbanization, economic migration and social transience that have come to dominate modern life have changed all that. We grow up in Huddersfield, go to university in Brighton, get our first job in London and move (or are moved by our employer) to Glasgow a few years later. At each step, we leave behind small groups of friends until time and distance eventually dim our relationships with them beyond the point of rescue. The effect of all this is that our networks of 150 people become increasingly fragmented, consisting of small clusters of friends who are forever associated with a particular time and place. These clusters rarely overlap; indeed, our social network only partially overlaps with even that of our partner, despite the fact that we live in the same house and share a life together. The core clusters of best friends and family may overlap, but we tend to have separate friends for work, hobbies and so on.'

It is this layering and fragmentation in people's networks that opens up the opportunity for a broader societal connectedness whose extent and power is truly awesome.

Gladwell and Granovetter

In nature's networks 'Birds of a feather flock together'. Malcolm Gladwell, in his book *The Tipping Point*,[6] points out that people not only associate with people they live close to (including family of course), but they also associate with people who have like interests and engage in similar activities: who work in the same company; who are in the same golf club; who move in the similar social circles, etc., and each of the people they

[6]Gladwell, M. (2000) *The Tipping Point: How Little Things Can Make a Big Difference.* Abacus. London.

associate with has his or her own extended networks too, just as Dunbar observes and network theory explains.

This was proved in 1973 by sociologist Mark Granovetter at Johns Hopkins University, in his seminal paper, 'The Strength of Weak Ties',[7] which explored the way people got jobs. He showed that the diffusion of influence and information in social networks happened through relatively loosely connected, dyadic (based on two) ties between individuals each of whom moved in different social circles. Granovetter demonstrated that networks link through acquaintances (the 'weak' ties) as opposed to the strongly tied family and close friends. Milgram's packets had leapfrogged over 2000 kilometres in only five or six steps because people were linking their weakly tied networks of acquaintances, not their families and close friends.

Social networks do not comprise a fixed number of nodes with an average number of links; they are dynamic systems that change constantly, adding new nodes and links and losing others as circumstances change. Animals, chemicals, cells, as well as people, link in ways that are neither straightforward, random nor democratic.

Evolution, the survival of the fittest, means that all living organisms exist in a competitive environment. There are winners and losers in the social process. Politicians strive for opportunities to be heard, companies compete for customers, people vie with each other for social links because it gives them greater influence and security. Unlike the spider's web or the fisherman's net with their broadly similar numbers of nodal links, social networks are 'scale free',[8] i.e. the number of their linkages follows the principle behind Pareto's 80:20 theory, also known as the Power Law, where the vast majority of nodes have only a very few links and a small number have a disproportionately large number.

Scale-free social networks tend to cluster, and these clusters become richer because they become more interesting and active, which makes

[7]Granovetter, M. (1973) The Strength of Weak Ties American Journal of Sociology, Vol. **78**, Issue 6, May 1973, pp. 1360–1380.
[8]Barabási, Albert-László (2002) *Linked: How Everything is Connected to Everything Else and What it Means for Everyday Life*. Plume, Penguin Group (USA).

them more able to grab more links and grow very quickly. The ability to make links relative to every other node in the community is called 'fitness'. Fitness, measured by the number of links a node has, is a quantitative measure of the ability to stay ahead of the competition and it doesn't necessarily favour those who have been around the longest. (Google's domination of the internet search-engine market and its trumping of the early pioneers such as Yahoo! and Alta Vista demonstrates this vividly.)

Fitness accounts for why a company is more successful than its competitors to attract and keep customers, or why someone has a greater aptitude for being liked and being more memorable relative to others. In business, the earliest into the market isn't always the winner.

It is likely that some of the individuals involved in both Milgram's and Granovetter's research were what Gladwell calls 'Connectors'. Connectors are super-networkers. They are naturally social creatures who, as Gladwell puts it, have big Rolodexes: they are extremely well-connected individuals who have mastered the art of Granovetter's weak tie. Connectors are often charismatic individuals who energize other people. They are memorable and influential and they have a talent not only at building large numbers of friendly yet casual connections, but for keeping in touch with them. As individuals, they possess fitness and are able to attract many connections.

Milgram's packets leapfrogged over 2000 kilometres in only five or six steps not only because people were linking their weakly tied clusters of acquaintances rather than their families and close friends; they were almost certainly facilitated by connectors who have always been around in society, and massively effective even in the days before we had the internet and social media connecting billions of people worldwide. Most of us don't posses that ability, but the social media has given it to us. By being part of these super-hubs, any one of us can now spread a message amongst many people in a very short time. Today, we are all, potentially at least, socially powerful connectors who can use the new technology for good or ill; especially when it comes to product, brand and service reputation.

Web 2.0 and word of mouth

Immediately after the so-called 'dot-com' bubble burst in the late 2001, a new term came into our vocabulary. 'Web 2.0' was a reappraisal of the way the web worked, its culture and its ethos. People were using the web differently, adapting it in ways that no one had predicted hitherto. User-generated content became widespread and the internet came to be seen as a service to the community. Amongst a number of observable characteristics of this new paradigm, emergent behaviours rather than predetermined ones became apparent, and under Web 2.0, massive decentralization of power took place and freedom of communication was born.

In a sense Web 2.0 has given birth to 'Communications 2.0' where the act of communication has taken on a new dimension, and that oldest form of human connection, word of mouth, has become massively leveraged.

Thoughts, ideas and views can now be shared openly, and passing these on is aided by the ability to 'tweet' and 'like' what you see. Technology now allows people spontaneously to broadcast what they feel and think, linking those comments and the people who make them.

People's opinions, shared hitherto at most with only a narrow social circle, are now one-to-many, and this is permanent. The perishable verbal social tittle-tattle of pre-web days is a thing of the past. Now we have written-word communication, with all its permanence, its easy searchability, undiluted by 'Chinese whispers', and capable of being read asynchronously when it suits the reader, or across time zones. Comments on company performance, for example, can last.[9] They are no longer 'nine days' wonders' – and they can flash around the world in seconds.

The days when organizations could control what information about them was disseminated to the public are gone. The brochure-ware websites of the early period of the web, where organizations of all kinds spoke

---

[9]The celebrated example of 'United Breaks Guitars' has an ever growing list of viewers on YouTube. Two years after it was published, the hit count stands at over 12.3 million and rising steadily.

to their markets in conventional ways, controlling and dictating what was said about them and their products, are a thing of the past. The control of brand reputation and image has largely been taken from their owners, and made or broken by people interacting with each other online. In this brave new world, customer service quality is becoming mediated in cyberspace, and organizations of all types need to beware. In a 2010 marketing trends survey carried out by the Chartered Institute of Marketing of the UK, more than half of respondent firms expressed themselves afraid of venturing into social media. Only the brave, the blind, or the squeaky clean are engaging with it.

Apostles and Terrorists

Intuit is one of the world leaders in accounting software, its product Quicken has millions of users across the world and it is famous for its attention to its customers. However, in marketing circles, its CEO Scott D. Cook is more famous for identifying what he calls 'Apostles and Terrorists' amongst customers. Apostles are customers who are so satisfied that they go out of their way to convert others to a product or service; they see themselves as converters of the uninitiated. On the other hand, there are customers who have had such a bad experience, who are so unhappy and disaffected, that they speak out against an organization at every opportunity – they become commercial terrorists who go out of their way to spread the bad news by word of mouth. Because they are so passionate, and because of the power of social networks, they can easily reach hundreds, and in many cases thousands and more, of people with their story of woe discouraging others even from trying a product or service.

As we shall see later, Service-Ability (or the lack of it in the case of United Airlines) is easily capable of producing these extremes of customer response.

Get your service delivery right and it can result in the creation of unpaid, voluntary marketers, apostles, who evangelize through-

out their networks; get it wrong and you might get commercially destructive terrorists who can wreak enormous damage far beyond imagining.

Feedback loops

Anyone who has used a microphone and amplifier will know about feedback. Get the position of the microphone wrong relative to the speaker, and sound will be picked up, fed into the amplifier, which feeds more sound into the speaker, only to be picked up by the microphone again, re-amplified and the whole cycle keeps repeating and growing until what is known as 'howl round' takes place: that painful screech of infinitely re-amplified sound that sets your teeth on edge.

Norbert Wiener, an American mathematician who died in 1964, formalized the notion of feedback, which describes how an output of information about an event will influence an occurrence of the same event in the future when it is part of a cause-and-effect chain: the event is said to feed back into itself. Today, social networking sites such as Facebook and Twitter leverage this effect enormously. So-called 'friends' become engaged in a constant feedback loop, updating their status in real time in a loop of information between 'friends'; a chain of action and reaction where one posting triggers another, which in turn triggers a third, and so on. Feedback in sound systems can produce a deafening and uncontrollable noise, and so it is with the social media if a viral feedback loop is induced. That's what happened to United Airlines in the Dave Carroll incident.

In a completely different context, Barack Obama used this multiplying power of social networking using the internet for the first time in history for political purposes when, in 2009, he engaged with the social media in his campaign to become President of the USA. At the height of the campaign, Obama had more than three million friends on Facebook, and his social media campaigning staff, largely drawn from the generation to whom this medium is second nature, were using Facebook, Bebo, Myspace, YouTube, Twitter and a host of other such sites in such an innovative way that they managed to create what ultimately became a viral campaign.

Creative fans of Obama were even re-editing official campaign videos and redistributing them using YouTube to friends who, because of their novelty, passed them on. Obama's people were acting like connectors but using viral marketing through the powerful hubs of the social media to leverage that enormously, and they were so successful, their work is widely attributed as being a major cause of Obama's election.

Reflection on United

Let us reflect on that salutary tale about United airlines. 'United Breaks Guitars' is the consumer fighting back with tools that are now available in power and abundance. That airline's incomprehensible lack of even a modicum of customer service not only perfectly illustrates the desperate need for what is being argued for in this book, but shows how even hard-won good practice developed over years through basic common sense, let alone experience and cleverness, can be frittered away in the kaleido-scope, anything-goes, culture of our current times. United's experience doesn't just show how far organizations can fall away from even the basics of hard-won good practice, developed over decades, and often born of bitter experience, it shows that organizations today are being forced to have their customer relationships mediated in the eco-system of social media that has leveraged word of mouth by factors of thousands or even millions. According to *The Times* of London on 22 July 2009, under the title: 'Revenge is best served cold – on You Tube', United's share price plunged 10%, wiping $180 million off its value as a result of this colossal service failure. This is equivalent to well over 50,000 replacement guitars for Dave Carroll.

Companies both large and small and in all sectors of our economy are trying to find ways to harness social media for marketing com-munications, but they should heed that old adage from the Indian sub-continent: 'He who rides the tiger is afraid to get off'. They must wake up to the downside of what it means to ride roughshod through their customers' needs and rights.

Poor or nonexistent service can result in reputations that have taken years to build being destroyed in days through the power and reach of the connector-hubs of the internet social networks. It is often said that we live in a small world: today, it is a frighteningly small world.

2

On the BBC News website of 28 May 2010, reporter Lucy Rodgers[1] published an article entitled 'Retailer W H Smith is ranked joint bottom in a customer satisfaction poll by consumer watchdog Which? So has the former High Street favourite fallen out of favour?' Apparently the consumer organization had named the company worst for service and quality alongside Currys.digital with a 48% customer satisfaction score[2]. A comment left on the BBC site by a reader said this:

> 'Smith's [sic] can't compete on price so has to compete on service but it doesn't. It used to do so; only a couple of years ago I sent a letter of praise about a particular assistant in a local branch to their manager but sadly that assistant has now gone (as has her welcoming smile and her small-talk which was friendly and not intrusive). This has been replaced with 'bargain offers' on chocolate bars and a charge on wrapping purchases. The latter is only a small fee but if it's raining outside I want my newspaper to stay dry and in any

---

[1] http://news.bbc.co.uk/go/pr/fr/-/1/hi/magazine/8708145.stm (published 28 May 2010).
[2] In the interests of fairness, we are not told what customer satisfaction criteria were sampled, and W H Smith did point out that the Which? survey had sampled only 171 respondents and commented that their own customer satisfaction survey, which used a larger sample size, showed the chain scored 'particularly well for . . . the service our colleagues offer in store'.

case if I've just spent £18.99 on a hardback book I want it protected from knocks & dirt. It's a cheap way to treat loyal customers – so like many others I'm no longer loyal and increasingly do most of my shopping for books, music & DVDs online.'

(Leigh Williams, Buckinghamshire, UK)

This is damning stuff for a long-established British firm: a household name, that was founded 218 years ago and built its reputation over 200 years to become a high street name equal to the best, and it serves to illustrate how easy it is to lose sight of core values in the pursuit of profit under a narrow strategy whilst ignoring the enormous value of serving and satisfying the customer.

Some years ago, the United States Chamber of Commerce[3] carried out a survey that sent shock waves through the business world. It showed that, of all the customers an organization loses, 1% die, 3% move away to another town, 5% develop other business transactions, 9% move to another product because of a recommendation, 14% defect because they are dissatisfied with the product or service, but a staggering 68% go elsewhere because they feel the business is indifferent to their needs.[4]

That consumers form opinions and make judgements about an organization based on the employees with whom they interact is just a simple truth. Psychologists know that humans are stimulated by the offer of attention and become much more vulnerable to false messages if the person they are dealing with is not attentive to them and focused on their needs.

The process is packed with all the basic issues that exist in human relationships and interactions and, in a world dominated by technology that is creating ever more distance between the organization and the cus-

[3]Source: US Small Business Administration and the US Chamber of Commerce.
[4]It also showed that for every complaint a business receives, there are approximately 26 other customers with unresolved complaints or problems. The report also concluded amongst other things that the lifetime value of a customer can be worth up to ten times as much as the price of a single purchase.

tomer, getting this right is more important than ever before. People do business with people, after all. Customer service is about how the customer experience is dramatized: how it is acted out on the stage of the customer interface.

Non-rational man

Economists study the behaviour of people through the lens of their economic behaviour. However, economics has at its heart a flawed assumption: that people behave rationally in markets; in particular, that their behaviour will always be directed ultimately toward wealth maximization given the availability of perfect information and low transaction costs. So-called Economic Man is deemed to be a rational calculator of his economic self-interest: a wealth-maximizing robot acting rationally and only for maximum economic utility. Not so. Marketers have know this for years in their appeals to the emotional aspect of the buying decision process.

Daniel Kahneman is 2002 Nobel Laureate in Economic Sciences for having integrated insights from psychological research into economic science. He is also co-recipient of the 2002 Bank of Sweden Prize in Economic Sciences in memory of Alfred Nobel, and he points out how judgements and decisions of individuals in uncertain situations can systematically depart from the common assumptions and predictions of traditional economic theory.

In the introduction before presenting his Prize Lecture on 8 December 2002, at Aula Magna, Stockholm University, the Chairman of the Prize Committee, Professor Torsten Persson, succinctly summed up Kahneman's thesis as follows:

> 'It [economic theory] always builds on very strong assumptions: agents are motivated by pure self-interest and are capable of making rational decisions also in very complex situations. This picture may have been reasonably accurate 20 years ago but nowadays it is becoming more and more of a bad caricature. In fact, many researchers today in the fields of behavioural economics and behavioural

finance are now working with models that are modified to incorporate things like limited rationality and intrinsic motivations, other than self-interest.'

Persson went on to explain how Kahneman had shown, through surveys and experiments, how judgements and decisions in uncertain situations might systematically depart from the common assumptions as well as the common predictions of traditional economics. Human judgement and decision-making under conditions of uncertainty do not follow the previously accepted patterns of behaviour. Kahneman had developed an alternative model, called Prospect Theory, to better explain observed decision-making.

The idea of 'Rational Man' may have helped economists formulate their theories in the past, but modern research is showing that it is not the real world.

Today we understand people as acting with bounded rationality. In other words, rationality in market decisions has its limits. From the early 20th century, observations of human behaviour began to reveal that people act for a myriad of other reasons than purely economic ones. Freud argued that humans were complex mixtures of conflicting drives. Certainly, we have an ego that is aware of reality and is concerned with higher thought processes such as reasoning and problem-solving, but he argued that this has to compete with the id wherein lies our primitive drives and which operates primarily on the maximization of pleasure or the avoidance of pain, and the super-ego where lie our values, morals and rules of right and wrong derived from our nurture. In a sense, the super-ego has a model of what we should be and is a counterbalance to the pleasure-seeking id.

In 1943, Abraham Maslow, in his paper 'A theory of human motivation', proposed a hierarchy of needs in humans. He conclusively demonstrated that people have higher needs once a basic level of security has been secured. At the top of his pyramid of needs (and hence motivations to act) lie esteem and self-actualization 'The desire for self fulfilment, namely the tendency for him [the individual] to become actualized in what he is potentially. This tendency might be phrased as the desire to become more and more what one is, to become everything that one is capable of becoming.' Later still, Eric Berne[5] talked about our three ego states, parent, adult and child (the expression of the id) and showed how humans can seamlessly slip from one to the other in their transactions with others, thus illustrating the complex fight between our natures that goes on within all of us. The emotional, child ego state is one of the most common.

The idea of Rational Economic Man may be a useful assumption to allow economists to develop their theories and practice, but it is artificial. In the real world, people act in far from rational ways, especially when they are customers of some product or service. Maximization of utility (i.e. minimization of waste and the quest for utility) is not the overriding motive that economists would have us believe it is. Wealth (relative wealth) is important but there is a lot more to buying behaviour (particularly consumer buying behaviour) than obtaining the best deal, or getting the best value for money.

The so-called 'buyer black-box' of buying decision making is well known to marketers and it is what its title suggests: a closed, mysterious, process often producing bizarre results that no one could have predicted. What is well known, however, is that marketing promotional effort always produces the best results when it plays to the emotional aspects of the human personality, not its rational ones.

People do not always act rationally in buying activity. They may act out of greed, or lust, or attention seeking, or pride, or social conscience, or a sense of fair play, or a desire for revenge.

People can seek instant gratification from purchasing an expensive item to improve their social status, or just because they don't feel so good that day, spending money for the pleasure it brings when they are feeling down (nowadays called 'retail therapy'). As economic consumers/

---

[5] Berne, E. (1964) *Games People Play*. New York: Grove Press.

customers, people are primarily purpose maximizers rather than profit maximizers: they are materialist, often choosing to spend their money and time collecting goods that they don't truly need.

The rational organizaion

Organizations are undoubtedly wealth maximizers. They exist to make a return on investment. (Even public sector and social sector organizations are doing much the same thing, except that this is translated into the most efficient administration of scarce resources, or the desire to have surpluses that can be ploughed back into more effective activity.) Getting a return on investment is a cold, hard-headed, rational process, often measured only in accounting (economic) terms, and this, all too often, results in them applying the same thinking to their offering in response to customers' needs. It is as though they think that because their corporate motives are rational, then so too should be those of the customer – that if they turn out a good-quality product or service it will be enough to satisfy – but, as we have seen, nothing could be further from the truth. The biggest marketing blunder made today is a belief in Ralph Waldo Emerson's famous phrase, 'Build a better mousetrap, and the world will beat a path to your door'. It will not.

Emerson, an American philosopher, lecturer and essayist, nicknamed the Concord Sage, and a leading voice of American intellectual culture in his day, was born in 1803 and died in 1882. He was a 19th-century man: a man of the Industrial Revolution which, by then, had spread to the USA and was in full swing. This was a time of increasing mass-markets, of increasingly large corporations and a time when economist Adam Smith's ideas were being put into practice. (We discuss these at more length later.) Consumers were experiencing innovation for the first time and they were hungry for it. This was a time when consumerism, 'the systematic creation and fostering of the desire to purchase goods or services in ever greater amounts' (Wikipedia), was only just being born. For the first time in history, products of all kinds were becoming available in large quantity and people were becoming intrigued by innovation. Hence Emerson's comment.

People don't buy purely on the rationalization of functional benefits. Buyer decision behaviour goes much wider than that. Customer satisfaction is now more important than ever, and for the organization that seeks to maximize its return on investment, it must understand that the quality of the experience is what leads to customer satisfaction. In turn, satisfaction is directly linked to customer retention and that is linked to return on investment. (Cisco, the American multinational corporation that designs and sells consumer electronics, networking and communications technology and services, says that a 1% increase in customer retention leads to a 3% increase in revenue.) It is not just delivering an innovative, quality product or service that matters anymore, but a quality of delivery that creates delight and makes the transactional experience pleasurable.

In a restaurant, the occasional delivery of lukewarm soup is far less important than the overall experience to the customer. Conversely, having someone really good who fixes a problem on the end of a helpline is not going to be as memorable as the long wait on hold the customer experiences before getting to speak to him or her.

Service is created as it happens between the service provider and the customer, and it's sole aim is to meet the customer's needs; it should be a pleasurable interaction that never creates stress in either party. The experience is dynamically co-created, with each party contributing to the interaction, as in a dance, and service providers need to be able to step into the customer's shoes, not operate in a different reality that commoditises and standardises the service-delivery process. People do business with people is a time-tested business axiom that seems to have been forgotten in the transition from a commodity to a service economy.

Service delivery, like a three dimensional product, is felt, smelt, heard and touched, but it is also experienced, and service providers must understand how much of an impact the experience of the service, rather than just it's intrinsic benefit, has on the customer: especially how he or she perceives the overall offer. Organizations need to understand the context of the service delivery and how that impacts on the perceptions of the customer. As Marc Stockdorn[6] puts it:

> The system design of an organisation, its inherent culture, values and norms as well as its organisational structure and processes are important issues for the design of services. Disparities between the corporate identity embodied by the organisation's management and staff and the corporate image perceived by the customers need to be ironed out.

In a very real sense, the entire organisation is on a stage, acting out the service delivery, stringing together service moments or touch points, delivering care, help and assistance with rhythm, progress and climax. Communicating in the way people do in a narrative way that induces pleasing responses both ways, and that means the players on the stage, the service deliverers, need to be skilled in the service-delivery process, just like actors are skilled in their profession.

All people, all levels

Furthermore, it is not just customer-facing staff that matter, but all staff, at all levels, at different points of contact over a spread-out process of customer service delivery. Every interaction is important. Even one bad experience can destroy the value of the rest. It is no good how personable the salesperson is, if the service engineer is surly and unhelpful. It is no good how excellent the product is, if the delivery driver is late and doesn't go out of his way to explain and make up with the customer. We could go on with more examples. Suffice to say that unless every employee is fully focused on the customer and makes sure the interaction is a positive one, the customer is unlikely to have any loyalty and is likely to leave at some time or another for any one of the many reasons we have already discussed. Service is built-in at the point of its production and, therefore,

[6]Stockdorn, M. (2011) 5 Principles of Service Design Thinking. *This is Service Design Thinking*. BIS Publishers. Amsterdam.

Service-Ability is needed throughout an organization, top to bottom and across, if the asset of a solid body of loyal customers is to be built.

Moments of truth

Commercial organizations (and indeed many third-sector ones too) spend fortunes on building brands because they can make a significant difference to the bottom line. Effective brand management can harden the asking price of a product or service in a competitive market, thus improving the return on investment through higher-than-market-average profitability, lower cost of goods sold, lower marketing costs through leveraged effectiveness of the marketing spend and higher customer retention. However, brands are not only about memorable designs of logos, or uniformity in corporate identity throughout advertising, websites, and letterheads. Brands are intended to increase the perceived value to the customer of the offer by implying a level of quality and trust that exceeds the competitors' offer and that will be consistently repeated in future purchases.

More than anything, brands promise enhanced, reliable, consistent customer experience and that can only be delivered by people.

It is emotionally uplifting human interactions that are the principal drivers of any brand, and how customers are treated that gives the brand its meaning. Brands are about how people feel when they talk about an organization, and it is personality in the delivery that ensures those feelings are good. The little touches, those 'surprise and delight' moments that challenge and change industry norms are what make the difference in the eyes of the customer, even in the delivery of what may otherwise be a mundane day-to-day activity no different in essence from anything the competition can offer. Customer experience is about dramatizing the brand i.e. acting it out on the stage of the customer interface.

Jan Carlzon understood this crucial point. In 1981, he took over as CEO of the problem-ridden Scandinavian Airlines SAS, and when he left the company 13 years later, he had managed to turn it around by focusing on what he later called 'moments of truth'.[7] These were defined as the points of interaction at which the airline's staff encountered its customers. In a 2006 interview[8] (in words that carry a particular irony in view of the United Airlines debacle), he said this:

> 'What I saw was that we had to change the culture of our company and leave behind the focus that we used to have on technical operation issues and, instead, turn our focus to the market and be customer-driven. The whole case that I was driving was to make this very proud and very successful technical operational organization become a business enterprise or business organization. The way I described it to people was I said "We used to fly aircraft, and we did it very successfully. Now we have to learn the difficult lesson, how to fly people." . . . When we questioned our passengers, it showed that 90 percent of them didn't even know what kind of aircraft they were flying. Where did they get their impression or perception of the company? We found out that they got the perception in those meetings with human resources, the employees working in the company: a salesman over the telephone; a girl behind the check-in counter; a stewardess on board the aircraft; the captain, the way he spoke over his microphone. And all these meetings really constituted the company as such. That's why I said that if those meetings are good meetings, our asset side on the balance sheet will increase. If those meetings are bad meetings, the value of our assets on the balance sheet will decrease. In other words, the only thing we have to do is to see that those critical meetings are as good as ever and that they exceed the expectations of the customers. Then we are going to be a successful company in moments of truth.'

---

[7]Carlzon, J. (1987) *Moments Of Truth: New Strategies For Today's Customer-Driven Economy*. Pensacola, FL: Ballinger Publishing.
[8]Published on CustomerThink (http://www.customerthink.com).

To build relationships with customers (and thereby gain sustainable competitive advantage), organizations must relate to them on a human, emotional level. The need for attention is operating in virtually all human interactions and if you understand this you understand the need to give good customer service. Carlzon again:

> 'The people who work in the front line, who meet the customer in the market, they not only represent the company, no, they really are the company. Because that meeting when the customer stands face to face with a salesman, a check-in lady, your scanner attendant or what have you, that's when the company appears. That is the company. They are the moments of truth. If those moments are good, then your equity on the balance sheet is increasing, if that [sic] moments of truth are bad, your belongings in the balance sheet are decreasing. That's why [sic] you build a long-term successful business: out of motivated employees, feeling responsibility, taking responsibility, and, on the other side, customers who receive a service that they demand in the moment when they meet the people. There are no service instructions that can help because good service is just you and me, here and now.'

In 1978, Idries Shah[9] said, humanity would do well by '. . . studying the attracting, extending and reception, as well as the interchange, of attention'. So, too, would the leaders and managers of organizations. Griffin and Tyrrell[10] say that the need to give and receive attention is a nutriment that feeds us and that this basic human need is rarely far below the surface of human transactions; social or commercial. If we understand this, we understand how vitally important it is to ensure a level of customer service that satisfies this deepest emotional need. We must understand what it is that causes people to feel that the organization cares about them.

The core-product benefit, whether it be tangible or intangible, is only one part of the satisfaction a customer obtains from an organization, the

[9]Shah, I. (1978) *Learning How to Learn*. Octagon Press, London.
[10]Griffin, J. and Tyrrell, I. (2003) *Human Givens*. Chalvington: H G Publishing.

tangible issues of packaging and presentation (and the domain in which brands are most visible) are another, but that most vital of ingredients, the nutrition of attention, lies in that outer ring of augmented value. Psychologists know that people are stimulated by the offer of attention (and, incidentally, they become much more vulnerable to the message if the person delivering it is focused and attentive).

Customer relationships built on trust

Customer relationships are not built on transactions, they are built on emotions, where trust is the greatest factor for success. It is necessary for organizations to understand this if customers are to become integrated, nurtured and held for future profitability.

Customer satisfaction through service quality and meaningful interaction with people leads to growth. It causes an existing customer base to remain loyal and to which more customers can be added. In declining markets, customer-satisfying service is what ensures that existing customers are retained during difficult trading conditions, when it is easily capable of causing so-called 'transfer growth', i.e. attracting footloose customers who owe little allegiance to their existing supplier.

Jones and Sasser[11] say this:

> 'There are four elements that affect customer satisfaction: the basic elements of the product or service that customers expect all competitors to deliver; basic support services such as customer assistance or order tracking that make the product or service incrementally more effective and easier to use; a recovery process for counteracting bad experiences; and extraordinary services that so excel in meeting customers' personal preferences, in appealing to their values, or in solving their particular problems that they make the product or service seem customized.'

[11] Jones, T.O. and Sasser, W.E, (1995) Why satisfied customers defect. *Harvard Business Review*, November–December.

Note these words. 'Extraordinary services' that make the product or service '. . . seem customized' to the '. . . personal preferences' of the customer and '. . . appealing to their values.' These are all phrases that speak of relationship. They are all about being attentive to the customer's needs: the sort of attentiveness that produces a sense of being valued and that induces loyalty.

Loyal, satisfied customers are the source of repeating business (and they are an organization's best salesmen and women because they tell others). The only way to get this is to rack-up customer loyalty to such a degree that it is very difficult for the competition to entice them away. The clever schemes invented by marketers to encourage customer loyalty will never work in the long run if they are not accompanied by the attention that customers really need. Product quality is no longer enough. Service process quality i.e. making sure the service itself is thought-through and effective, is not longer enough. It is only constantly feeding the customer, in the interaction with the organization through employees giving him or her the human attention that is needed, that will produce the real sort of loyalty that builds a business. It is only in rare instances that an organization has complete control over its customer.

This only happens in a monopoly situation where the customer is in effect a hostage, but even in markets with relatively little competition, providing customers with outstanding value may be the only reliable way to achieve sustained customer satisfaction and loyalty. Satisfying customers who are able to make choices is simply not enough. The only truly loyal customers are totally satisfied ones and, except in a few rare instances, only by ensuring complete customer satisfaction, through a consistently satisfying experience, can true customer loyalty be secured.

Totally satisfied customers

Jones et al.[12] have shown that it is not until you totally satisfy customers that you can be sure they will remain loyal:

[12]Jones, T.O. and Sasser, W.E. (1995) Why satisfied customers defect. *Harvard Business Review*, November–December.

'According to conventional wisdom, the link between satisfaction and loyalty in markets where customers have choices is a simple, linear relationship: As satisfaction goes up, so does loyalty. But we discovered that the relationship was neither linear nor simple. To a much greater extent than most managers think, completely satisfied customers are more loyal than merely satisfied customers. In markets where competition is intense, we found a tremendous difference between the loyalty of satisfied and completely satisfied customers. In the automobile industry, even a slight drop from complete satisfaction created an enormous drop in loyalty. This phenomenon is not limited to markets or manufactured products: It also occurs in services.'

Using data collected by the Xerox Corporation, Jones *et al.* shattered the conventional wisdom that high levels of customer satisfaction, as evaluated by customer surveys, indicated a healthy state. Their data showed that totally satisfied customers (as opposed to those who reported high levels of satisfaction) were 6 times more likely to repurchase in the next 18 months than 'satisfied' customers. As they put it:

'The implications were profound: Merely satisfying customers who have the freedom to make choices is not enough to keep them loyal. The only truly loyal customers are totally satisfied customers.'

So, the conventional wisdom that the link between customer satisfaction and loyalty is a simple linear relationship, i.e. as satisfaction goes up, so too does loyalty, is just not true. Completely satisfied customers are a great deal more loyal than merely 'satisfied' ones. In fact, according to Jones and Sasser (op. cit.), they are almost half as likely again (42%) to be loyal than customers who were merely satisfied.

Beware of customer satisfaction surveys: you may be valuing what you measure rather than measuring what's valuable. You may have 80% of your customers expressing high levels of satisfaction, but they may still be up for grabs by the competition because that satisfaction is not complete.

Beware also of mistaking false loyalty for the real thing. Take for example frequent-flyer plans – there is a known high incidence of customers defecting when they exhaust their frequent-flier miles – or take the example of a customer who builds a relationship with a particular trusted employee of a firm who goes elsewhere when that employee leaves. The loyalty in these cases is not permanent. It is false loyalty. In the second example, the individual employee may have had Service-Ability but unless the organization has it as a whole and practises it in depth through all employees, the customer is easily lost. There are other ways in which false loyalty may happen: customers tied in by artificial means such as government regulation that limits competition; the presence of high switching costs as between one supplier and another; the possession by a firm of proprietary technology protected by patent (e.g. drugs manufacturers), but Jones *et al.* showed that whenever these customers are free to make a choice, they act like customers in markets with intense competitive forces at work: they vote with their feet and their emotions.

Customer loyalty is the main driver of long-term financial performance for any commercial organization. It is directly linked to profit and, therefore, return on capital invested. (In the case of the public and third sectors, the investment may be less clearly defined, but ultimately is linked to the administration of scarce resources or social value.) Customer loyalty is not just driven by product quality or service-process quality that satisfies needs, but also by effective, attention-giving service that, uniquely, is capable of creating customer delight. Without these two essential ingredients, customers can all too easily become footloose in a competitive market.

Loyalty = profit

There can be no doubt, therefore, that there is a link between customer satisfaction and customer loyalty. In turn, there is an inextricable link between loyalty and profit, but how do we prove that link? In 2000, Reichheld, Markey and Hopton[13] observed that loyalty reliably measures whether superior value is being delivered. In other words, whether customers are obviously coming back for more. Crucially their research showed that just a 5-percentage-point difference in customer retention consistently resulted in 25–100% profit swings. Describing these results as 'almost unbelievable', they attributed this to what they call second-order effects as follows:

1. Revenues and market share grow as the best customers are swept into the company's book of business, building repeat sales and referrals.
2. Costs shrink as the expense of acquiring and serving new customers and replacing old ones declines.
3. Employee retention increases because job pride and job satisfaction increase, in turn creating a loop that reinforces customer retention through familiarity and better service to the customers. Increase productivity results from increasing employee tenure.

They go further and say that once these second-order effects kick in, third-order effects start to emerge. As costs go down and revenues go up, profits (the third-order effect) increase. This provides resources to invest in superior employee compensation (further reinforcing retention) and in new activities or features that enhance customer value, thus further increasing both customer and employee retention. Profits are important, not just as an end in themselves, but because they allow the company to improve value and provide incentives for employees, customers and investors to remain loyal to the company.

We can see here the enormous importance of employee retention in this dynamic. Organizations with high churn-rates in their staff (particularly the main customer-facing staff) cannot possibly build Service-

---

[13]Reichheld, F.W., Markey, R.G. and Hopton, C. (2000) The loyalty effect – the relationship between loyalty and profits. *European Business Journal* **12**(3), 134–9.

Ability. Like the centre of a whirlpool, it all revolves around the employee and his or her pride in the job which, in particular, is derived from job satisfaction.

Reichheld *et al.* go on to say that the best 10% of an organization's customers are worth 5–10 times as much as it's average customers in terms of potential lifetime profits, and this seems to correlate well with what Jones *et al.* say about the fact that it is only totally satisfied customers who remain loyal: these are the ones who are six times as likely to repurchase within 18 months. This is the measure of success of an organization, not customer surveys that transform an organization into what it measures. The true mission of a firm, they say, is to create value for three key constituencies: customers, employees and investors – which brings us back to the core issue: the importance of the people in the whole process and their potential for reducing friction if they have Service-Ability. Let us reflect on this extract from their paper:

> 'The opportunity for reducing friction in most businesses is immense. Shareholders now churn their holdings based on short-term speculation at the rate of 50% per year. Employees change jobs with increasing frequency; 15–25% turnover is common. and customers defect at the alarming rate of 10–30% per year. With this much friction, it is no wonder that productivity and economic growth are languishing. Business is being conducted amongst strangers, trust is low and energy is sapped.'[14]

'Business is being conducted amongst strangers.' What a telling indictment this is.

Consider the widespread trend amongst call centres these days where employees will not identify themselves (other than their first name, which is little more than a label of convenience for the purposes of the

---

[14]Reichheld, F.W., Markey, R.G. and Hopton, C. (2000) The loyalty effect – the relationship between loyalty and profits. *European Business Journal* **12**(3), 134–9.

conversation; it is not true identification) and all apparently part of what is undoubtedly a tribally cultural call-centre practice, approved by their bosses. Strangers doing business with strangers indeed! Or (and it has to be said) the downright stupidity of having a person living in a village in Britain and wanting to speak to someone in their local bank branch a mile or two away being put through on a local number to someone working in a factory unit on an industrial estate outside of Mumbai, more than 7000 kilometres away, all because the technology allows what amounts to exploitation of people in another less-wealthy economy halfway round the globe in the name of profit. This is institutionally induced 'strangerness' (as well as being the export of jobs vital to our economy) and is inimical to the whole idea of business common-sense.

However well meaning, the Indian employee is just not connected in any meaningful way with the UK customer: there is a massive distance between the two and it is not only geographical, it is cultural and psychological.

Internal service quality

Earlier, we referred to the work of Heskett *et al.*[15] in describing the incidence of commercial Apostles and Terrorists, but they also make the point that internal service quality (how the organization treats its employees, the conditions it provides for them to work in, reward, work enrichment, etc.) affects employee satisfaction. This affects employee loyalty which, in turn, affects employee productivity and that affects external service value, customer satisfaction and, ultimately, customer loyalty which, of course, leads to growth and profitability. It is a chain: what Heskett *et al.* call a 'service profit chain' (the title of their paper) that starts with the employee

[15]Heskett, J.L., Jones, T.O., Loveman G.W. and Sesser W.E. (2008) Putting the service-profit chain to work. *Harvard Business Review*, July–August.

and how he or she is involved, led, trained and housed (in the sense of the working environment) by the organization. At risk of overstating the point, let us consider what they say, which puts the process in reverse order:

> 'The links in the chain (which should be regarded as propositions) are as follows: Profit and growth are stimulated by customer loyalty. Loyalty is a direct result of customer satisfaction. Satisfaction is largely influenced by the value of services provided to customers. Value is created by satisfied, loyal, and productive employees. Employee satisfaction, in turn, results primarily from high-quality support services and policies that enable employees to deliver results to customers.'

This is a system: a process in which employees are the central theme, indeed the focus (or perhaps the focused lens through which the customer is viewed fully in frame). It speaks of a depth of relationship extending from the very centre of the organization to the loyal, satisfied customer through the loyal, satisfied employee. It is all about the people: that message at the heart of Service-Ability.

Heskett *et al.* say that a primary source of job satisfaction is the service workers' perceptions of their ability to satisfy customer needs. Those who felt they did registered job satisfaction levels more than twice as high as those who felt they didn't. Therefore the satisfaction in the transaction, as between customer and employee, is mutually rewarding and employee satisfaction is the glue, the culture, that binds the relationship and seals the transactional value. According to Scott Cook of Intuit:

> 'Most people take culture as a given. It is around you, the thinking goes, and you can't do anything about it. However, when you run a company, you have the opportunity to determine the culture. I find that when you champion the most noble values – including service, analysis, and database decision-making, employees rise to the challenge, and you forever change their lives.'

However, people cannot function like this unless the organization is structured in such a way that it facilitates them to give of their best (or, at least, doesn't militate against them as many organizations do). Service-Ability is not only an individual thing, it is also an organizational characteristic. Neither can it work unless we get the people right, and that needs effective leadership, clarity of purpose and a management process that fits the modern world, not one that is steeped in the paradigms of the past.

3

In 1911, only three years before his death of pneumonia at the age of 59, Frederick Winslow Taylor (1856–1915), the son of a Quaker lawyer from Philadelphia, was questioned at length before a Special Committee of the House of Representatives in the USA. He had been summoned to give account of his views on management, because widespread hatred had developed against them. One of his most often quoted sayings is this:

> 'Under our system, a worker is told just what he is to do and how he is to do it. Any improvement he makes upon the orders given him is fatal to his success. Hardly a competent workman can be found who does not devote a considerable amount of time to studying just how slowly he can work and still convince his employer that he is going at a good pace.'

Taylor was, and is known still, as 'The Father of Scientific Management', a system that relies heavily on work study and measurement, particularly the measurement of time, and it is significant that, in 1912, following the recommendations of the House Special Committee, the American Government passed laws banning the use of stopwatches for work study in the US Civil Service. It took until 1949 for those laws to be repealed.

Taylor was an engineer steeped in the paradigm of the Industrial Age. He had cut his management teeth in the iron and steelmaking industry and was convinced that productivity was far lower than it could be. He attributed this to 'systematic soldiering', a combination of deliberate malingering by the worker, and the lack of a scientific approach to the design of working practices by the supervisors and managers, whom he accused of just using a rule of thumb rather than thought-through ideas. He thought them amateurish and advocated the development of management as a discipline. He also realized that the factory system made possible the ability to control productivity. If anything characterizes the name of Frederick Winslow Taylor, then the stopwatch does.

In 1898, as a newly appointed supervisor at the Bethlehem Steel Works of Pennsylvania, he reduced the number of workers shovelling coal from 500 to 140 without loss of production, by optimizing the size of the shovel each man used, although he did this in the face of considerable opposition from the workforce about whom he said this:[1]

'As was usual then, and in fact as is still usual in most of the shops in this country, the shop was really run by the workmen, and not by the bosses. The workmen together had carefully planned just how fast each job should be done, and they had set a pace for each machine throughout the shop, which was limited to about one-third of a good day's work. Every new workman who came into the shop was told at once by the other men exactly how much of each kind of work he was to do, and unless he obeyed these instructions he was sure before long to be driven out of the place by the men. As soon as the writer was made gang-boss, one after another of the men came to him and talked somewhat as follows: "Now, Fred, we're very glad to see that you've been made gang-boss. You know the game all right, and we're sure that you're not likely to be a piecework hog. You come along with us, and everything will be all right, but if you try breaking any of these rates you can be mighty sure that we'll throw you over the fence." The writer told them

[1] Taylor, F.W. (1911) *The Principles of Scientific Management*. New York and London: Harper & Brothers.

plainly that he was now working on the side of the management, and that he proposed to do whatever he could to get a fair day's work out of the lathes. This immediately started a war; in most cases a friendly war, because the men who were under him were his personal friends, but none the less a war, which as time went on grew more and more bitter. The writer used every expedient to make them do a fair day's work, such as discharging or lowering the wages of the more stubborn men who refused to make any improvement, and such as lowering the piece-work price, hiring green men, and personally teaching them how to do the work, with the promise from them that when they had learned how, they would then do a fair day's work. While the men constantly brought such pressure to bear (both inside and outside the works) upon all those who started to increase their output that they were finally compelled to do about as the rest did, or else quit. No one who has not had this experience can have an idea of the bitterness which is gradually developed in such a struggle. In a war of this kind the workmen have one expedient which is usually effective. They use their ingenuity to contrive various ways in which the machines which they are running are broken or damaged – apparently by accident, or in the regular course of work – and this they always lay at the door of the foreman, who has forced them to drive the machine so hard that it is overstrained and is being ruined. And there are few foremen indeed who are able to stand up against the combined pressure of all of the men in the shop. In this case the problem was complicated by the fact that the shop ran both day and night.'

Taylor finally solved what must have been one of the earliest industrial disputes by the simple expedient of halving the piece work rate for the job and offering the men the option of either earning less or working harder. They chose the latter. From 1895 onwards, he produced many papers on incentive schemes, piece rates, shop-floor management and, in 1909, his major opus *The Principles of Scientific Management*, for which he is best known, was published and this underpinned much of industrial management theory in the 20th century. (Taylor's ideas have been much maligned for being at the heart of many of the worst examples of bad management in the years since he expounded them and there is no doubt that this way of thinking finally came to a head many years later in the industrial unrest of the 1970s in Britain.)

Much of Taylor's writing is heavily laden with negative bias toward the workman and it is this that brings disapproval on him and his ideas. However, he is on record as saying he wanted to get both worker and manager to understand that their respective interests lay in seeing things from each other's point of view, and he argued that his ideas demanded a massive change of thinking in both the worker and the supervisor if they were to establish '. . . an intimate and friendly cooperation between management and men'. Significantly, he not only advocated the selection of the right workman for the job, but also his education and development: a principle that was to become an integral part of good human resource management almost 70 years later (although for different reasons than the 'scientific' methods he advocated). The main problem, however, was that he was defining what a good worker was in terms of the needs of management, and took little account of the needs of the employee. The needs of the customer of course, were not even on the radar.

Taylor was an uncompromising man, as the transcript of his testimony to the committee of the House of Representatives shows, and his spirit has permeated a substantial part of management thinking ever since. He said this:

> 'Now it must be clearly understood that in these experiments we were not trying to find the maximum work that a man could do on a short spurt or for a few days, but that our endeavour was to learn what really constituted a full day's work for a first-class man; the best day's work that a man could properly do, year in and year out, and still thrive under.'

Many believe that Taylor recanted his 'one best way' of managing before the House of Representatives, but he didn't. During his testimony what he did was say that he did not think his name should be forever associated with what had, by this time, become known as 'Taylorism'. He preferred instead the term 'Scientific Management'.

Taylor was a man for the moment. His ideas were formulated at a time when industrialization had reached its zenith. It was steaming along – literally.

The Industrial Revolution

The Industrial Revolution of the 18th and 19th centuries was the result of a unique congruence of three factors: the availability of raw materials, the availability of power; and the availability of labour (including child labour). In its first phase, Britain moved from what was a largely peasant economy where most people worked the land in smallholdings, growing food for themselves and trading surpluses for things they needed. In 1700 Britain had enormous, largely untouched, reserves of coal (hitherto, people had burned wood for heat and cooking) and many worked on larger farms owned by the landed gentry. What industry there was comprised cottage industries where people made things for daily life and spun yarns for clothing (usually the job of the single women in the household, hence the term 'spinster'). Smiths would shoe horses and make small mechanical devices, and commerce would be conducted by merchants who operated regionally.

However, things were about to change. Advances in farming practices were being made, landowners were appointing tenant farmers and the agricultural land was being redistributed from general use by a rural peasantry to enclosures with hedges and ditches. This unofficial practice progressed throughout the century but finally became law with the passing by Parliament of the General Enclosure Act, 1801 which sealed the fate of those people who had hitherto used the land for small-scale, unofficial production of food. It also reduced the need for farm workers, which added to the decline of the cottage industries. Science was emerging, and reason rather than religion was taking over in people's consciousness. As the century developed, the 'putting out system', a means whereby emerging manufacturing operations were able to subcontract work to artisans working under their own roofs, providing an income for skilled craftsmen, went into decline as factories began to emerge.

Britain had increasing access to raw materials such as cotton and pig-iron from her colonies, particularly America. Her markets were opening up for her emerging textile industries, both domestically and in places far further afield through her trading activities in India and the Far East. The industrialization of cotton textiles production, using raw cotton imported from America was a significant early development. Between 1796 and 1830, cotton production tripled through the invention of machines that vastly improved the process. John Kay's Flying Shuttle (1733) effectively doubled a weaver's production of cloth. Richard Arkwright's Water Frame (1769) used the power of water to produce an even stronger yarn. Also in 1769, James Watt patented the steam engine, powered by coal which by now was being mined. James Hargreaves invented the Spinning Jenny (1770), allowing many threads to be spun at once, and Samuel Crompton's Mule (1779) combined the benefits of the Jenny and the Water Frame to produce large amounts of fine, strong yarn, which was being increasingly worked into cloth by Edmund Cartwright's Power Loom (1783).

We most easily associate water power and then steam power as the principal drivers of the Industrial Revolution; in fact it was children.

From the 1720s onwards, thousands of young adults left their rural homes to move to the denser centres of population to find work in the factories and mills that were being built to house emerging industries. Wages were pitiful, but this young population was mobile and adaptable to change. Hitherto, land owners and farmers had kept their young workers single, using their economic and social power to restrict early marriage to ensure longer productivity. Young couples often had to ask permission of their master to marry. Now, people were released from this social restriction. The freedom young workers had, meant they were able to marry and start families sooner and the marriage registers of the time show that the average age of British brides dropped from almost 27 in the early 1700s to 23½ by 1800. Young women were more fertile at this age and could produce far more children, and the 1700s saw the population of Britain double, from around 5.7 million to 8.7 million.

Jane Humphries, Professor of Economic History at Oxford University and Fellow of All Souls College, says the great manufacturers; the inventors, engineers and entrepreneurs – the great and the good of the Industrial Revolution – all owed their success not to capitalism, but to the greatest resource the country had at that time: children. By the time Britain took its massive leap into the machine age, it had its largest population of youngsters, ever. As Humphries puts it, 'The country was awash with children' and, as the century progressed, the war with revolutionary France meant that many able-bodied men were away abroad. Skilled adult labour came at a premium and when William Pitt, the then prime minister, was warned that businesses were becoming unable to pay their taxes to fund the war, he is famously on record as saying 'Yoke up the children!'

By 1820, 40% of the population of the UK was under 15 years of age, and most were sent to work. In 1800 there were no cotton weaving machines in Lancashire, England; by 1830, there were 30,000, most of them manned and worked by children. These were the true 'Children of the Revolution'; many being auctioned to the highest bidder in a collusion between mill owners and local parish authorities' work houses. Poor children ended up as 'parish apprentices' and mill owners shipped them to distant parts of the country, far from where they were born and brought up, to be indentured until they were 21. It was little better than state-organized slavery.

The Enlightenment, which started at this time, was the social milieu in which all this happened. Born of a spontaneous emergence of the idea that reason should be the primary source of authority and legitimacy, it spread throughout Europe. Rationalism and science, philosophical debate, publishing and the arts all began to flourish as this thirst for knowledge and a striving for a better society took hold. This was a time of the Coffee House Movement in England: 'Penny Universities' as they came to be called, where you paid a penny to enter and drank as much coffee as you wanted whilst you talked and traded, and mixed with others of a like mind.

Many businesses were created at this time and by the last third of the century, the merchant, the handicraft artisan, the journeyman was no longer the main economic agent of the economy. Instead the industrialist with his investment in machinery, the routinization of production and division of work took over. Mercantilism gave way to industrial capitalism. A new group of economic theorists emerged. In his 1776 book *An Inquiry into the Nature and Causes of the Wealth of Nations,* Adam Smith (1723–1790), a Scottish philosopher, pioneer of political economics and leading figure in the Scottish Enlightenment, theorized that the pre-existing system of individual craft operatives, operating in cottage industries through the putting out system for example, represented significant transaction costs every time a job was undertaken.

Smith reasoned that firms were the answer to the inefficiencies of the craft system.

By bringing people together and dividing work into specialist tasks, he demonstrated that production could rise by several orders of magnitude from the level of the individual generalist operator, driving down cost of production, eliminating the cost of many market transactions, dramatically increasing profit and achieving a much higher return on the capital employed in the enterprise.

For example, Smith pointed out that a group of specialized workers, each performing one single task in the making of pins, could produce far more pins in a day than the same group where each individual made a whole pin. He wrote:

> 'One man draws out the wire, another straightens it, a thirds cuts it, a fourth points it, a fifth grinds it at the top for receiving the head; to make the head requires two or three distinct operations; to put it on is a peculiar business, to whiten the pins another; it is even a trade by itself to put them into the paper.'

Smith went on to say that by bringing the skills, resources and time of the employees together in one place, under one contract of employment and coordinated under strict authority, firms could grow vertically as more of these elements were brought together under this overarching system. Division of labour translated into the creation of formalized operating procedures, with rules for employees to follow, lines of authority, reporting procedures, etc., and this thinking undoubtedly underpinned F.W. Taylor and his Scientific Management (and those of Max Weber in his ideas about bureaucracy, to which we refer later) ideas a century later.

The industrial era was emerging, and people were experiencing loss of control over their means of existence, leaving them with only the ability to sell their time and physical strength for a wage, and also no doubt leaving them with no small degree of resentment. This was a time when the trade union movement started: when working people sought reform in their socio-economic conditions. The British Labour Party was born out of this movement.

The next century, the 19th, saw the second phase of the Industrial Revolution. This was the age of the engineer. Isambard Kingdom Brunel, the builder of ships, bridges and railways, and Joseph Bazalgette who built the sewerage system in London that is still in use to this day, are just two of the many examples of superstar engineers of the time whose skills were undoubted, but who were working with increasingly outmoded means of organizing labour for maximum output.

In the early phase of the Industrial Revolution, the management of children was a coercive process aimed only at getting them to work as hard as possible, often on a piecework payment basis, using Adam Smith's principle of division of work. There is no doubt that this management mindset still exists in many of our modern organizations.

There was no management theory, everything had been done by rule of thumb; no one had really developed a form of understanding about how to organize and manage for the new way of working. Then, around 1880, along came Taylor with his Scientific Management ideas, declaring 'In the past the man has been first; in the future the system must be first.' Taylor was closely followed historically by Max Weber.

Weber & bureaucracy

As the 20th century dawned, the sheer size of organizations meant that the control of efficiency became the imperative for those who owned the means of production and there emerged another man for the moment: Max Weber (1864–1920), a German sociologist and political economist, left a lasting effect on our understanding of organization.

Weber is universally regarded as the pre-eminent theorist of Modernity, the era that emerged following the Enlightenment of the late 17th and early 18th centuries and in which society in the developed world became industrialized.

The 'Modern Era', or the 'Age of Reason' as it is also known, is generally held to have lasted some 200 years. In very broad terms, it started with the fall of the Bastille in 1789 and ended with the fall of the Berlin Wall in 1989.

This was a time of massive change: in outlook, beliefs and values; a time when it is said 'man invented himself'. Before the Enlightenment, the prevailing idea had been that man was the reflection of God and His nature, and the rationality of existence was based on 'theologic', informed by dogma issued by the church. The Enlightenment replaced this with a rationality based on scientific logic, and heralded an era in which a new way of thinking and new ways of socialization emerged. Industrial life with all its norms of rationality, efficiency and desire for progress that became operationalized in the Industrial Revolution began at this time. So too did capitalism, and Weber's ideas, like Taylor's were formulated in the full expression of all of this.

In his famous 'Protestant Ethics' theses, Weber debated about the origins of capitalism, but it is more appropriate to interpret him as a theorist of 'Modernism': that combination of rational thought, asceticism, secularization and the bureaucratization of economic, political and military practice combined with the idea of monetization of value.[2] For Weber,

[2]Turner. B. (1990) The rise of organizational symbolism. In: J. Hassard and D. Pym (eds) *The Theory of Philosophy of Organizations*. London: Routledge. Also in J. Hansard and M. Parker (eds.) *Postmodernism and Organizations*. Sage. London (author's source).

the element of authority and how it is institutionalized was fundamental. He was suspicious of organizing under 'charismatic authority', as in families and religions where authority grows from the charm of an individual personality, or 'traditional authority' such as feudal, fatherly arrangements where power derives from traditional rights to rule in an individual. Instead, he advocated the principle of 'rational/legal authority', i.e. the way a modern state is run, under a rule of law accepted as legitimate by those subject to it, suggesting that only this method was able to bypass the personal idiosyncrasies of people and circumstances.

The internal allocation of roles in any corporate group, Weber argued, must always be with respect to an authority charged with the responsibility to bring about order, and that possesses the power to enforce that order. When this rational/legal form of authority exists over an administrative staff, Weber says, the organization takes the form of a 'bureaucratic' structure.

Bureaucracies are usually seen as pyramids with one person at the top, underneath whom is a number of heads of department, who themselves have subordinates, each in charge of sub-departments or sections in which there are people who in turn are divided in rank order according to job title and pay-scale,[3] each doing only part of the whole job and each restricted in his or her ability to exercise initiative: 'Precision, speed, unambiguity, knowledge of files, continuity, discretion, unity, strict subordination, reduction of friction and of material and personal

---

[3]The reader may have noted here the absence of the term 'hierarchy'. This is deliberate. For the purposes of dealing with leadership as a separate issue, I have very much taken on board Birkinshaw's (ibid.) distinction between bureaucracy and hierarchy. In support of the legitimacy of such a distinction, he argues that bureaucracies are about managing activities across layers in the organization, whereas hierarchy is about the rule of those who have some specialist power or knowledge that gives them the ability to rule over people through rank. It is true that hierarchies exist in bureaucracies, but I draw the distinction here so that we may deal with its implications in Service-Ability: the creation of initiative in people through trust in their leaders, dealt with in Chapter 8, Effective Leadership.

costs – these are raised to the optimum point in the strictly bureaucratic administration.' Weber said.

In one of his major works 'Wirtschaft und Gesellschaft' (Economy and Society), first published posthumously in 1922, Weber said this:[4]

> 'Experience tends universally to show that the purely bureaucratic type of administrative organization – that is the monocratic variety of bureaucracy [one person at the top] – is, from a purely technical point of view, capable of attaining the highest degree of efficiency and is in this sense formally the most rational known means of carrying out imperative control over human beings. It is superior to any other form in precision, in stability, in the stringency of its discipline, and in its reliability. It thus makes possible a particularly high degree of calculability of results for the heads of the organization and for those acting in relation to it. It is finally superior both in intensive efficiency and in the scope of its operations, and formally capable of application to all kinds of administrative tasks.'

Weber's principal concerns, and his thinking, ooze with the imperative of control for efficiency. Today, we need to be concerned with the empowerment of people for productivity, which is a massively different thing.

Control became the prevailing ethos of industrialization, and it still informs the way modern organizations of all types are managed and structured. However, in his introduction to the English translation of 'Economy and Society', Talcott Parsons[5] observes that Weber had a tendency to overemphasize the coercive aspect of authority and hierarchy in human relations.

---

[4] *Wirtschaft und Gesellschaft* (Economy and Society). Tübingen: J. C. B. Mohr (Paul Siebeck). First published posthumously in 1922.
[5] Weber, M. (1964) *The Theory of Social and Economic Organization* (T. Parsons, ed.). New York: Oxford University Press.

In a bureaucracy, fitness for office is determined almost exclusively by technical competence, tested by a long period of formalized training as a condition even of eligibility for a job. This impersonal, rational/legal culture is embedded right from the start. Bureaucracies pay little cognizance to the person in their recruitment processes, the emphasis is heavily on qualifications and technical competence. Weber himself said this:

> 'The purest type of exercise of legal authority is that which employs a bureaucratic administrative staff . . . Candidates are selected on the bias of technical qualifications. In the most rational case, this is tested by examination or guaranteed by diplomas certifying technical training, or both.'

The problem is, however, that standardization of process and regulation of operation tends to depersonalize employees who work in organizations like this; detaching them from the overall aim of the organization, and isolating them from the result of their work in such a way as to render them unaccountable and broadly indifferent to the outcome of what they do. We still see this today. Bureaucracy still rules in many organizations that see neither their staff nor their customers as people.

Contrast this with the principle of modern strategic human resource management that we examine in the Chapter 6, Getting the People Right, whereby people are recruited to the culture of the organization: implying that certain attitudes and attributes beyond the purely technical qualification are very much taken into account. Examine it also against the approach of Southwest Airlines also referred to in that chapter, whose 'Hire for attitude, train for skills' policy is the diametric opposite of the bureaucratic. Note also the idea of 'Googliness' also discussed there.

Weber's weakness was his concentration on the idea that the economy is a system of abstract market relationships, rather than seeing it as a society of people who bump and scrape off each other in a myriad of ways and in which organizations are themselves mini-societies. This blinded him to the reality of the way people in organizations really function, each with different roles, certainly, but cooperating, collaborating, in complementary roles in the way that recent sociological study has identified.

Parsons (ibid.) singles this out as one particular 'blind-spot' in Weber, and notes that with the passage of time, inadequacies and one-sidedness in his arguments would emerge:

> 'This emphasis on the economic rather than the occupational perhaps tends to account for one of Weber's conspicuous blind spots in the field, his failure to bring out the structural peculiarities of the modern professions and to differentiate between the organization of professional services and what may be called the 'administrative hierarchy' of occupational structure types.'

As we saw in our quotation of Chuang Tzu in the Preface, 'He who does his work like a machine grows a heart like a machine, and he who carries the heart of a machine in his breast loses his simplicity. He who has lost his simplicity becomes unsure in the strivings of his soul.'

Fordism

At the time Taylorism was becoming established and the principles of Weber were taking hold, another towering figure of 20th-century industrialization emerged.

Henry Ford was born on a farm in Michigan in 1863. He left home at 16 to go to nearby Detroit to become an apprentice machinist, qualifying as an engineer three years later at the Edison Illuminating Company. In 1893 he became Chief Engineer and, working in his own time, produced his first petrol-propelled vehicle, the 'Quadricycle', three years later. After two unsuccessful attempts to incorporate his own company, he finally founded The Ford Motor Company in 1903, with him as Vice-President and Chief Engineer, and started making cars from components bought in from other manufacturers. However, Ford was a man with a vision. In his autobiography,[6] he said:

> 'I will build a car for the great multitude. It will be large enough for the family, but small enough for the individual to run and care for. It will be constructed of the best materials, by the best men to be hired, after the simplest designs that modern engineering can devise. But it will be so low in price that no man making a good salary will be unable to own one – and enjoy with his family the blessing of hours of pleasure in God's great open spaces.'

The Ford 'Model T' was born in 1908. It was rugged, easy to operate and maintain, handled well on rough roads and was affordable. Truly it was a product for the time and it was a staggering success. By 1918, almost half the cars produced in the USA were Model Ts.

Ford was famous for saying 'Any customer can have a car painted any colour that he wants so long as it is black'.

Ford's Model T was made with pioneering production techniques based on division of labour. The Ford Motor Company introduced continuously moving assembly lines, with carefully timed delivery of parts by conveyor to the exact point where they were needed, so men could remain in one place, adding one component at a time to each vehicle as it passed them by. Now it was possible for men to earn high wages, if they were prepared and able to work hard. By the early 1920s, the massive Ford Rouge Plant on the banks of the Rouge River was a completely self-contained unit. It had a steel mill and a glass factory. Iron ore and coal were brought by ship from the Great Lakes and the railroads, where rolling mills, forges and assembly shops transformed the raw materials into springs, axles, engine blocks and car bodies. By 1927, all the steps in the production of the Model T took place at this vast plant, which was Mass Production incarnate.

[6]Ford, H. and Crowther, S. (1922), *My Life and Work*. New York: Garden City. Various republications. Original is public domain in USA.

There is much debate about whether Taylorism informed 'Fordism', as it came to be known. Many believe that Henry Ford was out on his own in terms of his production ideas and that he is reported to have had a considerable contempt for experts who claimed they had the answer. Instead, he is said to have relied on common-sense ideas of how to improve efficiency. One thing is sure: Adam Smith's ideas on division of labour, described a century earlier, lay at the heart of Ford's thesis.

Fordism was the acme of the division of labour, but this new expression of the industrial age was causing much concern and soul-searching in society at large.

In 1936, Charlie Chaplin, believing that the efficiencies of modern industrialization had caused the Great Depression of the early 1930s, produced the film 'Modern Times'. The film is the story of Chaplin's iconic little tramp character and his mostly futile attempts to become rehabilitated into the modern world, after being stripped of his dignity on a constantly accelerating assembly line where he endlessly has to put nuts onto pieces of machinery; to such an extent that he suffers a mental breakdown and runs amok.

Fayol and the human relations school

Around the time when Ford was in full stride, Taylor was expounding his ideas in America, and Weber his in Europe, on the other side of the Atlantic Ocean another engineer, the Frenchman Henri Fayol, was putting forth his ideas about management too. Born in Turkey in 1841 to a father who was himself an engineer working on civil engineering projects, Fayol trained as a mining engineer and, like Taylor, cut his management teeth in one of the biggest iron and steel producers of the time in France. He became managing director of the firm in 1888 and stayed in the top position for over 30 years, producing his book *Administration Industrielle et Générale* (1926) in which he made the first comprehensive statement about a general theory of management. Today this is known as 'Classical Management Theory'.

Fayol concluded that there were six primary functions of management and 14 principles. The functions are forecasting, planning, organizing, commanding, coordinating and monitoring; all of them much what management does anyway. However, it is in the 14 principles that we find the earliest hints that there is more to management than simple command and control. Fayol's principles show an understanding of the need to see people not as machines, or parts of a machine, but as people who have human needs at work. It is true that he refers to division of work in true Adam Smith fashion, and he echoes Ford in saying that people and materials need to be in the right place at the right time. He insists that discipline, authority, centralization of decision making and submission of the individual to the collective whole are essential, all very much in the spirit of the industrial age.

However, he also states the need for a person to have just one boss and not to be the recipient of orders from many different people, and he talks about fair remuneration and equity in the way bosses treat subordinates. He also talks about stability of tenure of personnel, because high turnover is inefficient, and orderly planning: the need to have people trained and ready to fill vacancies when they arise.

Crucially, Fayol talks about 'unity of direction' (all organizational activities having the same purpose, using one plan) and the need to allow employees to exercise initiative because that will motivate them to carry out the plans of the organization with high levels of effort. These are very much in the spirit of modern management thinking.

Above all, and most importantly, Fayol talks about the need for 'esprit de corps': that team spirit that promotes harmony and unity within the organization. Team spirit is also known as morale and achieving that is at the very heart of Service-Ability. Even in the tumultuous shriek of industrial activity of the early 20th century, in Fayol we have a voice of understanding about this most crucial of elements of a successful organization.

Fayol was not the only dissenting voice to the prevailing industrial zeitgeist. Sometimes referred to as 'The Mother of Scientific Management',

Mary Parker Follett (1868–1933), a contemporary of Taylor and Fayol, and another of the early management consultants, talked about 'reciprocal relationships' and the need to understand the dynamics of interactions between individuals in organizations. A pioneer in organizational theory, she challenged 'bossism': the tendency to over-manage people in the workplace (today we call it micromanagement), and she advanced an understanding of the importance of creating cross-functional relationships in bureaucracies; a major tenet of this book. She also challenged the use of power, arguing that it should be non-coercive and integrative: another vital component of effective leadership for Service-Ability. Psychologist Lillian Gilbreth was another voice of caution. Although time and motion consultants, cast very much in the Taylorist mould, with her husband, Frank Bunker Gilbreth, she produced a constructive critique of Taylor's ideas, arguing that they fell far short of understanding the importance of the human element. The Gilbreths introduced the study of fatigue factors in the workplace, recognizing that you simply cannot continue to drive people endlessly for productivity.

Follett's and Gilbreth's work informed many of the thinkers of the time including Elton Mayo, an Australian psychologist, sociologist and organizational theorist at Harvard University. His famous 'Hawthorne Experiments' (1924–1932), carried out at the Hawthorne Plant of the General Electric Company near Chicago (See Huczynski & Buchanan[7] for a description) found that people's work output continued to rise regardless of variations in working conditions, principally the influence of higher or lower levels of light. Initially regarded as perplexing, the 'Hawthorne Effect was later understood to be due to the very selection of a group of human guinea pigs who regarded themselves as special because they had been selected for the experiment and formed into a special group that worked in a different part of the factory.

It was the sense of specialness and the attention they were receiving that was the main motivation to work harder for the Hawthorne guinea pigs, not better or worse working conditions.

[7]Huczynski, A. and Buchanan, D. (1985) *Organizational Behaviour: An Introductory Text*. Hemel Hempstead: Prentice Hall.

Jump 70 years

Let us now jump forward some 70 years, to a time just before the ICT explosion of the mid 1990s, and explore the ethos of people management that had emerged by this time. In the ever-expanding economic climate of the post-Second World War years the ideas of Taylorism and Fordism had been the prevailing ethos of industrial organization. As we have seen, the thinking was that people were employed to do a job exactly the way their managers required it to be done and were not considered capable of anything else. The overriding management style was still Taylorist (as defined by Douglas McGregor[8] in 1960 in what he termed 'Theory X'), i.e. that people are basically lazy and need to be driven and that they will, therefore, dislike work and require high levels of control, discipline and direction in the workplace in order to get them to carry out their duties. Managers were deemed to know best and although this was evidently not always the case, the constant expansion of markets, both domestic and export, covered up any deficiencies in their abilities.

The onset, however, during that period, of general long-term recession in the developed world in the 1970s (given impetus by the Arab oil embargo on the US and Europe that brought an abrupt end to the era of cheap oil and the consequent rise of hyper-inflation) caused companies to cut back on pay and to downsize to meet reducing demand. This in turn revealed the flaws in the prevailing management system. The result was a return to the resentments of the past.

An increasing antagonism between worker and management emerged in the 1970s and the old, deep rooted capital-vs.-labour divisions sown in the Industrial Revolution reared up with a vengeance.

In the post-Second World War era, Trade unions had steadily become more powerful and now they were flexing their muscles over managements. Production lines were being sabotaged and stopped by spanners literally being thrown into the works, and shop-floor intimidation of

[8]McGregor, D.M. (1960) *The Human Side of Enterprise*. New York: Routledge.

workers not to be 'scabs' and go against the union, was widespread. The resulting industrial unrest and conflict between the trade unions and the managements of companies attracted the (mostly ineffective) attention of successive governments and this reached a climax in the late 1970s with the now infamous 'Winter of Discontent' in the UK.

The increasingly aggressive stance of the unions was constraining the ability of managers to manage to a point where there was little or no freedom to take strategic decisions in response to the rapid change in markets both at home and abroad and, after a decade or more of apparently insoluble strife, a Conservative government headed by Margaret Thatcher was elected on a mandate that included curbing the unions by strong legislation. Despite a few rearguard actions by some of the stronger unions, the government prevailed.

The miners strike of 1984–85 broken by the Thatcher government was a defining moment. A new awareness emerged of the 'right to manage' by those in charge of companies emerged.

Things had changed, however, not only in the attitude of managers, but also in that of the workers. A new spirit of cooperation appeared, spurred on by the example set by the newly arriving Japanese companies who were starting to invest heavily in the UK, probably as a result of this newly created political climate (interestingly, certain trade unions were instrumental in espousing the new thinking).[9] Goss[10] sums this up perfectly when he says:

[9]Ron Todd of the TGWU in December 1986, in announcing a recruitment drive aimed specifically at temporary workers whom the TGWU saw as being an increasing and worrying trend, announced, 'The nature of the labour force has been changing dramatically and will continue to do so. We cannot afford to be tied to the employment patterns of yesteryear. It is our intention to take the initiative and shape events, not to sit back and let them happen.' (Reported in Wickens, P., 1987, *The Road to Nissan: Flexibility, Quality, Teamwork*. London: Macmillan, p. 60.)

[10]Goss, D. (1994) *Principles of Human Resource Management*. New York: Routledge, p. 1.

'The development of HRM [Human Resource Management] as a body of management thought in the 1980s can be linked to a conjunction of socio-economic factors – in particular, changes in international competition, the restructuring of industrial sectors and organizations, and the rise of a renewed confidence in the power of managers to manage.'

The Japanese were showing the way to the future in their clearly articulated and practised concept of product differentiation through Total Quality. This was based on the work of Deming and Juran in the USA, whose ideas they had completely absorbed. Total Quality Management, or TQM as it came to be popularly known, requires high workforce motivation and involvement to get the product 'right first time' and HRM with its emphasis on teamwork was already a highly developed Japanese management practice designed to support this aim.

In the vanguard of this benign invasion in the UK was Nissan Motor Manufacturing UK whose human resource strategy of 'Flexibility, Quality, Teamwork' is concisely articulated by Peter Wickens,[11] their Director of Personnel, in the title of his book *The Road To Nissan* published in 1987.

New approach to management

This new approach to the management of people for better results, especially in the use of worker teams, was the practical culmination of many years of academic research into the motivation of people in the workplace dating back as far as the 1920s, to Parker-Follett, Gilbreth and Mayo, who were seminal influencers of the human relations school of management. This work led to the birth of the 'behavioural science movement' whose leading members and their work in the 1950s and 1960s is summarized by Armstrong and Long,[12] as follows:

[11] Wickens, P. (1987) *The Road to Nissan: Flexibility, Quality, Teamwork*. London: Macmillan.
[12] Armstrong, M. and Long, P. (1994) *The Reality of Strategic H.R.M.* London: Institute of Personnel Development, p. 20.

- Maslow (1954), whose hierarchy of human needs placed self-actualization at the top of the pyramid.
- Likert (1966), who developed his integrating principle of supporting relationships. This stated that organization members should, in the light of their values and expectations, view their work as supportive and as contributing to the building and maintenance of their sense of personal worth and importance.
- Argyris (1957), who believed that organization design should plan for integration and involvement and that individuals should feel that they have a high degree of control over setting their goals and over the paths defining those goals.[13]
- Herzberg (1957), who advocated job enrichment as a means of improving organizational effectiveness.

Herzberg, in particular understood the drivers of motivation in the workplace. It is he who observed what he called 'hygiene factors', such as pay and benefits, company policy and administration, working conditions, supervision, status, job security, etc., had a limit to their motivational effect and that there were higher factors such as relationships with co-workers, achievement, recognition, personal growth, responsibility and interest in the work itself, which often resulted in increased performance.

The most important of Herzberg's findings was that, whilst the absence of hygiene factors could be a serious demotivator, they had limited power to motivate beyond a certain level. Money, in particular, had a limit. Paying people more didn't necessarily mean they would produce better results.

A pivotal moment came in 1989 when Konosuke Matsushita, Japanese industrialist and founder of Matsuhita Electric with brands such as Panasonic and Technics, famously said: 'Business is people'. In his address to a conference of business leaders he also said:

[13]In other words, 'empowerment' – the discovery of the 1990s – although it was not called that in 1957.

'We are going to win and the industrial West is going to lose out: there's nothing much you can do about it, because the reasons for your failure are within yourselves. Your firms are built on the Taylor model; even worse, so are your heads. With your bosses doing the thinking while the workers wield the screwdrivers, you're convinced deep down that this is the right way to run a business. For you, the essence of management is getting the ideas out of the heads of bosses and into the hands of labour. We are beyond the Taylor model. Business, we know, is now so complex and difficult, the survival of firms so hazardous in an environment increasingly unpredictable, competitive, and fraught with danger that their continued existence depends on the day-to-day mobilization of every ounce of intelligence.'

What was behind what Matsushita was saying is the idea that people should be treated as human beings in the workplace in a way that recognizes that they have abilities, hopes and aspirations beyond those required for the job in hand; that they have a contribution to make to the way an organization should be run for improved efficiency; and that they have a basic need for an increased quality of working life.

In the immediate post-Second World War period, reconstruction of the Japanese economy produced an economic miracle. This was in no small part due to the fact that they started again from a clean sheet. The ways of the past had been swept away in national defeat and indignity, and this allowed a complete rethink about how to organize and manage for success. In particular, western capitalism, with its sole emphasis on shareholder value creation, was tempered by the adoption of the idea of stakeholder companies where not only the shareholders, but also the employees, customers and even wider society were given emphasis. The idea that companies should be for the overall benefit of the nation prevailed and the idea of 'national service through industry' came to the fore. This idea, the first of seven spiritual values of the Matsushita Electric,[14] underpinned

[14]Company philosophy at Matsushita Electric Company. Given as Exhibit 5.1 in Morgan, G. (1986) *Images of Organization*. London: Sage, p. 115. Source reference: Pascale and Athos (1981: 75–76, 73) and reprinted in Morgan by permission.

Matsushita's earlier company that eventually became the international giant, Panasonic.

Here we see the outcome of several decades of emerging understanding about the management of people for maximum output. McGregor's (ibid.) 'Theory Y' – that work is as natural as play; that people like to work and to feel useful and that they will, if given the opportunity, become involved with their work and develop a high sense of responsibility and commitment – underpins this new thinking. Gone was the controlling, spirit-sapping Scientific Management of Taylor and replacing it was a more human and humane approach to employees, their motivations and their untapped potential; especially when motivated by team spirit.

Modern human resource management theory was finally being put into action in the intelligent management of people, designed to improve their output through gaining their cooperation.

The old paradigm of authoritative, coercive management of personnel was finally overturned and a new one had emerged for the benefit of everyone – or so we believed, until the advent of the technological era.

4

M any people believe our economy is weak because we don't make things anymore, but this is not strictly true. We pay our way by selling our inventiveness, our ideas, especially abroad. The factories, the ordinary production lines churning out endless numbers of assembled product may have moved abroad, but in many cases, our manufacturing skill remains with us, and we still gain from that economically.

Although we don't necessarily sell large volumes of manufactured product abroad, we still gain enormous value-added by selling our intellectual property. When other countries churn out tangible products, such as electronics from the Far East, in true mass production redolent of the early 20th century, or raw materials, such as oil and gas from the Middle East, or agricultural produce from Spain for example, our industries sell brainpower, such as leading-edge pharmaceuticals and technology, or film-making.

In the period after the end of the Second World War, it is true that manufacturing as a proportion of Britain's economic activity declined (from around 46% in the 1950s, to just 12% today), and services of one kind or another increased to around 78%. It is equally true that our manufactured goods are approaching 30% more than they were a few decades ago, simply because of another British skill: manufacturing technology.

Britain is constantly inventing even more efficient ways of making highly complex things, and that shows through in massively increased efficiency, which leads to competitive prices.

We even, now, have what is being called 'manu-services'.[1] These are areas of our industry that have moved beyond simply making things: where what we make is combined into packages that deliver solutions rather than simply something in a box.

Rolls-Royce's aero-engine facility constantly monitors between eight and ten thousand in-service jet engines on a 24/7/365 basis. Using satellite telemetry, the vital operating parameters of engines fitted to customers' aircraft are continuously streamed back to the company's UK base and monitored using computers that flag up any variance in performance, such as overheating in individual components, or unusual vibrations. There, a team of engineers, each of whom is qualified to assess the implications, liaises with its engineering and maintenance counterparts in the airline, advising on maintenance, repair or parts replacement, often well in advance of any failure. Apart from the obvious safety implications, the ability to plan interventions in advance allows the minimization of engine (and therefore, 'plane) downtime, which has equally obvious benefits to the airline in keeping to its schedules, and in turn, to the passenger.

In the race for advancement, competitive advantage lies in being first, in innovating; and Britain is good at that

Professor Keith Baddely[2] of the Open University Business School describes what happened in the second half of the 20th century as a 'hinge in history': a period that saw the demise of the industrial age and the birth of the new technological era. This is how he sums it up:

> 'The years since the Second World War have seen the fabric of Britain disintegrate and with it the widespread emergence of urban decay. In its place, on greenfield sites and science parks, new knowledge-based businesses have arisen: part of a counter-

[1]Sissons. A. (2011) More than making things: A new future for manufacturing in a service-economy. *The Work Foundation, a wholly-owned subsidiary of Lancaster University*, London, UK.
[2]'Intellectual Capital: The New Wealth of Nations', 1996 RSA Lecture.

revolution with effects potentially far greater than the Industrial Revolution itself . . . The "Knowledge Revolution", born of the computer age and global digital communication, creates a bridge with earlier knowledge-based societies and heralds a new era based on the value of intellectual capital: the knowledge that people possess, and the wealth that this creates.'

Many of our companies, such as GlaxoSmithKline, illustrate the transformation. In the 1930s, Glaxo made baby food, but the Second World War, when the discovery of penicillin became a major way of combating disease from injury, changed its philosophy. The British government asked companies to find a way of making this wonder drug in bulk and this prompted GSK as it is now known to invest heavily in research and development.

When the National Health Service was founded in 1948, GSK became a major pharmaceutical supplier, and in the post-war era it never looked back. Today it is the fourth largest pharmaceutical company in the world, and one of Britain's biggest spenders on R&D. GSK reflects our economy as a whole.

We have moved along the value chain from the physical manufacturing of goods to manufacturing innovation.

Other advanced nations have done that too. So-called 'teardown' analyses of Apple's iPod Nano reveal that each unit costs only one-third of its retail price and the bulk of that it taken up with the myriad of components used in it. Of the remaining two-thirds, approximately one-third goes to the retailer (many stores are owned by Apple of course), and Foxconn in China gets less than $5 for the final assembly. The balance to Apple, broadly speaking, is the value of creativity and branding.

Here in the UK, we have one of Apple's major suppliers. ARM Holdings, situated in 'Silicon Fen', that cluster of some 1400 high-technology companies that trade from a variety of business parks in and around Cambridge that collectively employs over 40,000 people. ARM is a major international revenue earner. Starting in the 1980s designing chips for microcomputers, the company has positioned itself securely in the centre of one of the world's fastest growing industries. Nokia was the first to adopt ARM technology, then Apple and, since then, many others have come to the company for its cutting-edge ability to design the complex circuits that make microprocessors work.

If you look on almost any microchip, you will see ARM's three-letter brand stamped somewhere. ARM receives a licence fee from every chip manufacturer that uses its designs, wherever they are in the world. A few cents earned from every one of 6 billion chips made worldwide amounts to a lot of money.

As we become more affluent, so we want more sophisticated products. As our basic needs are fulfilled, we worry less about quantity and functionality, and care more about the aesthetics of the products we buy, and what we buy becomes driven by the meaning that ownership of the product gives us. We buy products that appeal, that add colour to our lives: that give us identity. Marketing, packaging, branding and advertising therefore become even more important in this process, and there is a massive amount of economic value in these activities. British advertising and branding specialists are very good at turning standard commodities into something special.

Rowntree is one of our best brand inventors. In 1988 it was bought out by Nestlé after a vicious takeover battle between that company and Suchard. The successful bidder paid in excess of £4.5 billion when Rowntree's asset value (its manufacturing plant and machinery, etc.) was only worth around half a billion. In the balance lay the value of its brands such as Kit Kat, Smarties, Aero and Black Magic. The money paid for these brands came directly back into the UK economy and Britain still benefits from worldwide sales of these products. Kit Kats, for example, are still made in York. There is good logic in Britain's specialization in high-end value. Britain was the first country in the world to industrialize, but other countries caught up. At one time we were the workshop of the world, but others became just as good at making things and started to copy us, so we simply became more inventive to stay ahead of the game. This is a normal part of the evolution of nations. As economies generate the resources to spend on research and education, they become more advanced. It is called progress.

A difficult birth

Professor Baddely observes, however, that the transition, the birth of the new era, has not been without a struggle. The industrial mindset has been hard to change, and that has slowed us down. The old industrial paradigm was hard fought for, especially by the Labour left who quite naturally (because they essentially represented industrial workers from whom their power derived), sought to stem the tide using their political power.

The two governments of the 1960s under Labour's Harold Wilson swung hard towards the left of politics. In their first period in office after more than 13 years, Labour introduced a tax on capital gains (CGT) for the first time ever in November 1964. They also introduced swingeing increases in income tax aimed at the better off, and this was added to by a tax on unearned income. Industrial tension was still high, however.

Despite Wilson's famous association with trade union leaders and late night meetings with them over: 'beer and sandwiches' at 10 Downing Street, London, his attempts to control prices and incomes still did nothing to calm the seething unrest. Even shortly after he was elected in 1966, there was an extremely damaging seamen's strike that lasted for six weeks, crippling the nation's economy.

When Conservative leader Edward Heath challenged Wilson in that year, he lost. Four years later he won, and immediately went to work to try and redress not only the economic situation, but the political balance. In 1971 he introduced the Industrial Relations Act that curbed union practices by limiting wildcat strikes, and he established a National Industrial Relations Court empowered to grant injunctions to prevent strikes that were injurious to the economy.

Heath also introduced a prices and incomes policy that angered the unions to such an extent that he was forced to adopt a national three-day working week to conserve electricity when the miners went on strike and cut off supplies. Using the slogan 'Who Governs Britain?', Heath called a general election in February 1974, but that resulted in a hung parliament and, unable to broker a deal with the third party, the Liberals, he had no choice but to concede defeat to Harold Wilson who took over again as Prime Minister, securing a narrow majority at another General Election just months later.

Britain's woes were not over, however. At this crucial time, the Organization of Arab Oil Producing Countries, who were angered at the West's resupply effort of Israel during and after the Yom Kippur War of 1973, imposed an oil embargo against America and Europe. This resulted in massive hikes in the cost of crude oil and inflation was sent spiralling.

The UK economy, that had seen remarkable growth in the post-war era, went into free-fall in the 1970s. Tensions rose in British industry and the old Capital -vs.- Labour antagonisms emerged with a vengeance.

Even under the Labour government of James Callaghan matters weren't resolved. He attempted to control inflation rates (in excess of 30% at the time) by introducing pay freezes in the public sector as an example to private employers to do the same, but widespread strikes, particularly amongst public sector workers, ensued and matters came to a head in 1978–79 in the infamous 'Winter of Discontent', which brought about the fall of Callaghan and his Labour government, and the election of Margaret Thatcher who had secured leadership of the Conservatives five years earlier.

Mrs Thatcher declared herself determined to reverse the precipitous national decline. She deregulated economic policy, created flexibility in labour markets and sold or closed down state-owned companies. However, union reform was the centrepiece of her policy platform. She introduced secret ballots for strikes (hitherto, votes had been taken at mass union meetings on a show of hands: a system vulnerable to peer pressure to vote with the crowd); she ended the closed shop where everyone in the workplace had to be a member of the union that represented that particular industry, and she introduced legislation to ban secondary picketing (joining other workers' disputes as a show of solidarity).

In particular, she accelerated the process of decline in the traditional industries such as coal mining, and the miner's strike of 1984–85 in which her government stood firm and prevailed was the defining moment. The traditional pride of the working class succumbed to the inevitable, and a new era began. A new political climate emerged in which inward investment to Britain accelerated, and the move to the 'brave new world' of an economy based on knowledge and technology began. As she later put it:

> 'So, as we have redundancies in the declining industries, so we are getting new jobs in the new industries, and new jobs in some of the service industries; and they are being created by our dynamic economy...let us not belittle our achievements.'

The new innovative industries given birth at this time have created new jobs and have replaced those of the industrial era. Britain still uses that very special talent to invent that was its hallmark in the days of the Industrial Revolution when it led the world, and now we sell that talent rather than use it to make things ourselves. However, this strategy hasn't been enough completely to offset the economic effect of the decline of industry and the passing of our industrial era.

As predicted 25 years ago, the British economy has changed. Yes, Britain can no longer be called a manufacturing economy, but instead of making things for money, we do things instead.

Our old industries have gone and we have proved ourselves able to respond by focusing on high value-adding parts of the supply chain. British designers are versatile. They are excellent at problem solving, and as the world changes, they are eminently capable of adapting to new problems that are in search of solutions. We remain in the top division of science and creativity and that will continue to be a major source of our competitive edge in the world. It will continue to earn us international revenues but we can never be entirely reliant on our intellectual capital alone. By strategically shifting our place in the value chain, we have substantially offset the effect of our enforced move out of manufacturing. However, not all of us can wear lab coats, or be power dressers in advertising agencies. We don't need just to be clever, we need to be good at the other major part of our strategic shift: our service industries, where three quarters of us work.

The service economy

Nevertheless, it is true that, today, eight out of ten of us work in service industries of one kind or another and the majority of our wealth is being generated by knowledge/service. Although the 1980s was the last time Britain's balance of physical exports to imports was equal, we now export about £160 billion of our expertise, and that goes a long way to replacing the deficit in the balance of exported goods to imported ones.

UK services come in all shapes and sizes. Our construction expertise is in demand worldwide. British architects and civil engineers are responsible for enormous construction projects in the Middle East amounting to £2 billion per year recently, and in many other places they are actively designing, managing, advising, consulting clients who use local labour to do the manual work.

As Evan Davis,[3] a British economist, journalist and presenter for BBC TV, puts it, 'Services are everything you can't put in a box, but it doesn't mean they are not valuable'.

Another way to look at it is, a service adds value to you but doesn't add to your assets. Domestically, one of our main service industries is higher education. Currently, British universities teach 1.96 million stu-

---

[3] *Made in Britain*, BBC TV.

dents a year (a quarter of a million of whom are foreign nationals who pay top dollar for their courses – British universities are the most sought-after institutions after those of the US and foreign students are worth some £5 billion of foreign exchange). These act as hubs for other services, such as landlords offering rented property to students (these in turn of course use local services such as estate agents, surveyors, plumbers, carpet fitters, decorators, etc.).

More specifically, the City of London, the so-called 'square mile', is the financial capital of the world. It has an unrivalled ability to make money, not by risky trading, but by providing the infrastructure and the services that allow trading to take place. The City of London has earned more for Britain in export revenues than the whole of Wales, or Northern Ireland, or the north-east of England put together, and much of this is by offering services to people who take the risks. A small percentage made on a very large number of transactions amounts to a very large number in itself – and it is steady business, relatively free of risk.

Then there is London, a service-industry powerhouse in itself that not only attracts tourists, but businessmen and women who choose it as a place to do business because it lies conveniently between America and Europe, and the East. They stay in hotels, buy meals, hire cars, and many of the mega-wealthy buy property that continues to change hands many times providing business for estate agents, household service firms, interior designers, architects and all the things properties need for their upkeep and maintenance.

Outside these services hotspots, Britain is peppered with a wide diversity of service offerings: pure services such as professional firms of lawyers, accountants, surveyors, architects, etc., whose product is simply expertise; hybrid services such as restaurants, web designers, painters and decorators, plumbers, etc., that provide a tangible product but with a heavy element of personal attention as part of the overall package; and there is a vast array of organizations of all kinds, commercial, public and third sector (including social enterprises as well as charities) such as bus companies, train companies, local authorities, quangos and most notably our National Health Service that exist solely to deliver what may be an intangible product separate from the service delivery.

Perhaps the most appropriate definition of a service provider comes from the Equality and Human Rights Commission, who for the purposes of their legislative framework offer the following list as being service providers:

- Advice agencies
- Charities and voluntary organizations
- Churches or other places of worship
- Courts
- Emergency services
- Employment agencies
- Housing Associations, estate agents and private landlords
- Financial services providers such as investment companies, banks and building societies
- Accountants
- Hospitals and clinics
- Hotels, guest houses and hostels
- Law firms
- Libraries and museums
- Mail, telephone or online retailers
- Parks and other public spaces
- Petrol stations
- Post offices
- Property developers and management agencies
- Public utilities (such as gas, electricity and water suppliers)
- Pubs and restaurants
- Railway stations, bus stations and airports
- Rented business premises
- Services provided by local councils, government departments and agencies
- Shops and market stalls
- Some types of clubs
- Sports and leisure facilities
- Telecommunications and broadcasting services
- Theatres and cinemas

They also give a useful definition of a service provider as follows:

'A service provider is any organization that provides goods, facilities or services to the public, whether paid for or free, no matter how large or small the organization is.'

The term 'service' embraces a wide range, but one thing is common to all: the need for interaction with consumers who may or may not be the customer as well; and that is where we are signally lacking in Service-Ability.

Unlike our exemplary manufacturing and design industries, in our core service industries, where service quality is so much needed, we are lamentably bad.

This is where our reputation for outstanding performance in innovation and sheer cleverness is tarnished: where our industrial history, our social history and the culture of the British come together in a perfect storm of mediocrity that pulls us down, and makes us the laughing stock of the world; where our comics and social commentators such as those behind the 'Little Britain' television series, can become successful by showing us with their acid observation, how ridiculously unprofessional we are, in that most vital part of our economic activity-giving service.

Today, at best we now service customers rather than give service.

Commercially dangerous

These are times when customer service needs to be exemplary but, paradoxically, good service is a rapidly vanishing phenomenon. Where it exists, it often falls far short of even acceptable standards and this is commercially dangerous. People today are increasingly discerning, demanding and much less tolerant of bad treatment. They are also better informed, better connected and more powerful than ever before.

Organizations are increasingly being forced to have their customer service quality mediated in public through social media such as Twitter and Facebook, as Leah Milner[4] observed in *The Times* on 29 January 2011:

> 'Customers who air their grievances on the social networking site appear to be getting a much prompter response than usual. Frustrated customers are hanging up on premium-rate customer service helplines and turning to Twitter as their first port of call when making complaints – with impressive results. A growing number of insurers, telephone and broadband providers, and other retail names are monitoring the social networking site for all mentions of their brand, making it an ideal forum for unhappy customers to get their voices heard . . . Times Money has heard from many consumers who have vented their frustration on the Twitter website after failing to get their problems resolved through other channels. Companies often rush to engage with customers to stem the negative feedback and put the issue right, sometimes with the offer of a refund or freebie as a sweetener.'

Even in that paragon of good service, the USA, standards are slipping, as witness the tale of United Airlines and Dave Carroll quoted in our introduction. Carroll's plaintive message 'United Breaks Guitars'[5] has now had 12.3 million hits and the cost to United's reputation must be incalculable.

The effect of technology

Why should this be? Why is poor or indifferent treatment of customers so widespread? Why, with a few notable exceptions, are interactions between organizations and their customers becoming so standardized

---

[4]'Should you be using Twitter to complain about poor service?' http://www.thetimes.co.uk/tto/money/consumeraffairs/article2892126.ece
[5]http://www.youtube.com/watch?v=5YGc4zOqozo

and characterized by indifference? There are many reasons for this: historical, generational, demographic, cultural and shifts in society's attitudes. However, one of the major reasons is the advent of technology.

Just as in the Industrial Revolution, that last major socio-economic-technical upheaval of the 18th and 19th centuries, the technological revolution of the late 20th century has reached a stage of consolidation where its applications are penetrating every aspect of our lives, altering them and affecting them in ways we could hardly have imagined only 20 years ago.

One of the principal effects of technology is to deprive us of the very thing this new era demands: relationship, not just connection.

In their gold-rush fervour to implement the benefits of computerization, organizations of all types are failing to realize that in using technology to mediate their relationship with the outside world, they are negating the human nature of the transaction with the customer. Customers are incorrectly being forced to engage with mechanical business processes: the push-button phone systems that offer the caller a labyrinth of pre-recorded options, many of them seeking to redirect the call to a list of frequently asked questions (FAQs) on a website or pre-recorded messages with false voice inflexions do nothing to recognize the customer's need for personal attention.

On the other side of this increasing technological chasm, the personality of the employee is also becoming suppressed by cold technology, inappropriately used. The systemized, script-driven responses of 'customer service' employees, that force both them and customers into predefined patterns of behaviour that are unnatural and deny the expression of the individual; the target-driven time allowances for customer interactions, all work progressively to reduce what should be a human interaction to a mechanical process and represent systemized depersonalization right at the point where the very thing that is most important in business – meaningful, human interaction with the customer – is lost.

The Industrial Revolution spawned organizations and management practices that depersonalized people, reducing them to components in a machine order. The technological revolution is doing that too. Whereas people once served the means of production housed in factories, they now serve computers: employees are becoming the servants of ICT. For all practical purposes they are machines sitting in front of machines. Just another part of the mechanism, responding to and acting upon expert systems, interpreting them to the outside world, following pre-programmed behaviours without the human freedom to decide things for themselves, or do things in their own way, and relaying data not meaningful information in their interactions with customers.

How many of us have witnessed the 'if-it-isn't-on-the-screen-it-doesn't-exist' syndrome when booking a holiday or trying to get a public utility to deal with an account error? How many of us have been the victim of expert systems put on computers that make broad-stroke decisions on credit worthiness, insurance risk and a myriad of other things, yet have been left with the distinct feeling that a decently trained, experienced and motivated human with an infinitely greater ability to make fine judgements in individual cases could have made better choices; choices that would be in the interests of the business, let alone the customer?

How many of us, when lost in this technological snarl, have longed for the restoration of humanness and personalized service: a relationship with a human being in which we can transact in a human way?

British disease

The ICT explosion has undoubtedly been a factor in changing our service mentality for the worse, but it is not the only factor militating against good service in Britain. There is another constraint that goes deep into the national psyche.

In America they thank you for your custom and say 'Have a nice day!' – and they mean it! This is because they have a clear understanding that service is what makes money and they are happy to give it. In Britain, it is different.

In Britain, service is seen to be servile. People in organizations often seem to regard themselves demeaned by having to give service – they resent it – and this is probably due to a combination of a historical British issue and our national temperament.

Napoleon Bonaparte is once said to have disparagingly described England as 'A nation of shopkeepers' indicating the she was unfit for war against France, but this idea seems also to embody something of a lack of imagination that constantly transfers itself into our business world: the British are inherently transactional in their approach to business; and systems and processes are often used as a surrogate for personality. Deep down, well beneath the social skin, Britons don't really do service because they really don't do servant-hood.

Unlike many other countries, particularly those with a Confucian culture like Japan and China, where there is an acceptance of unequal social power, ranks in society and different responsibilities that go with rank, the British have an intensely egalitarian spirit. The words from Rule Britannia, that unofficial national anthem (at least of England), with its defiant stanza '. . . Britons never, never, never shall be slaves', sums this up perfectly. These stirring words, always sung with such fervour at the Last Night of the Proms in the Royal Albert Hall in London speak of far more than just a nationalistic pride – they articulate a deep national characteristic of individualism and equality. The British consider themselves the equal of anybody (and arrogantly, it has to be said, the superior of many).

In business the attitude that the supplier is the equal of the supplied is why our business interactions are so transactional.

We also have a powerful heritage to contend with that has left us with another negative customer-service legacy. Notwithstanding the individualistic common nature, Britain has always struggled with class-conscious tensions and social power-broking. Even just a hundred years ago service meant to be 'in service', which meant that you were lower class and reliant on the largesse (and whim) of the upper classes who treated their servants as being of low status, giving them little more than an institutionalized contempt. This idea doesn't sit comfortably with the British temperament and as our service economy progresses, it is becoming even more an issue, not less.

The loss of pride in the artisan that we saw in pre-industrialization era is another problem. As the Industrial Revolution gathered pace, the social power of the traditional land-owning aristocracy gave way to a new industrial–commercial oligarchy: the entrepreneur–industrialist, and the businessman; new dimensions were added to the status of people in society. This was the time of the emergence of the middle classes who, in their social mobility and increased wealth, often emulated the aristocracy in their superior, distant, aloof, unfriendly approach to the craft worker.

The 'tradesman', with his traditional pride in the job and hard-learned skill, was now considered lower in the social order and, therefore, considered obliged to offer deference and respect.

Industrialization also brought us the concept of the 'working man': the industrial worker operating under division of labour and mass production whose 'working class' status was widely accepted to be of an even lower order. In a sense, industrial workers became the new feudal servants to industrialists who rarely considered even the welfare, let alone the well-being, of their employees; and who were seen as getting rich on the sweat of the workers' labour. In response, the workers formed trade unions to give them a collective voice and bargaining power to redress the power balance, and the well-known capital-vs.-labour division took root. This inherent tension remains with us, and it undoubtedly contributes to a lack of commitment to organizations and corporate objectives.

The effect of all this is the general belief that serving people is demeaning, and there is little or no pride in the job, or the organization.

Employers treat service-sector employees with indifference, often paying them lowest rates and working them hard, with the result that they become resentful or even hostile to customers.

This clashes with customers' expectations that are rooted in middle-class superiority that demands a servile approach, and there is little wonder that the whole situation in such a mess.

Demographics

Demographics have changed as well. In 2006 the first of the 'Baby Boomers', that generation of children born in the decade or so after the end of the Second World War, reached the age of 60. They changed the world in their youth and they will continue to do so in their old age. This is an innovating generation that all its life has reinvented and challenged existing ways of doing things. It is a wealthy generation, being the first in history to inherit property from its parents on a widespread basis. It is also a tech-savvy generation that, unlike its parents, uses the internet, which it invented, using the personal computer, which it also invented, with ease.

The Baby Boomers see the internet as a part of everyday life. Most of them are now using it every day they are comfortable buying online and they have massive spending power to play with and there is nothing to suggest that as they get old these habits will change.

They are a force to be reckoned with because the Boomers are a demanding generation who know what they like and what they don't like. The cheapest is not the best for the baby boomers, and they expect good service.

At the other end of the age spectrum we have the emergence of Generation Y who, in many respects, display similar characteristics to the Boomers. Born after 1980, this generation is now entering the workforce in a big way and it is bringing with it a different set of expectations and skills, not least a second-nature facility with technology. Gen Y grew up sitting in their bedrooms in front of games computers for hours on end. Like the Boomers, they are challenging existing paradigms. For them, existing ways of doing things have little meaning, especially in their view of organization for business. Like the Boomers, Gen Y people want freedom in everything they do, but unlike their forebears, they are not so bound with the sense of societal structure which that previous generation inherited. They love to customize and personalize and, again much like the Boomers were in their youth, they are into collaboration and relationships.

The unique characteristic of Gen Y is a deep-seated need for speed.[6]

This is the Facebook generation and it is the driving force behind the development of new organizations like Google that operate in a different way to traditional organizations. Gen Y is reinventing the way we do things: it is even prepared to work for nothing, just for the intrinsic reward of being able to do it, as witness the rise of Linux. Gen Y is seriously techie and it is applying computer software solutions to everything it comes across. This is bringing enormous benefits to our lives, but all in the garden is not roses. These people are now staffing the callcentres and bringing with them their own culture and way of connecting that is conditioned by the technology with which they grew up. Gen Y doesn't see slavery to the machine as a problem.

Lower pay/inequality

Wages of service workers (particularly the young) outside the commercial hot-spots have been held low as a result of the use of computer technology. Whereas service sector jobs in the capital and other commercial hot-spots may attract salaries of £50,000, there are many more in the provinces that attract just £15,000. Regional services cannot get into the big league.

[6]Tapscott, D. (2009) *Grown up Digital*, New York: McGraw Hill.

There is a pronounced weakness in regional service economies and too often regional service jobs are characterized by over-work, low pay, poor conditions of employment and poor working conditions.

Contrast this with the massive increase in the gradient between the average pay of the ordinary worker, and that of senior executives. According to Bill Seddon,[7] chief executive of the Methodist Central Finance Board, in the 1970s chief executives were being paid around ten times the average salary of their workers; today it is of the order of 100 times. However, this masks some striking individual variations. For example, Sir Terry Leahy is a former CEO of Tesco Plc, had a salary ratio of 550 : 1, whilst, Willie Walsh, the CEO of British Airways, was paid to a ratio of 15 : 1.[8] Ajay Kapur the former strategist to Citigroup, argues that the economies of the USA, Canada and the UK have become 'Plutonomies' where growth is powered by, and largely consumed by, the wealthy few, whilst the averagely paid worker in whatever industry or service has to work for wages that barely cover living expenses.

Inequality, the ratio of the top 20% of earners' average income to that of the bottom 20%, has almost doubled in Britain since 1980 and is now at over seven times. In America it is almost nine times. Such steep social gradients are known to be correlated with low levels of trust in society, as well as increased levels of general anxiety, a general lower-ing of people's self-esteem and sense of security, lowering of pride, increasing shame, an increased sense of status and a move from a sense of community to mass society.[9] All of these things introduce stress into people's lives, which inevitably affects personal relationships and inter-relations with others. It is hardly surprising, then, that motivation and

[7]*Church Times* (2010) Report recommends tighter formula for executive pay. *Church Times*, 19 March.
[8]'A just wage and executive salaries'. Zenit News Agency, 25 April 2010. Permalink: http://www.zenit.org/article-29029?l=english
[9]Wilkinson, R. and Pickett, K. (2010) *The Spirit Level: Why Equality is Better for Everyone*. London: Penguin.

general belief in giving the best service to the customer is at an all-time low.

Employment 'contract'

Not only has the social contract changed, but the employment contract has too; at least the psychological part. There has been a rapid increase in free-agency[10] – knowledge workers who possess their own means of production, i.e. a laptop and internet connection are now working in significant numbers, in loosely affiliated networks of flexible workers, on flexible supply contracts and in portfolio careers. Often they are clustered around larger organizations that retain only an essential core of jobs and people in the 'inverted doughnut' structure described years ago by Charles Handy.[11] This is happening both in commerce and the public sector, and it signals a change from the traditional psychological contract, whereby an employer offered security in return for loyalty from the employee and a wage or salary was the consideration. Nowadays, organizations offer opportunities in return for skills on a purely transactional basis, using either short-term contracts or fee-based considerations.

Loyalty by the employee has been replaced by disengagement, and security from the employer by distance.

Opportunity

The personality of the individual employee is undoubtedly becoming suppressed by cold technology, inappropriately used. This not only leads to an improper depersonalization of the individual, but to a deperson-

[10]Pink, D. (2001) *Free Agent Nation: The Future of Working for Yourself*. New York: Warner Business.
[11]Handy, C. (1994) *The Age of Paradox*. Boston, MA: Harvard Business School Press.

alization of that most crucial of areas, the interface with the customer. Just as in the Industrial Revolution, technology is turning employees into automata, dominated by the rigidity of systems driven by programmed machines; serving as extensions of the computer rather than as individuals.

If you turn people into impersonal organizational machines, you cannot avoid them coming to regard customers in the same way. The effect of technological depersonalization is passed on in a viral way and, if left unchecked, this culture, as with all so-called 'Dark-Side' cultures (those that emerge spontaneously within organizations as a result of the corruption of accepted values and which are not necessarily driven by management or corporate ethos), becomes embedded as '. . . the way we do things here', and the customer relationship, that fulcrum around which everything balances, gets corrupted. Far from being a sustainable cost advantage, this is a major threat to business profitability and long-term business success.

The time-honoured business axiom that 'people do business with people' is undoubtedly being dangerously ignored as we move into the 21st century. This is not just a nostalgic plea for bygone times, it is the articulation of a serious issue that will become increasingly important as we move further into the new millennium. Customer focus and care are undoubtedly being sacrificed in favour of cost savings, increased control and a form of efficiency that the new technology brings, and this will become worse as companies and organizations in all sectors, both large and small, become even more sold on what ICT can offer them in cost savings.

Organizations need to use the technology, certainly, but they need to find ways of using it more intelligently, putting it behind customer-facing employees as a facilitator, not between them and the customer as a barrier. If they don't, they will lose out in the long run because an opportunity is opening up for those organizations whose strength lies restoring the personal touch: that ever so important, personalized, problem-solving capability. That is the reality of business today and it is the single most important issue facing UK organizations.

It doesn't matter what field of business or sector they are in, organizations that give a high level of personal attention to their customers will win out over those that treat their customers as pawns in their machines: seeing them as only there to be serviced, not served. Customer focus, and a genuinely personal approach to customers in a climate where there is increasingly a widespread lack of it, will be the key differentiator for competitive advantage in the next 20 years or so; it will stand out like a beacon in the storm.

5

Years ago, the story goes, when people travelled in Pullman railway sleeping cars, a passenger found a bed bug in his berth. He wrote a letter to George M. Pullman, president of Pullman's Palace Car Company, informing him of this unhappy fact. By return, he received the following:

> 'The company has never heard of such a thing and as a result of your experience, all the sleeping cars are being pulled off the line and fumigated. The Pullman's Palace Car Company is committed to providing its customers with the highest level of service, and it will spare no expense in meeting that goal. Thank you for writing and if you ever have a similar problem, or any problem, do not hesitate to write to me again.'

Enclosed with this letter, by accident, was the passenger's original letter to Pullman, across the bottom of which the president had written a note to his secretary: 'Send this S.O.B. the standard bedbug letter!'

It has to be said; many of our organizations treat customer complaints like this. They are fantastically internally focused with many customer-facing employees acting as though customers are an unwarranted intrusion into their daily affairs, and are clearly not aware of how serious an offence this really is. Even today, we see this process in action. Letter after letter being sent out from customer service departments of large organizations in response to a steady stream of complaints from customers, mostly about how the organization has treated them badly; and all of them written to a formula, i.e. acknowledge the complaint, show concern, validate the customer's anger, express sorrow, indicate a positive course of action within the company to prevent a future recurrence, leave the door open for future complaint – end of story. The letters are obviously template files on word processors, and that speaks volumes about the industrial nature of the process and the systemic insincerity behind the operation.

This is not customer service and it will do nothing to generate the customer loyalty that is at the heart of good customer service delivery.

Total customer satisfaction demands a relationship with the customer that must be genuine, otherwise people will spot its inauthenticity.

Porter's value chain

In 1985, Professor Michael Porter of Harvard University Business School published his world best-seller: *Competitive Advantage: Creating and Sustaining Superior Performance,*[1] a book on corporate strategy that became a world best-seller and standard reading on MBA course across the world. In it, he described what he called 'the value chain', an idea that offered a generic model for understanding the components of a business.

Porter's value chain, linked as it is with his thesis on corporate strategy, has become the industry standard of organizational diagnosis for management consultants and senior business executives ever since. Indeed, I have used it countless times as an organizational diagnostic tool and found it an invaluable framework for thinking and analysis. However, it is a diagnostic tool, not a framework for organizational design. The way

[1] Porter M. (1985) *Competitive Advantage: creating and sustaining superior performance.* New York: The Free Press; Simon and Shuster, Inc.

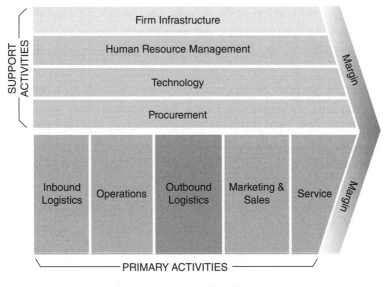

Porter's generic value chain

Professor Porter shows the value chain as being made of discrete units of activity has misled us to think that that is how they are in reality. They are not.

Service is not something you bolt on at the end of everything else in the value chain: neither is it only 'after-sales service' (very much the emphasis that Porter places on it).

Certainly after-sales service is what it says it is: after sales. It is an important component in the value offering to the customer and it cannot be neglected. It would be inconceivable that maintenance of product performance, spare part availability, repair, failure rectification would not be offered. That is the barrow-boy mentality, and no one would buy expensive product from a company on that basis.

After-sales service is a servicing operation designed to stand by product quality, and obviously it has to be the responsibility of some department in the organization. Even in a service context customers will have queries that need to be dealt with. Take a bank, for example: queries and issues from customers crop up from time to time in the course of the regular relationship the bank has with the customer; these need to be attended to.

However the point being made here is that, to see service only as 'after sales' – to see it as something that is done by a customer service department – is to cause organizations to neglect their service soul. This is where so many organizations go wrong, because they reduce the whole idea of customer service to a mechanized, analyzed, systemized thing that sucks the life out of its very nature. Politeness, focus, attention to detail and so on are important in these interactions, and that demands Service-Ability. Let us remind ourselves of Jan Carlzon's message:

> 'The people who work in the front line, who meet the customer in the market, they not only represent the company, no, they really are the company. Because that meeting when the customer stands face to face with a salesman, a check-in lady, your scanner attendant or what have you, that's when the company appears. That is the company. They are the moments of truth . . . There are no service instructions that can help because good service is just you and me, here and now'.

Those organizations that have customer service departments where people '. . . do customer service' are, frankly, completely and utterly missing the point.

Customer service is not a specialist activity, and it is carried out by everyone, at every point of interaction with the customer (and, incidentally, that includes internal customers too). Organizations that have a customer service department are almost certainly only servicing their customers, not serving them. (And many, particularly where the product is a pure service delivered by people, are probably functioning only as apologists for, and rectifiers of, bad service in the first place.)

True customer service, the sort practised by those companies who do it well and who add value not only to the customer, but to their shareholders/stakeholders, is built-in at the point of delivery, and it comes from an alignment of everyone in the organization toward the customer and his or her needs. It winds like a thread through all stages of the value-adding process, and it must be built-in at the point of production at all levels and at all stages.

Rather than our thinking about service delivery as being based on the joined links of the chain, a better metaphor is the DNA double helix: with one strand the product or service being delivered, and with the other the value-adding ability to deliver that product or service consistently and effectively, intimately bound up with it.

Balanced scorecard

The balanced scorecard is a strategic performance management tool that not only fully integrates the customer's needs with the customer-serving people of the organization, but also with the internal systems and processes and the broad strategic aims of the shareholders. Abernethy *et al.*[2] consider this approach to be effective because:

> '. . . it articulates the links between leading inputs (human and physical), processes, and lagging outcomes and focuses on the importance of managing these components to achieve the organization's strategic priorities.'

Kaplan and Norton,[3] the originators of the idea, argue that there is too much emphasis placed on financial measures of performance in organizations. They say you get what you measure, but that may not

---

[2] Abernethy, M.A., Horne, M.H., Lillis, A.M., Malina, M.A. and Selto, F.H. (2005) 'A multi-method approach to building causal performance maps from expert knowledge', p. 136. (Cited in Wikipedia: http://en.wikipedia.org/wiki/Balanced_scorecard#cite_note-1).
[3] Kaplan, R.S. and Norton, D.P. (1998) The Balanced Scorecard – measures that drive performance. In: *Harvard Business Review on Measuring Corporate Performance.* Boston, MA: Harvard Business School Press. Originally published in *Harvard Business Review,* January–February 1992. Reprint 9205.

necessarily mean that what you get is what is needed and that a broader focus is required: a more balanced presentation of business performance. In particular we need a measure that links the operational to the financial and one that incorporates customer satisfaction as well as measures of internal process efficiency in achieving that aim.

There are four aspects to this:

1. How do customers see us?
2. What must we do to excel?
3. How do we actually create value?
4. How does this relate to shareholder value?

Ultimately, it is not just financial performance but customer value that drives the future value of the organization. That value can be expressed both in terms of the value of the offer to the customer and the combined value of retained customers – what used to be called 'goodwill'. The balanced scorecard approach distils the elements of the organization's competitive agenda: customer orientation, response, quality, teamwork, new product development and long-term stability. It demands the translation of the general mission statement into specific measures to reflect what really matters to customers.

However, it also has an internal perspective because it forces ongoing examination of the processes that have the greatest impact on customer satisfaction, such as employee skills and productivity: linking the strategic drivers of the organization as a whole to what actually goes on, on the ground, and that adds to the corporate mission. The balanced scorecard puts strategy, not control, at the centre of the agenda and that represents a fundamental shift of attitude. Industrial-age thinking was that management specified actions to be taken by employees and then measured the outputs to see if they had been carried out: systems controlled behaviour. Under the more enlightened management approach of today, using ideas like the balanced scorecard, goal setting takes precedence – the assumption being that people will adapt their behaviours to meet the ever-changing conditions in which they have to operate to meet those goals.

The balanced scorecard idea forces cross-functional integration, customer–supplier partnership, continuous improvement and team rather than individual accountability all, of course, focused on delivering customer value.

Car body repair shop story

A short while back, I stupidly cut a corner in a car park and ran over a tree stump, severely damaging my car. As it was relatively new and still under manufacturer's corrosion warranty, I took it back to the main-dealer body shop. When the work was finished, it was amazing. It was impossible to tell the car from new. The repair was no different from the original build quality and there is no doubt that the standard of work, controlled by excellent quality management, was the highest it could be. On completion and handover, the service technician offered me a quality questionnaire and asked me to fill it in. I was able to score top marks to every question; however, I explained that I would never use the firm again because my experience overall had been far from satisfactory.

Initially upon arrival, and feeling rather silly at having damaged such a new car, the service receptionist did nothing to sympathize or even empathize with my situation. He was clearly someone who had been promoted from the shop floor and was only interested in the practicalities of how the repair could be carried out. No doubt he was clever at his job of devising repair specifications, but there was no conversation, no explanation of what needed to be done, no recognition of how I was feeling, and no expression of understanding or interest in what had happened; only the estimate and the job specification. Then there was the 'courtesy car' that was not courteous. Apart from being dirty and with a flat tyre for a spare, it had the firm's details signed all over it that announced to all and sundry, including my neighbours and clients, that I had had a crash. When I asked when the car would be ready, I got the reply 'When it is finished': an obvious statement, but particularly unhelpful when one has to plan one's business and life around the event. Upon completion, no one offered any thanks for the business or even showed appreciation of my decision to use them, and yet I was able to give them top marks to the questions they were asking!

The point is, they were valuing what they wanted to measure: they were not measuring what was valuable to the customer. Their focus was wrong. For them, build quality was enough, but they were meeting their own requirements out of some form of professional pride rather than meeting their customer's requirements and needs. It is true, high build quality ought to pay back in the long run, all other things being equal, but in this case, the company's investment was being largely wasted because the service quality was so lacking in what I also needed: a sense of care and attention; recognition of me as a human being; that nutrition of attention to which we referred earlier. The product quality was exemplary, but the overall package fell woefully short of what the customer needed. In marketing terms, they had the core product right and, to some extent, the tangible product too (their premises are spectacularly modern and their staff all wear nice uniforms), but the augmented product area, in which reside most customers' buying decision criteria, was a closed book to them. They just didn't get it that real quality is not just product quality, but service quality too, intimately coiled together with the core product that the organization delivers. Just as in Jan Carlzon's 'moments of truth', both have to be delivered at every stage of production and be inextricably linked with the orientation of the whole organization toward the customer. Put simply, this organization totally lacked Service-Ability.

Product quality and service quality must weave together like the strands of the DNA double helix; it has to be built-in at every stage of the production process.

(Incidentally, this firm ultimately became absorbed into another body shop in the region because they couldn't sustain the low levels of business they were getting for such a high investment in quality plant, machinery and workmanship.)

The customer is king

Obviously service and customer value mean having nice premises and presentable staff, nicely presented information and so on. Naturally, it is about avoiding mistakes and the need to rework or rebuild product. Or, as in the case of a hotel, for example, not losing bookings because they haven't been properly recorded on efficient systems, or a charity that gives incorrect information on a helpline and has to spend staff time and expense when dealing with the consequences, let alone the damage to its reputation. Service quality is undoubtedly product based, i.e. about superior product and service-product attributes, and it is user based, providing customers with what they need. It is also operations based, aimed at achieving conformity with a design specification, and it is value-based, so that not too much cost is incorporated into the offering. However, these are no longer enough because these things are now taken as a given by consumers. They are no longer differentiators for strategic competitive advantage.

Today, product and service quality is about excellence in every aspect of both the production and the delivery. Slack *et al.*[4] say 'Quality is about consistent conformance to customer's expectations'. It is a holistic idea that, as Feigenbaum said, sees the 'customer as king' and starts '. . . with customer requirements and end[s] only when the customer is satisfied with the way the product or service of the enterprise meets those requirements.'

Especially with services, quality is perception-based and those perceptions are exclusively the property of the customer, who alone will decide by which set of criteria the total offering is to be judged. Total service quality is more than just getting the product right. It is about getting the whole customer experience right and has to be seen and practised as

[4]Slack, N., Chambers, S., Harland, C., Harrison, A. and Johnston, R. (1988) *Operations Management*, 2nd edn. London: Pitman.

an integral way of doing the business. For all these reasons, that is why an organization needs Service-Ability.

The cost of quality

There is, of course, a cost to quality. Bank[5] suggests as much as 20–30% of a company's revenue may be spent on the cost of ensuring product quality, but this needs to be weighed against the opportunity cost of poor or inadequate customer service. Where things are being made to a quality standard it is relatively easy to measure the cost of failure (returns and repairs, for example), whereas in a service delivery context, we don't have the luxury of knowing when we've got it wrong because customers vote with their feet and usually don't tell us why. On the rare occasions they do, it is often too late to do anything meaningful to recover. The cost to the car body repair shop was that it had to close its doors as an independent entity and the loss of income streams, as well as the cost of lost investment, can be calculated, but the cost to United Airlines of well over twelve million repetitions of 'United Breaks Guitars' is incalculable.

Service failure is the most difficult cost to quantify, but is potentially the most damaging to an organization, especially a service organization. In manufacturing or retailing, bad product that gets through can be recalled and replaced; indeed, doing this effectively can be seen by the customer as excellent service. However, in a service context, where the product is intangible and, once delivered, cannot be recalled or repaired, the cost of external failure in terms of bad feeling (or bad-mouthing) from the customer can be immense and long lived, especially if the service failure involves disinterest or rudeness because, as we saw early on in this book, the overwhelming reason a customer leaves is because they feel the organization is uninterested in them.

There is a third cost of service quality failure and that is the cost of dealing with customer complaints; a topic to which we shall now turn.

---

[5]Bank, J. (1992) *The Essence of Total Quality Management*. Hemel Hempstead: Prentice Hall.

The Bottom Line interview

In a BBC Television episode of the programme *The Bottom Line*,[6] broadcast on 17 October 2010, the presenter Evan Davis interviewed three CEOs on their approach to customer service:

- Ian Mason, Group Chief Executive since 2001 of Electrocomponents Plc, a business to business company founded in 1937 and claimed to be '. . . renowned for delivering high service levels';
- Tim Steiner, CEO and founder of the online supermarket OCADO that in partnership with Waitrose since 2002, has grown from three people in a single-roomed office in central London into a business with several thousand people, serving millions of customers around the UK – Ocado openly states quality is the key to its success; and
- Nick Wilson, Managing Director of the UK arm of the mighty Hewlett-Packard, the multi-national technology giant offering computer solutions from handheld devices to supercomputers, and whose corporate web site states, amongst other things a 'Passion for customers' and a desire to '. . . earn customer respect and loyalty by consistently providing the highest quality and value'.

Here is the transcript of the discussion:

> *Evan Davis, interviewer:* 'Here are two philosophies that I'd like you all to comment on. First a philosophy of zero tolerance of failure. Treating every customer as too important to upset. Or, secondly, a philosophy of economic realism: the idea that it is not sensible or cost effective to try to satisfy everybody 100%. Companies generally like to tell us that customer service is really what matters to them, but is it sensible to spend any amount of money on keeping customers happy?'

[6]http://www.bbc.co.uk/programmes/b00vjdqf.

Ian Mason, Electrocomponents: 'I think yes, we aim for the first model, but you can't go too far. I think customer service is an area where the cost–value equation is something you need to think about all the time. There's lots of people that know the cost of everything and the value of nothing to use that old phrase, but the costs of doing the service are very clear, they're very hard, they're very "now". But the value of having someone there to take that phone call, the value of having your people properly trained, you can see the cost. You're aiming for a very high standard of service.'

Interviewer: 'I'm going to look at Tim [Steiner, OCADO] now because you sometimes go to ludicrous expense to satisfy customers. On one customer you'll spend an enormous amount. It must be a huge drain on the ability of the business to earn money?'

Tim Steiner, Ocado: 'I think the key is we ship over 100,000 orders a week and actually to do the perfect order is the best order, it's the best economically, to do it right first time. If it arrives on time, everything's fresh and the order is perfect, they tend not to phone, so your operator doesn't need to answer the phone. You don't need to give them a refund and they're most likely to shop with you again. When occasionally a small number of those orders aren't right, your reputation is also incredibly important, and a reputation is something that's very hard to earn and very easy to lose, and so we strive very, very hard to maintain that.'

Interviewer: 'It's expensive to maintain!'

Mason, Electrocomponents: 'You mustn't focus on the cost all the time. It's the value.'

Interviewer: 'Let's talk about HP, Nick, because it's not difficult to find complaints about HPs customer service. Just a cursory search on the web . . . [choosing an example from his papers] "Does anyone have Mr Wilson's email address, I would be delighted to tell him what I think of him", "Ramshackle customer service", another one, "I've been trying three weeks to get a part replaced under warranty, I haven't had it yet", "Phone calls are all premium lines at 12p a minute . . ." You get the point? What is your philosophy? Do you essentially assume that you always have to have a level of discontent and it's just not economic to get rid of it?'

Nick Wilson, HP: 'We do try to satisfy every customer. Are we going to make it perfect every single time shipping a PC every two seconds, and a printer every two seconds? No. Hopefully, though, what we strive to do is fix it when we get something wrong quicker and better. Do we fix it all perfectly first time? No. I have a dedicated team for escalated complaints of eight people. They can write to the MD and I make sure I do have a look at them all. I have a weekly call with the customer services team looking at the complaints that get escalated, etc.'

Interviewer: 'But just tell me this, it is a common complaint of technology companies, not just HP in fairness, that it is almost impossible to find a telephone number to call them on. Which is deliberate, right?'

Wilson, HP: 'No, there is a customer services number prominent on the web site and they have to get through to an individual that will try and help them. We have a customer services centre specifically for handling enquiries, and we have an escalation process.'

Interviewer: 'It's sometimes seen like it is a revenue centre for the company.'

Wilson, HP: 'Errm. It shouldn't come across like that. It's not designed to be like that . . .'

Mason, Electrocomponents: 'But it's short-cycle, it's short cycle.' [Referring to the revenue from premium rate lines.]

Interviewer: 'But is it a revenue centre?'

Wilson, HP: 'No it's a customer fix. The service assumes that we'd like the clients back.'

Interviewer: 'Why would you then have a premium phone line number on? Not obviously a very expensive one, but a 10p a minute one?'

Wilson, HP: 'They shouldn't be . . . most of our customer service lines aren't premium ones, no . . . my email address is actually on the web so they can get to me. It's . . . I have a specific email for customer complaints which I look at weekly.'

Interviewer: 'And you've got eight staff who sit there basically dealing . . . ?'

Wilson, HP [cutting in]: 'Just doing installations and nothing else. Errm. Which ones that get through . . . they call them "The MD complaints" which go above that, but we do have a customer services centre.'

Interviewer [turning to Steiner, OCADO]: 'I mean you make a huge effort, Tim, to keep everybody satisfied, you still get complaints presumably?'

Steiner, Ocado: 'Yeah we do and I think we do things a little bit differently, so we do aim in our call centre to try and answer the phone after the first ring, rather than some companies that leave you at least 20 [minutes], in the hope that you will give up and drop off.'

Interviewer: 'And that's deliberate is it?'

Steiner, Ocado: 'But that's because people are not phoning us to cancel a subscription to a phone service or television service or something like that, they're phoning us because they've got a problem with a live situation normally with our order. Our call centre's very small because very few of our customers have a requirement to call. It's in our office, on the same floor as my office so it's about a few hundred feet from my desk, so the customers know when they're calling in they're talking to our head office, which helps the first-time resolution rate go up because customers are reassured it is being dealt with properly. And that actually reduces the cost of operating that call centre from when it was previously outsourced and operated in Ireland. So, bringing it back to base actually was a good thing. And, yes, we do get some complaints and a few get escalated to me, probably about half a dozen a week. I don't have a team of eight dealing with it, they'll come in with it and either myself or my founding partner Jason will actually respond to the customer directly because there are very few of them that actually come to us. We hope to resolve them before that is required.'

Interviewer [addressing Wilson, HP]: 'To be honest, it does sound like a phenomenally expensive business. I mean eight staff in your office handling basically personal emails to you, Nick . . .'

Wilson, HP: 'Not there for me, they're basically serious complaints that we view on top . . .'

Interviewer [addressing Steiner]: 'You're spending Chief Executive time on dealing with, you know, individual customer complaints.'

Steiner, Ocado: 'Attention to detail is important. Sometimes you find something out when somebody complains. If they've actually got that upset that they want to complain to me or to Nick, there is sure to be something in it that you might want to learn so, sometimes it's really interesting to look at these complaints.'

Mason, Electrocomponents: 'With complaints though . . . in restaurants [for example when you are asked] "was the food alright", I mean [you say], "yes it was" but you ain't going back . . . you know, you've got to independently verify. I'm sure you all do the same, but we do independent research to say how was the customer service, how do you compare us to our competitors, how do you compare us to other companies? I think it's very important you get that independent voice, it's not just the complaints you should listen to.'

Interviewer: 'Well, I think that's all we have time for. Thank you to my guests . . .'

Reflecting on this exchange, the reader will no doubt form his or her own opinion about which organization has the most cost-effective approach to customer service: which of the CEOs are listening to the voice of the customer; to what extent each sees customers as central to the whole operation; and, crucially, which sees customer service as a cost rather than an investment.

Call centres

In much the same way as in the early part of the Industrial Revolution, when ordinary, unskilled people working in factories and mills were used for long hours and little pay and the owners and leaders of the means of production grew rich, the technology revolution has had a very similar effect.

Call centres are the classic example. Often referred to as the 'sweat shops of the 20th century', here we find staff who are controlled, unmotivated, underpaid and whose loyalty to and engagement with their employer is low, because their employer's loyalty to and engagement with them is equally low. (Shop workers, incidentally, are the same.)

On 25 February 2001, the *Independent* newspaper published an article by Hester Lacey entitled 'Sweatshop slaves of the virtual age', about how the UK Trades Union Congress had set up a helpline for call centre workers. Here is an extract:

> 'Over the past fortnight, the TUC has been running a hotline for workers in call centres who want to report horror stories. In the first week alone the helpline received more than 400 calls; there was an even higher volume last week. Staff have been complaining of bullying, impossible sales targets, not getting wages on time, and hostility to unions. Some have told of being forced to go into work to report in sick instead of being able to phone in, having to put their hands up to go to the lavatory and then being monitored over how long they spend there, being given only a three-second break between calls and not being allowed to take more than three days' leave in one go.'[7]

They may be a modern phenomenon, but call centres are straight out of the bureaucratic, industrial era mindset. They represent the worst thinking, the worst aspects of controlling, mind-numbing, disempower-

---

[7] Lacey, H. (2001) 'Sweatshop slaves of the virtual age'. *The Independent*, 25 February.

ing management of people for minimum cost and maximum output. It is an amazing feat of technology and a truly wonderful thing that the information available on a screen to the average call centre operative today would only a few years ago have needed a small army of clerks to assemble and make available, but all that has happened is that ICT has allowed the number of people processing information to be cut drastically; it has added nothing to the quality of the service.

Under the title 'Mumbai isn't calling anymore' an item in the magazine *The Marketer*[8] said this:

> 'Language problems arising from call centre outsourcing to India are such a national bugbear in the UK that NatWest based an advertising campaign on the promise that its operators are based in Cardiff not Calcutta. Swift Cover insurance promotes its online services with a headset-wearing hen, advising customers to "click" online instead of talking to "clucking" call centres. Attempts to surpass culture clash by briefing Indian operators on UK lifestyle and traditions has been the source of much humour – in *Slumdog Millionaire* a character secures a job in India as a telemarketer where his attempt to feign British nationality goes terribly wrong: "I live near Loch . . . Big . . . Big Ben, Loch Ben." While the cost saving advantages of outsourcing are clear – the average call centre hourly wage in Britain is £6.73, compared with [sic] 90p in India – outsourcers pay the price: only 4 per cent of those polled by YouGov say they've had a good call centre experience.'

It is now axiomatic that customers hate dealing with call centres, especially foreign-based ones. Yet, today, many companies are still structuring themselves like this, outsourcing their customer-facing function to call centres in foreign parts. It is beyond common sense to subcontract this vital role to another organization with a different corporate culture, in a different world culture and with different values, operating from a

[8]*The Marketer*: official magazine of the Chartered Institute of Marketing of the United Kingdom, June 2010.

factory unit on an industrial estate on the outskirts of Mumbai. It just doesn't make sense to redirect local calls about local issues halfway round the world to people in another culture just because they are cheap by western standards. This is knowing the cost of everything and the value of nothing.

All call centres have done is add a better means of coercion to their staff and more control over a standardized output. Call centres only exist because the technology has allowed them to exist. They are only there because they can be there. They are not the product of the pull of customer need: demand hasn't shaped their provenance, the push of the technology has; but this is blind use of technology that in turn has blinded organizations even to common sense.

Although not necessarily highly vertically structured, the call centre movement has within it the spirit of the bureaucracy and the disempowerment of the employee that so characterizes that form of organization. Parsons (ibid.) says this about that spirit:

> '. . . a system of rational/legal authority can only operate through imposing and enforcing with relative efficiency, seriously frustrating limits on many important human interests, interests which either operate independently of particular institutions in any society, or are generated by the strains inherent in the particular structure itself. One source of such strain is the segregation of roles, and of the corresponding authority to use influence over others and over non-human resources, which is inherent in the functionally limited sphere of office.'

The obvious lack of flexibility allowed to staff who simply cannot do anything else but what the computerized systems they are operating allow them to do is testimony to this. (The 'Computer Says No!' television sketch is a classic example.[9])

Neither is it sense to isolate customer-serving employees from the rest of the organization in highly specialized centres, even in the same country,

[9]http://www.youtube.com/watch?v=0ZAoMv_QnAU.

hamstringing them from contact with other parts of the organization often by thousands of kilometres: cutting them off from colleagues who have ownership of that part of the organization in which they work, and an intuitive understanding as well as local knowledge that makes satisfying customer needs efficiently and holistically easy to do (notwithstanding NatWest's 'innovative' idea – Cardiff is still a long way from Cornwall, culturally!).

If your customer-facing employee doesn't know (or can't even possibly know in the case of call centres located abroad) anyone else in the organization with whom he or she can have a personal, or even acquaintance-like colleague association, sufficient to be able to deal with customers' issues internally in a spirit of teamwork, how can things get done properly?

If you're not even in the same organization, how can you represent the interests of that other organization to its customers in a meaningful way? Whose customer are you serving?

Why can't we create a mini call centre function at local centres of activity within our organizations? ICT can surely facilitate that rather than dictate the process? Why can't humans answer the phone? People are not all great talkers. They mix up their words and express their needs in their own unique ways. They even don't always know what they need. 'Option 7' may not be the one they think will be appropriate to fix that particular mistake on their bill; 'Option 4' may not seem the right one to change their order, or their flight, or whatever.

What customers need is a person who is focused and able to get them to speak to that person who can get things moving for them; and give them what they want, not what the organization thinks they want: someone to help fix their needs. Why can't a customer ring accounts? Why can't he speak to delivery? They are the people who know what is going on in their areas of activity on the ground where it happens and have access to short-circuited lines of communication that get answers quickly and things done efficiently. That's why it's great when a human answers the phone.

The answer to all these questions, of course, is the blind use of technology as a financial quick-fix without thinking through (perhaps not even caring about) the consequences. The economics of technology is driving organizations and customers alike up blind alleys. We must release customers from these imprisoning funnels that in reality serve no one. Technology used this way puts distance (psychologically as well as physically) between the customer and the need-satisfying resource. It may be clever, but customer needs are not being met and that is why there is so much tension created when customers interact with call centres – why they shout and get upset.

Yet the response of organizations to these problems is not to recognize the cause of the problem and engage with it. Instead, they police their staff and even their customers, using the self-same technology, i.e. recording conversations: '. . . in the interests of security and training'; announcing this practice to the customer whilst on hold in its weasel-word-warning to watch out, to be careful how they conduct themselves in their interactions with the organization. This is not only inappropriate treatment of human beings, it is basic arrogance toward the customer who, as Feigenbaum once said, should be king.

The truth is that call centres and labyrinthine telephone systems are only symptoms of a deeper malaise that has inexorably crept into our daily lives: the idea that customers are there to be serviced, not served. This is the subtle shift that has happened. It is cold, rational industrialization of what is essentially a human interaction and it is utterly ill thought through in its concept, as well as its practice. Someone, much sooner rather than later, needs to think the unthinkable about call centres and their enabling technologies, number-selecting telephone systems.

Customer value triad

Earl Naumann, who specializes in the strategic implementation of customer value, argues that there has been a fundamental shift in economic power from the producer to the consumer in recent years and, in the preface to his book,[10] he says: 'Unfortunately, many firms act as if they still have power, as if they need to only give lip service to customers. But it is the customer who now clearly dictates what constitutes appropriate product quality, appropriate service, and reasonable prices.' He goes on to say that the only way firms can redress this imbalance of power is through an increased ability to satisfy customer needs by getting even closer to the customer and offering the three factors: product quality, service quality, and value-based pricing in a 'customer value triad' which, he says, is the only foundation for future success. That way, they will be able to engage in 'value-based pricing', i.e. charging more than their low-service competitors for what is essentially the same product but delivered in such a way that it is better value for money. McNealy[11] repeats this theme by saying customer satisfaction is the critical strategic weapon for any enterprise as we move into the 21st century, stressing that customers are an organization's most valuable resource and that every organization must understand the value of retaining and delighting its customers if it wishes to be successful.

Rather than thinking of service as just another component of the value chain, those firms that will have the most economic power in the future (through higher profits and retained earnings) will achieve it by combining product quality and service quality that will delight the customer.

David Hall[12] describes this as a process in which everyone in the organization becomes committed to delighting the customer not just by satisfying expectations but also by exceeding them. He coined the term 'Customerizing' because he felt that the term 'marketing' was simply

[10] Naumann, E. (1995) *Creating Customer Value: The Path to Sustainable Competitive Advantage.* Cincinnati, OH: Thomson Executive Press.
[11] McNealy, R.M.(1994) *Making Customer Satisfaction Happen: A Strategy for delighting Customers.* NJ: Chapman & Hall.
[12] Hall, D. (1992) *The Hallmarks for Successful Business.* London: Mercury Books.

not enough to describe the activities of those successful companies that he had observed doing this. They focused on customers, not markets, because, as he puts it, 'In the history of business, a market never bought anything'.

Summary

Organizations that deliver true customer satisfaction will have a Service-Ability built on a philosophy espoused throughout the organization, driven by management but practised by every employee at all levels, not just by specialist staff. Underlying this is the idea that everyone in the organization, at all levels and in all roles, not only wants to but is able to get close to the customer to offer a personalized product delivery service that is right first time, fit for purpose and built-in at the point of contact, not checked or coerced into existence either during or after the event by customer-service surveys, recording telephone calls, or whatever other controlling, authoritarian methods those organizations who do not understand its true nature get up to these days. We must stop merely servicing customers and get back to offering customer service.

It is essential for organizations to become refocused on the customer, and offer not only good products, but also outstanding service quality too. Those who don't will lose out. It was not until the hearts and minds of the people, that central idea behind Total Quality, came to the fore in industry in the latter part of the 20th century that cracked the problem of unreliable product quality. So too will it be in the 21st century when the hearts and minds of senior managers as well as the rank and file are fully harnessed in the pursuit of total service quality through an innate Service-Ability. This is the baton that Service-Ability will receive from TQM to be borne high into the future.

6

More than 65 years ago, a young German soldier stepped onto the wide, flat bridge deck of the bridge over the Lower Rhine at Arnhem in Holland. It was still littered with the smoking debris of battle, and he had a white flag of truce in his hands. He spoke good English, and his orders were to deliver an honourable invitation to surrender to the shattered remnants of the beleaguered British First Parachute Brigade under the command of Lt. Col. John Frost, who had failed to take the bridge and were now up against overwhelmingly superior German forces.

The battle for the bridge at Arnhem in September 1944, immortalized in the film '*A bridge too far*', was a bold attempt by Field Marshall Bernard Montgomery to make a quick dash into the heartland of Germany through Holland, and finish the Second World War early. The attack on this last bridge failed when the remaining 740 men out of a 10,000 strong force had to withdraw after holding out for more than four days, instead of the planned two. The German invitation to surrender was refused by the British Paras. Their last radio message was: 'Out of ammo. God save the King!'

Only months earlier, on 6th June 1944, young American men 19, 20 and 21 years old had slugged onwards up Omaha beach in Normandy, finally achieving their objective, but suffering heavy casualties under withering enfilade fire as they disembarked from the landing craft right into the jaws of the German machine guns. (Enfilade fire is where one high-velocity bullet passes through five or six men in file, just as these American soldiers were at the moment the doors of the landing craft fell open and spewed them onto the beach.)

What is it that inspires this sort of spirit? What is it that keeps people motivated and moving forward against all odds? The French call it 'Spirit of the corps' (*esprit de corps*), in English it is known as morale: that spiritual glue that binds people together in the face of adversity and which inspires them to achieve the apparently unachievable.

Some ten years ago, I was driving to Durham University Business School where I was doing some research and postgraduate teaching as an associate, when I was listening to the early morning 'Today' programme on the radio. There had been some inner-city unrest the day before and they were interviewing a senior army officer about it. I don't remember his name and neither do I remember the details of the riots, but I will never forget his answer. He said that the only difference between a platoon of young soldiers and a group of disaffected, angry young men was discipline born of high morale, and he went on to say that morale was predicated on four things: trust in your leaders, trust in your mates, pride in the job and belief in the cause. I reflected on this for days afterwards and it began to dawn on me that good service needs high morale in the organization and that could be found within a team spirit based on trust, belief, and pride in the job: we could really use this idea in business – in the world of organizations.

SERVICE-ABILITY is a structured idea, based on the understanding of morale (*esprit de corps*, or team spirit), which it uses to underpin the rationale for a much wider and deeper organizational approach to customer service delivery. High organizational morale is necessary for success in any venture. It sustains and underpins the body corporate, giving it identity, coherence and purpose; and its creation is a matter of strategic intervention by senior management. It is the organizational expression of high morale in service-delivering employees that derives from a culture in which there is:

- **Trust in your leaders.** This is vertical trust and it derives from the senior management acting as leaders and being trustworthy, supporting and facilitating the individual's efforts, and backing decisions made in customers' interests by employees.
- **Pride in the job**: the desire to do things properly and well. This is the result of the personal self-confidence that comes from an employee

being well fitted to the job through intelligent recruitment, effective development and training, and meaningful support.

- **Trust in your co-workers** (colleagues). This is horizontal trust across the organization between co-workers, acting collegially, and it is characterized by people co-operating and supporting one another: working together in a common bond of purpose: focusing on things that need doing rather than on things to be avoided, and always acting in customers' interests

- **A belief in the cause** by the employee: in the mission, vision and, above all the values of the organization, as well as the value to the customer of the product or service being delivered.

SERVICE-ABILITY can be defined as:

> The ability of the whole organization, through its individual members, to deliver consistently what the organization seeks to do: in a culture of initiative, professionalism, engagement and involvement that resonate with the customer and create delight and satisfaction in both parties.

It is a contiguous strategic system (as distinguished from a collection of mere functional specialisms working independently). Rather than simply ensuring staff are trained in customer-service skills and quality checked to see that they are delivering them, it is a much wider and deeper organizational approach to customer service delivery. It is a culture as well as a set of processes that seeks to engage with the loyal satisfied customer, through the loyal satisfied employee, and it originates from senior managers at the strategic level, who take it upon themselves to ensure that the whole organization is enabled to consistently deliver the product or service-product, not just rely on front line staff to blunder on in an environment that neither supports, nor facilitates them in their interactions with the customer.

The four core attributes of trust in leaders, pride in the job, trust in co-workers and belief in the cause are the visible manifestation of high morale and they respectively result in initiative, involvement, professionalism and engagement in the individual employee. The argument is that these attributes are needed in every employee, at all levels, not just those in customer-facing roles, if the organization is to achieve overall Service-Ability.

Drawing on latest thinking on leadership, management, organizational design and strategy, these four attributes are inferred back into the organization, and classified under four core dimensions: 'effective leadership'; 'getting the people right'; 'appropriate organization'; and 'clarity of purpose'.

EFFECTIVE LEADERSHIP leads to trust and then initiative in the individual employee and it derives from the emerging understanding of the servant leader: one who leads not from in front, not from behind, or from above, but from within the body of the people; and who acts at all times also like a colleague, as first among equals as it were.

GETTING THE PEOPLE RIGHT results in professionalism. It comes from a strategic management approach that encourages pride in the job and draws on modern thinking about recruitment that takes account of attitude and personality, rather than just the hard technical criteria of job specification and person specification into which people are shoehorned. Getting the people right also means continuous development and a reward system that takes account of intrinsic motivation, not just relying on extrinsic reward. It also takes an appropriate, measured approach to less-than-expected performance. Individuals need to take responsibility for their work if they are to have pride in it.

APPROPRIATE ORGANIZATION leads to involvement in employees born of trust in co-workers and colleagues. It is characterized by 'form following function', in which people are facilitated by an organizational design that encourages them, not works against them, to work effectively together in trust and teamwork. Key in this is the elimination of bureaucratic structures that induce a silo mentality and prevent free and open communication across the organization. In a sense, the whole organization needs to have a sense of working as one team in the customers' interests.

CLARITY OF PURPOSE leads to engagement in the employee who believes in the cause. Engagement is not only with the organization, but also with the customer. It is achieved by having a strategy based less on specific performance benchmarks and more on oblique ideals, such as the expression of values, that seek the same result but by more indirect means.

These values need to be clearly articulated and communicated effectively, so that the people become imbued with them, and engaged. All this leads to a clear sense of direction that adds purposefulness to the daily work of the organization.

SERVICE-ABILITY, therefore, emerges from an organization-wide team spirit based on a culture of trust, a belief in what the organization stands for and for what it seeks for itself, and pride in the job: all embedded within a supporting and facilitating set of initiators, facilitators and core values under each of the four dimensions. These are all nested in layers or orbits in which the issues spiral, are interrelated, interconnected and ultimately become focused on the people (who are the organization after all) who deliver the service-product.

To borrow the technology metaphor, SERVICE-ABILITY is about reprogramming the organizational operating system to refocus on the loyal, satisfied customer, through the loyal satisfied employee. A quadrant model illustrates the whole idea. Studying it gives a clearer picture:

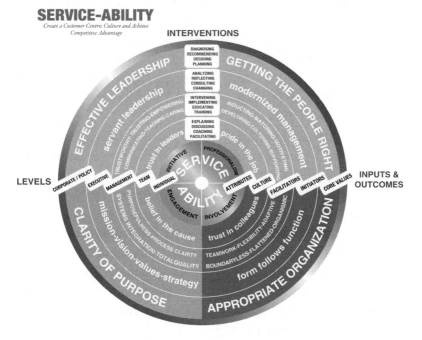

Service-Ability as a diagnostic consultancy tool

Engagement

Before employees can truly offer customer service, they have to have a sense of engagement with the organization. In other words, they need to feel part of it and have identity with its future direction and development. Without engagement, employees will not be motivated to give good service.

Engagement comes from a belief in the cause and this derives from understanding what the vision, mission and values of the organization are, so that employees identify with its core values and have a sense of common purpose. Many organizations put their mission statements on posters and plaques but communicating and embedding the true message is a complex process far beyond wall-mounted exhortations.

The process of engagement starts with the induction of the employee into the organization after recruitment. This leads to clarity of purpose and the whole organization buying-in to corporate objectives.

It also comes from sharing the formulation of strategy with them. Best-in-class world companies not only seek the views of their employees about future direction and opportunities, but they involve them in the decision-making process through cross-functional quality circles, action learning groups and works councils. By doing this, they secure employee ownership of the overall aims and strategy and increase the sense of engagement in the employee.

A belief in the service-product and its inherent value to the customer is, of course, fundamental to ensuring that the employee believes in the cause. No employee can fully engage either with the organization or the customer unless he or she feels that the outcome of his or her work is of proper quality, and fit for purpose.

Ultimately, communicating, teaching and inculcating these things is a matter of strategic intervention by senior management: those charged with the responsibility of being the directing mind of the organization. One of the key ways to achieve this is by communication up, down and across the organization, remembering that communication is as much about listening as it is about telling.

Initiative

No two customers are the same. Their expressed needs and wants are often idiosyncratic, and this requires a flexible approach by the customer-facing employee who must know that he or she can act on initiative to satisfy the customer's needs when necessary. A timely decision taken at the point of need can secure the customer's loyalty and avoid expensive rectification later if there is a problem.

Initiative needs empowerment. The two go hand-in-hand. The ability of the employee, interpreting the common values and aims of the organization rather than sticking to a rulebook, to act on initiative in the best interests of the customer, is an essential part of the employees' cultural, psychological, operating contract under Service-Ability.

Employees cannot comfortably act on initiative unless they know that any decision they make is within the bounds of what is allowed. It is the legitimate role of leadership to decide on what boundaries should prevail, but those boundaries should be very carefully considered so as not to inhibit appropriate customer-satisfying action at the point of delivery.

Being able to act on initiative also requires trust in one's leaders that they will support the outcomes. The employee must trust the leaders and that means the leaders must be trustworthy. Those who do not gain trust cannot exercise leadership. Trust is earned, it is not a given and success or failure in this arena is directly attributable to the attitudes of the leaders.

A reliance on a blame culture or an over-reliance on procedures and systems (particularly the misuse of technology or other means such as mystery shoppers to police employees' behaviour) will result in managers finding it difficult to engender the trust needed from their employees for initiative to blossom. Servant leaders leading from within the body of those who are led, acting as *primus inter pares* ('First among equals') rather than as authoritarian: 'Do as I say' leaders, are most likely to achieve this.

It is not only the skills and abilities of the managers, but their attitude, which is instrumental in creating the general organizational culture of mutuality, trust, loyalty, honesty and communication, all of which are essential for the development of initiative. For this reason, management education, rather than mere training in the skills of management, is the area where attention and expenditure needs to be applied in the Service-Ability model.

The interrelatedness of the issues in the orbits of the Service-Ability framework holds particularly true in this area because this becomes the foundation for trust in colleagues in a team culture, which we examine later.

Professionalism

Professionalism, facilitated by training, support and employee development for maximum effectiveness, is an essential component of effective Service-Ability. Strategic human resource management – getting the people right – ensures this. It results in self-confidence and pride in the job, in the people.

The strategic selection and recruitment of those types of people who fit the culture of the organization, and who have the necessary personal attributes and skills that suit them for the job, is vital to engendering professionalism. The American expression: 'hire for attitude, train for skills' sums this up very well indeed. Personal competence, i.e. self-management, interpersonal skills, personal values, etc., all fall within this area, and serve to build that confidence which is the hallmark of professionalism.

Following on from this, thoughtful induction, support and on-going motivation of employees, complemented by the appropriate training to equip them with the competencies necessary for effective customer service delivery, all serve to build pride in the job. All these factors are an integral part of modern strategic human resource management.

Involvement

The Service-Ability culture must include involvement: not only with the job in hand but with the customer, colleagues and the organization as a whole. Meaningful customer interactions must be capable of being delivered holistically by the organization. No one member of it can ensure it happens, and neither can a so-called cstomer service department. Organizations that have such an approach are completely missing the point. They are probably servicing customer enquiries and problems, not giving value-adding customer service in the service-product delivery.

Service-Ability calls for a spirit of co-operation, derived essentially from teamwork, and that is a matter of appropriate organization. The form of the organization must follow its function. Team working involves the development of flexibility and understanding through group learning and development, particularly in the area of customer needs, profiles and service issues. This could manifest itself in many ways. The most obvious example would be co-operation between workers in the same team but also cross-organizationally, for example between sales and production departments or accounts. So the design of the organization must be relatively boundary-less to facilitate cross-functional teamwork and Service-Ability. The bureaucratic form of organization is inherently inimical to this because its purpose is to reduce an organization to functional silos, and to induce a mechanistic rather than an organismic culture.

Knowing the needs of colleagues in other departments, understanding how their jobs fit in with the overall aims of the organization, and being flexible as to job boundaries, avoiding demarcation arguments and inappropriate internal competition; all these are beneficial outcomes of acquiring Service-Ability.

This, briefly, is the Service-Ability framework. By studying it and understanding the issues contained in it, it can be seen that organizations that simply try to bolt-on customer service by sending their staff on training courses, are probably wasting their time and money. Concentrating on the individual whilst failing to pay attention to the whole organizational framework and culture in which that individual has to function is never going to work in the long term. At best it is a quick fix. Before deciding on staff training courses, senior managers must first ensure that all factors of the model are in place otherwise the change will not stick.

Service-Ability is a multi-layered model, much like an onion. The outer level is the corporate/policy level where the core values driving customer service are laid down. At this level, it is all about diagnosis, decision making and planning. It is also about very senior management, through effective leadership, ensuring that those values are clearly articulated and transmitted into the organization.

The next level inwards (or downwards if you like to consider it this way) is about executive management putting in place structures, policies, procedures, etc., that initiate the process of Service-Ability. In a real sense, this is the internal consultancy phase concerned with analyzing, reflecting, consulting and initiating change.

At the day-to-day management level, the emphasis is on facilitating what the senior management have set in train. Herein lie the normal management activities of intervention and implementation through educating and training.

At the team level, it is about building and sustaining the culture of service to the customer. There is a strong coaching and facilitating element to the activities in this area. Team leaders operating as servant leaders, acting as *primus inter pares* (first among equals), form a key element in ensuring the people realize their true potential and develop the four personal attributes of professionalism, involvement, engagement and initiative.

Service-Ability is strategic: it requires in-depth thought and intervention starting at the top and cascading down through the organization. Much like the proverbial swan serenely moving across a placid lake in the moonlight, an organization with SERVICE-ABILITY is paddling purposefully beneath the water.

7

At 8:46 am on September 11, 2001, a fully-fuelled Boeing 767 belonging to American Airlines and carrying 76 passengers, 11 crew and 5 hijackers crashed into the North Tower of the World Trade Centre, New York. In a fireball of fuel, mangled metal and masonry, all on board were killed together with dozens more at the point of impact. Seventeen minutes later, an identical aircraft with another 65 people on board smashed into the South Tower. In a few minutes, hundreds of lives were taken, and by the end of that terrible day, the remains of 2741 people, including at least 200 who chose to throw themselves to the ground rather than burn to death, were lost in the dust and debris of what remained of the two collapsed giant towers.

Those of us who were around at the time will never forget the images of that appalling event as they unfolded on our television screens, and will still feel the shock, revulsion and fear that swept out across the world from that one small place, in one of the most famous cities on earth. In that horrific act of terror, Lenin's revolutionary slogan 'Kill one, frighten a hundred' took on a degree of meaning far beyond anything we could imagine.

This most horrific terrorist attack had a devastating effect upon the American consciousness – and on the American economy. In particular, the American airline industry was badly hit. People were simply too afraid to fly, and those who already had purchased tickets were causing severe cash-flow crises for the carriers by asking en masse for refunds. Many airlines had to go deeply into debt in order to survive 9/11, but not

Southwest, a low-cost, no-frills airline founded in 1971 by Rollin King and Herb Kelleher. In those exceptional circumstances Southwest no doubt had to draw deeply on its financial reserves, but it also had another resource upon which to draw: its substantial bank of customer loyalty.

In her book, *Lessons in Loyalty*, Lorraine Grubbs-West,[1] former executive with Southwest, says this:

> 'Imagine making a one-time decision to place the fate of your entire company in the hands of your customers. If your well-placed faith in the good relationship with your customers is right, you get to stay in business, If not, you're history. Such was the case for Southwest Airlines, post 9/11. We began to get requests for refunds from customers who had purchased tickets but were now afraid to fly. Our competitors decided to allow the refund, but tack on a "refund penalty" to cover their cost and lost revenue. Not Southwest. We put ourselves in our customer's shoes. We thought, "Why should we penalize people who had become fearful of flying due to circumstances beyond their control?" So, we took a risk and decided to offer full refunds to anyone who asked, with no penalties. We were counting on our customers not making a "bank run" refund request. Why? Because we had developed a great relationship with our customers and trusted they would have faith that we could get through the tough times following 9/11. And, they proved us right. In fact not only did many of them not ask for a refund, we were overwhelmed when many sent their tickets in with notes saying 'Southwest Airlines, take this ticket and keep it. I don't want my money back . . . I just want you in business in five years and today you need the money more than I do.''

Today, Southwest is the fourth-largest airline in the USA, flying to some 58 cities, and it is financially sound when most of its competitors are not. That is because it maintains high levels of passenger numbers on

[1]Grubbs-West, L. (2005) *Lessons in Loyalty: How Southwest Airlines Does It – An Insider's View*. Dallas, TX: Cornerstone Leadership Institute.

its flights. It does this by operating a low-cost, no-frills business model, but its competitive edge comes from being dedicated to the highest quality of customer service delivered with warmth, friendliness, pride in the job and a strong company spirit.

> *Southwest puts the message 'Provided by our Customers' on every employee's pay cheque.*

Southwest's slogan is: 'If you get your passengers to their destinations when they want to get there, on time, at the lowest possible fares, and make darn sure they have a good time doing it, people will fly your airline', and they reinforce this policy by rewarding and promoting people who demonstrate their commitment to good customer care. For Kelleher and King, customer service is not just a mantra or a flavour of the week, it is an integral part of their value offering. It is not only built-in to the company's mission statement, it is also celebrated in its meetings and its successes. Their employees learn to ooze customer service. As Grubbs-West says (striking a remarkable resonance with Jan Carlzon whose views we quoted in our chapter linking customer service to profit), 'We were taught that we were in the customer service industry; we just happened to fly airplanes'.

Southwest may have driven cost out of its operations, but it hasn't driven out the value for the customer, and here we are reminded of the work of Heskett et al.[2] and their paper 'Putting the service-profit chain to work', (*Harvard Business Review*, 2008), in which they say:

> 'Top-level executives of outstanding service organizations spend little time setting profit goals or focusing on market share, the management mantra of the 1970s and 1980s. Instead, they understand that in the new economics of service, front-line workers and customers need to be the centre of management centre.'

[2]Heskett J.L., Jones T.O., Loveman G.W. and Sesser W.E. (2008) Putting the service-profit chain to work. *Harvard Business Review*, July–August.

Southwest's management believes that by looking after the staff they will look after the customer; Grubbs-West again:

> 'If they're happy, satisfied, dedicated, and energetic, they'll take real good care of the customers. When the customers are happy, they come back. And that makes the shareholders happy.'

This is a mindset built-in to the company from its birth. It is a living, breathing philosophy that manifests in all facets of the business: it is even inculcated at the start of every employee's time with the organization. The airline selects its people on their ability to exercise humility, altruism and compassion, whilst at the same time being able to lead and be tough when needed, as for example in an in-flight emergency. Its people are its focus and the basis of its value offering, not just heavily discounted air fares.

Southwest's principle is: 'Hire for attitude, train for skill'.

To be at the centre of management concern, customer-facing employees must have the necessary aptitude, the appropriate interpersonal skills and service-enabling knowledge; and be properly motivated to perform effectively this most basic of functions for the organization that employs them, and that they represent. Employee satisfaction is the glue: the culture, that binds the relationship and seals the transactional value, and in Southwest we see an excellent example of how their employee satisfaction translates into a level of customer service that secures extraordinary customer loyalty: even in the most difficult of circumstances. Southwest knows the value of the 'economics of service' and they know how important people are in that economic system.

It is all about the people: that message at the heart of Service-Ability, and the way people serve each other within the organization, as well as how the organization serves them, that translates into the way customers are served. It is about a depth of commitment extending from the very centre of the organization to the loyal, satisfied customer through the loyal, satisfied employee and that is obtained by motivating people appropriately, leading them, training them (especially in the delivery of service) and, above all, selecting them correctly in the first place.

Recruitment

Getting the people right starts with recruitment, and we could learn much from Southwest Airlines' 'hire for attitude and train for skills' approach. It is, of course, axiomatic that recruiting skills an is essential and that qualifications demonstrate competence. Skills are important, but our service industries pay far too little attention to the personality of the candidate, searching for those qualities that make people responsive and empathetic to the customer. For example, when we want to hire people, we start by drawing up a job specification, then we draw up a person specification to fit that job, and then we go out trawling for the candidate who best fits our criteria. Our current recruitment practice is far too steeped in the industrial/bureaucratic legacy. It has become dominated again by the idea that technical competence and qualifications are the be all and end all; even of eligibility for an interview where those attributes in their absence would become clear.

Standardization of process and regulation of recruitment using bureaucratic principles will, from the very beginning, reap what it sows: depersonalization and detachment of the employee from the aims of the organization; and indifference to the results of their work in such a way as to render them unaccountable and broadly indifferent to the outcome of what they do. The whole process seems to have defaulted back to trying to fit square pegs into round holes: to filling posts with functionaries rather than people with personalities, and this approach inimical to creating a culture of customer service. It also stands in stark contrast to the principles of modern strategic human resource management where wider skills, interests and attributes are factored in right from the beginning.

Skills and qualifications are important but we must upgrade the importance of people-orientated attributes in our selection procedures.

The HR profession would do well to learn from their fellow professionals in marketing in this; understanding the reality that employers need to consider themselves sellers as well as buyers and realize that candidates are buyers as much as they are sellers. Organizations need to be able to construct and effectively articulate their offer for a given vacancy, and then pitch that offer to resonate with the needs and wants of the talent they need for success. Talent knows its value these days – and its price – and we must be aware of cultures, attitudes and practices that block the recruitment of excellence.

This should prompt us to examine how appropriate our recruitment practices are in a changing world, and whether we need to realign to better ways. The dynamics of the employer and candidate decision-making process need to be understood and rethought, and we need a new approach to recruitment. It is no good anymore trying to fit square pegs into round holes. Service-Ability is a culture and people need to be recruited to that culture. We need to be able to think customer focus right from the start.

Intellectual capital

Today, modern companies are having to recognize the importance of people, not just as a cogs in a machine, but as valuable assets: the sum of their know-how becomes 'intellectual capital', and a clear link between intellectual capital and wealth creation for shareholders is now being established.

Keith Baddely[3] of the Open University Business School says 'The recipe for success is taking the idea from the person's brain and giving it form'. A composer, for instance, with an idea for a tune in his mind has no possibility of making a living until he puts it down in notation that is capable of being replicated and used by someone else. Without giving form to intellectual capital there is no chance of realizing a return on the investment.

The biggest issue about intellectual capital is that it can easily drain away.

[3]'Intellectual Capital: The New Wealth of Nations', 1996 RSA Lecture.

Ideas and practical know-how are the property of the individual, not the organization, and that individual can take his or her knowledge anywhere he or she likes. Professor Charles Handy rather wryly says this:

> 'You know, Karl Marx was right? He said the world would change when the people owned the means of production. He meant they should have the shares but of course it didn't work like that. Now they literally own the means of production in organizations that rely on intellectual capital: on knowledge and intellectual skills, because the people have them in their brains, in their heads, and they can walk out of that organization at any time. So it makes nonsense to say that the people who provide the money own the people who have the means of production, because you can't own other people can you? Either morally or literally? So that's going to change the nature of capitalism. Secondly, it's going to change the nature of management because you can't actually boss these people around in the same way if they don't like what you're doing. They have a market price: they can walk out – most of them. The world is not insecure for people who have intellectual capital in their heads. It's only insecure for the people who don't have it.'

So, in this emerging context, remembering always that loyal satisfied customers come from loyal satisfied employees, how do we retain intellectual capital? How do we link the people to a large organizational structure in a way that secures their engagement, their involvement: their loyalty? How do we ensure that employees are engaged with the organization for whom they work? How do we ensure that staff become familiar with the needs of customers even if, as in a large organization, that could not be on a personal basis?

Inappropriate management

Out of date, inappropriate, amateurish management is a chronic disease, due in no small part to the philosophy that management is something anyone can do and that it is just another part of your real job. This belief is steeped in the British psyche, and it owes far too much to the equally British tradition of the amateur: someone who does things for the love of the pursuit, which all too often becomes translated to mean 'as good as the professional'.

The thinking goes like this: if you are good at a job you get to supervise others doing it. If you are good at that you get to supervise the supervisors, and so on. Reduced to its essence, it means that management is something you get to do because you are good at doing something else.

Rarely are newly promoted managers properly selected (many don't even have the aptitude for management), or properly trained and educated into their new profession. Many are forced to learn the job, on the job, or by 'sitting alongside Nelly', absorbing traditional ideas that are straight out of the industrial paradigm and passed down by others who have learned their management style the same way in 'Chinese whispers' fashion. But it is the blind leading the blind. It all results in a style of management based on supervision that becomes management-by-policing, when management should be the act of getting people together to accomplish desired goals and objectives. If you don't educate managers in all aspects of business (and that includes the basics of marketing as well as finance), you cannot expect them to motivate their people to be customer focused, and if you don't have a day-to-day process whereby this is managed, you can't expect it to happen on its own.

Many managers, of course, haven't got a clue about the value of customer service (as we saw in the Evan Davis BBC interview). They fail to create a culture of service because they see it as incidental to the work of the organization, just an add-on to the main product/service delivery, a cost not an investment, and their concern for efficiency through control blinds them to the reality that they need to invest in their people if those people are going to be able to deliver customer-satisfying service. This concern for control prevents them freeing up employees to offer service: empowering them to act in way that serves the customer, not just the shareholder; and they signally fail to engage in exemplary conduct themselves.

This situation is compounded by another popular notion: that higher pay and career progression means you go into management. It is not like this in other countries. Take Germany, for example: there, it is perfectly possible for someone to rise to the highest levels of pay and recognition by being a better engineer. Management is a career in itself, just as other careers are, like engineering. Furthermore, managers' career development often just happens in an evolutionary way, not a planned and structured one.

The results of this are plain to see. Today, many people, especially in service organizations, have become a commodity again to be used and exploited in the machine by managers who exercise arbitrary power and signal lack of creativity or humanity over people and resources. Massive salary differentials between workers and executives have emerged. Distance has been created between very senior management and the workforce, and a return to 'us and them' rather than just 'us' is prevalent again. The 20th century saw giant strides in the area of management of people through enlightened management, so where did it all go wrong? Why has all of this hard-won knowledge been abandoned by so many organizations as we charge forward into the new millennium? Why are we back in what is essentially a command-and-control paradigm?

The answer, of course, lies in the major societal shifts that have happened in the last 20 years or so. The explosion of the technological revolution with its depersonalizing, mechanistic, cost-minimizing fervour that, at the time when better management practices were burgeoning, crashed upon us, stifling the initiative, sucking the life out of our organizations. Almost a century of development of management and motivational theory was swept away like flotsam in the flood that, like that tsunami, just keeps on coming; and all because of the cost savings to be derived from using technology. The baby was undoubtedly thrown out with the bathwater.

Rules and regulations

Over-regulation – proscription rather than principles of behaviour; procedures rather than processes – is rife in many of our service industries today. Often driven by heavy external regulatory regimes (the financial services industry, for instance), many of our service industries place a disproportionate emphasis on rules and regulations, and that actively removes purposefulness from their people: it sucks the life out of them. This is the issue that comes up time and again, of doing what is right, not just doing things right, because it is perfectly possible to do something strictly according to rules and processes that are intrinsically immoral or unethical.

Over-regulation can so easily cause organizations to lose sight of moral values. It takes away the judgement from those who need to make judgements. We saw this in our reference to the experiments carried out by Professor Milgram, who found it possible to induce ordinary people to administer pseudo-electric shocks to others because he placed them in a situation where they believed they were acting according to acceptable rules of behaviour. We see this time and again in customer-facing activity: scripts (which are rules in narrative form) that force staff to speak to customers only in prescribed ways; procedures in call handling that force the interaction to the same pattern in every instance, and the current, extensive and frankly iniquitous use of 'mystery shoppers': the secret police of organizations, as this extract from an article by Miles Goslett in the *Sunday Times* of 30 January 2011 under the title 'Rapid rise of the citizen shopper spies for hire'[4] shows:

> 'Public sector bodies including the police, London Underground and the City's financial regulator, are spending millions of pounds a year hiring people as 'mystery shoppers' in an effort to tackle poor levels of service. In some cases, ordinary members of the public and out-of-work actors are being paid £100 a day to pose as customers

[4]http://www.thesundaytimes.co.uk/sto/public/sitesearch.do?querystring=rapid+rise+of+the+citizen+shopper&sectionId=2&p=sto&bl=on&pf=all

in places such as banks, train stations and jobcentres [sic] . . . Figures released to the *Sunday Times* under Freedom of Information rules reveal that London Underground spent £933,000 in 2009–10 hiring fake passengers to observe the 'ambience' at stations and to test the knowledge of staff. Four years earlier it spent £384,000 . . . The undercover passengers give marks to employees for helpfulness, appearance and accuracy. They also record how often and how reliable announcements are, keep an eye on litter and graffiti, and secretly test disabled facilities.'

All these take away the freedom of the individual to act in a spontaneous way and the enjoyment of the interaction for both parties, and do nothing to produce satisfaction of need, either in the employee or the customer. Organizations that seek to standardize and control the activity of their people these ways will drain purposefulness from their people.

Of course, some rules are needed to give guidance on practice in eventualities, or to provide a framework of acceptable or desirable behaviour, but it is the degree to which rules are relied upon to direct and control the individual that is the issue. Too many rules (even those introduced in protective response to external threats) create a hostage to fortune that leads to more customer dissatisfaction because the pressure to break rules is like water, it will always find the cracks and weaknesses in a structure, and the more rules you create, the more you open yourself up to attack and criticism for not following them. This is especially true if the criteria of acceptability are based not on ethics or legality but, as they all too often are, on 'company rules' or 'company policy' (an excuse all too frequently used as an apology for bad customer service). When the rules get in the way of doing what is right, then the rules are wrong and need to be rethought.

Too many rules spare people the need to think, but customer-facing staff need to be able to think about what they are doing and adapt to customer needs. They need the freedom to vary their actions according the circumstances. Schwartz[5] quotes the story of Aristotle,

[5]http://www.ted.com/talks/lang/eng/barry_schwartz_using_our_practical_wisdom.html

who observed some stonemasons on the island of Lesbos and noted how, as skilled craftsmen, they adapted and improvised to get the desired result. They were making round columns and, of course, needed to check consistency of circumference to ensure they were all the same. It is difficult to use a rigid ruler to do this so the stonemasons created a flexible rule, one they could wrap around a cylindrical object: by creating a tape measure, they 'bent the rule'. Just as we shall see in our example about the hotel concierge in the chapter on leadership, the stonemasons used practical wisdom in the practical application of what they were doing.

> Serving customers needs the ability and freedom to exercise practical wisdom and to 'bend the rule'.

For Service-Ability, we need people are able to exercise initiative: who are able to know when, and how, to make the exception to rules in the best interests of the customer, which can never be anything else but in the best interests of the organization in the long run. The more rules you have, the less leeway exists for initiative. People need to know how to improvise in situations that are ambiguous and cannot be clearly defined: they must be able to use initiative in the pursuit of what is right, rather than doing things right according to rules and procedures.

Greed and financial incentives

There can be no doubt that many of our corporate managers are failing to lead, motivate and inculcate their people in good service. This is largely because they are too concerned with control, financial measures and ensuring cost savings and efficiencies (often using information and communications technology to do this, as we have already observed). Nowadays, a substantial part of senior managers' earning ability is deliberately linked to financial performance (as witness the recent banking crisis) and that forces them to act in a performance-based mode, but there are massive dangers in linking performance to extrinsic reward. It stifles the inner satisfaction people get from a job well done: that reward of professionalism and pride in the job. This is the culture of knowing the cost of every-thing and the value of nothing.

Julian Birkinshaw,[6] professor of Strategic and International Manage-ment and Deputy Dean of for Programmes London Business School, observes that extrinsic rewards, whilst valuable in linking and rewarding outcomes to effort, have drawbacks in that they drive out intrinsic interest in just doing the job (which is rewarding in its own right), replacing it with greed, and Dr Barry Schwartz[7] goes much further, arguing that extrinsic incentives such as bonuses introduce an ethical weakness into human activity. He argues that the principle of rewarding someone for doing a certain thing boils down to encouraging them to be selfish: they may do good for someone else, but that is only because they are doing good for themselves; selfishness can and should never be the motive for doing the right thing:

> 'We can certainly see this in response to the current financial crisis. Regulate, regulate, regulate; fix incentives, fix incentives, fix incen-tives. The truth is, neither rules nor incentives are enough to do the job . . . What happens is that as we turn increasingly to rules and incentives, they may make things better in the short run, but they create a downward spiral that makes us worse in the long run. Moral skill is chipped away by an over reliance on rules that deprive us of the opportunity to improvise and learn from our improvisations. And moral will is undermined by an incessant appeal to incentives that destroy our desire to do the right thing.'

Birkinshaw[8] throws this into further stark reality by citing the heavily incentivized investment bankers in the recent world financial crisis, who became so focused on their bonus earnings that they forgot the basic principles of their profession; often taking risks that were anathema to the ethics of investment banking, and unleashing a financial firestorm through

---

[6]Birkinshaw, J. (2010) *Reinventing Management*. Chichester: John Wiley & Sons.
[7]Schwartz, B., with Kenneth Sharpe (2010) *Practical Wisdom*. New York: Riverhead Books.
[8]Birkinshaw, J. (2010) *Reinventing Management*. Chichester : John Wiley & Sons.

greed. Take Lehman Brothers, for example: Dick Fuld, the head of Lehman Brothers at the time of the crisis (described by Andrew Gowers[9] of the *Sunday Times* as a '. . . textbook example of the command and control CEO') had put in place an incentive system for employees that he knew would appeal to greed. As Birkinshaw puts it:

> 'It [Lehman] had perverse incentive systems. Lehman's employees knew what behaviours would maximize their bonuses. They also knew that these very same behaviours would not be in the long-terms interests of their shareholders – that's what made the incentive systems perverse. For example, targets were typically based on revenue income, not profit, and individual effort was often rewarded ahead of teamwork.'

Managers of too many of our modern companies seem to be defaulting to the idea that money is the only motivator despite the progress that was made throughout the 20th century, during which the idea that workers could be encouraged to work through the application of ever more refined reward/threat 'incentives' became mediated by the human relations school, which added social science to Taylor's mechanistic management 'science'. Abraham Maslow and his followers, such as McGregor, introduced psychology to the mix, so that we understood that people in the workplace were motivated by emotional satisfaction not just money and coercion; that they had a need to be seen as individuals, influenced by social interactions, and yet today, where the understanding of reward and motivation is so well understood, too many or our organizations are increasingly reverting to the industrial management paradigm of old.

Pink on reward and motivation

Daniel Pink[10] reminds us that, once people are paid sufficiently, additional units of money yield relatively few additional units of satisfaction or

---

[9]Gowers, A. (2008) Lehman: consumed by the death spiral. *Sunday Times*, 14 and 21 December (Referenced in Birkinshaw, op. cit.)
[10]Pink, D.H. (2009) *Drive: The Surprising Truth About What Motivates Us*. New York: Riverhead Books/Penguin.

performance. He says people are no longer responding to being treated as 'better-smelling donkeys', they are increasingly seeking to direct their own lives and be creative in their work, and that is what is producing higher levels of output and the best service in today's enlightened companies:

> 'What motivates Wikipedians, as well as high-performing organiza-
> tions of all kinds, is a sense of purpose. Businesses with a transcend-
> ent purpose – whether it's Google's aim to organize the world's
> information and make it accessible or Apple's desire to "put a dent
> in the universe" – will, over the long haul, outperform those driven
> only by profit.'

Pink refers to three built-in drives in humans: the biological drive which causes us to eat, drink and procreate; the reward and punishment drive which is the response to work harder on the promise of a bonus (or turn up on time under threat of dismissal for being late); and the drive to do things even when they don't satisfy our biological urges. For example, we play musical instruments simply to master something that is challeng-ing, or we give up a highly paid job to take up one that is less lucrative because it is more meaningful to us. These are the intrinsic motivators in us that now need to be applied to the world of work.

In the past, all too often organizations stopped at the second drive, using extrinsic rewards in trying to motivate their people; they structured their approach to motivation around an elaborate mixture of carrots and sticks attempting to reward the behaviours; they sought to punish the behaviour they disliked. Whilst this approach worked well enough in the industrial era, when people were doing relatively simple, routine, rule-based work, that sort of work has now all but vanished. Pink argues that, these days, work is often its own reward as the Wikipedians and the Apples of this modern world are showing.

People are increasingly becoming purpose maximizers not just profit maximizers: mastery of something is intrinsically satisfy-ing, even if no pay is attached, and as long as sufficient financial compensation is gained somehow, that reward often transcends pay and conditions.

Today many workers, particularly service workers, do jobs that involve knowledge and creativity where job enrichment and flexibility are increasingly important, and the carrot-and-stick approach simply has no place. It just doesn't work. In fact, as Pink observes and Schwartz confirms, it can actually do harm to people: to their moral/ethical stance as well as their relationship with their employer, and more importantly, to their employer's customer; and yet in very recent experience, we have seen the extent to which money has re-emerged as the key motivator in some quarters of our economy.

Strategic HRM

The picture is not all bleak, however. Today, the best companies place a powerful emphasis on intrinsic reward, rather than extrinsic: all in line with McGregor's Theory Y, i.e. that people like to work and to feel useful and will, if given the opportunity, become involved with their work and develop a high sense of responsibility and commitment. As we move into the early decades of the 21st century, our humanity is re-expressing itself through Pink's 'third drive'.

The concept of strategic human resource management, developed in the post-Second World War period of the 20th century, is a better way. This modernized management approach is needed to achieve focus on the job in hand, professionalism, initiative, and involvement with the organization. All these elements are essential for Service-Ability: they are the bedrock upon which Service-Ability stands.

Strategic HRM encompasses a clear recognition of the need to ensure that the people in an organization are not only fitted for their jobs, but also fit into the organization's culture: that they are recognized as having motivations that need to be satisfied in their work, and equipped with skills beyond those required for the job in hand; that those skills can be used in different jobs when needed; and that this will produce greater output and productivity. It also recognizes that people need to be treated as human beings and not just automata, albeit in a culture which recognizes the harsh fact that people need to fit in and produce or be removed. Strategic HRM demands that that the whole process be viewed holistically, and that people must become an integral part of corporate planning aimed at achieving sustainable competitive advantage in fragmented, short product-life-cycle, markets.

Professor Michael Porter,[11] the Bishop William Lawrence University Professor at Harvard Business School, and strategy specialist, describes this approach as '. . . consisting of activities involved in the recruiting, hiring, training, development, and compensation of all types of personnel' and explains that 'Human resource management supports both individual primary and support activities and the entire value chain'. A further, usefully clear high level view of what strategic HRM is given by Michael Armstrong[12] as '. . . a strategic and coherent approach to the management of an organization's most valued assets – the people working there, who individually and collectively contribute to the achievement of its objectives for sustainable competitive advantage' and Rosemary Harrison[13] sums this up with her description of a set of policies and practices, which she says comprise HRM. She argues that each practice and policy must be present, that each must interact positively with the others and that the whole process must be formally incorporated into the strategic planning of the organization, if the desired standards of performance are to be achieved.[14] She offers a useful diagram which gives a good overview.

[11] Porter, M.E. (1985). *Competitive Advantage: Creating and Sustaining Superior Performance.* New York: The Free Press.

[12] Armstrong, M. (1992) *Human Resource Management: Strategy and Action.* London: Kogan Page, p. 13.

[13] Harrison, R. (1993) *Human Resource Management: Issues and Strategies.* Wokingham: Addison-Wesley, p. 40.

[14] Harrison, R. (1994). 'Teaching Note Part 1: What HRM Is And What It Offers To The Business'. Durham University Business School MBA Foundation Course in HRM.

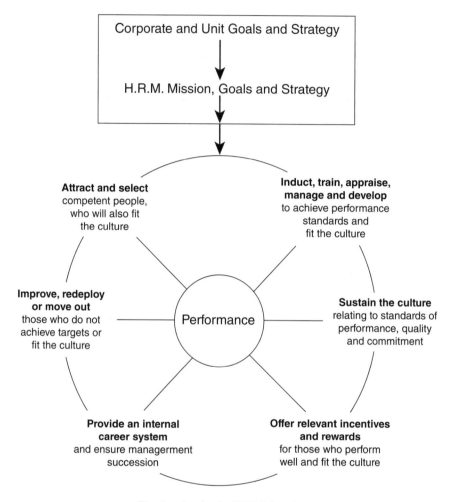

Harrison's wheel of HRM functions

Were we to be ever in doubt about the importance of the additional 'P' of people in the extended marketing mix, this will bring it into sharp focus.

Strategic HRM is emphatically not personnel management (or 'HR', a title personnel management has inappropriately assumed: the name may have changed but ideas have not). It is not just another name for past practices and beliefs, it is far wider and more far reaching than that. Getting the people right through strategic HRM represents a major shift away from the mechanistic methods of personnel management so prevalent in the 1960s and 1970s, and from the earlier 'Scientific Management' views in which the dispassionate management of personnel has its provenance.

The concept of Strategic HRM was born out of the changing economic and political circumstances and increasing global competitive pressures that forced companies to strive for sustainable competitive advantage in the increasingly globalized and fragmenting markets from the 1970s onwards. Its emergence and widespread adoption at that time, in tandem with Total Quality Management, led to high product quality, and it was effective in creating and maintaining competitive advantage in the last two decades of the 20th century.

As Terry Lunn, Personnel Director of Joshua Tetley lc, put it in 1993, 'Organizations wanting to survive are having to face facts: survival depends not just on securing competitive advantage but on establishing a sustainable advantage' and Geoff Armstrong, then Director General of the Institute of Personnel Management, echoed this at the time, saying 'As organizations move into increasingly competitive markets, the people they employ are going to be the key differentiating factor'.

The distinction between strategic HRM and personnel management is clearly drawn by Prokopenko, (1993):[15]

Some general differences between personnel management and human resource management

Personnel management is usually a centralized, specialist activity where specialist staff execute operational functions.	Human resource management is usually a decentralized activity where line managers are responsible for coordinating all their resources – including people – and HRM specialists give support.
Links between personnel activities and business planning often appear remote; personnel management is often a fragmented set of processes.	Business strategies and human resource strategies are closely aligned so that HRM processes need to reinforce each other.

(Continued)

[15]Harrison, R., ibid.

Some general differences between personnel management and human resource management

The purpose is operational: to ensure the right people are matched to given jobs at given times.	The purpose is strategic: to ensure the continuous availability of human resources with the skills and flexibility to help the business achieve its changing goals through time.
The workers are cost factors that need to be managed in order to achieve efficiency.	People are an organization's key asset and need to be retained and developed in order to achieve effectiveness and long-term growth of the business.
Emphasis is on top-down management of subordinates and on producing clearly defined job descriptions and performing relatively unchanging tasks.	Emphasis on development of self-managing teams and individuals and on being able to take on changing tasks as the needs of the business change.

Armstrong,[16] in his attempt at describing Strategic HRM, also refers to the comparison between it and Personnel Management, and cites work by Pettigrew and Whipp (1991) as follows:

Element	Personnel management	Human resource management
Employee relations	Adversarial	Developmental and collaborative
Orientation	Reactive and piecemeal	Proactive and business focused
Organization	Separate functions	Integrative function
Client	Management	Management and employees
Values	Order, equity, consistency	Client and problem focused; tailored solutions
Role of line management	Passive ownership	Active ownership
Overall output	Compartmentalized thinking	Linking various human resource levers to business needs

[16] Armstrong, M. (1992) *Human Resource Management: Strategy and Action*. London: Kogan Page, p. 36.

Empowerment, de-layering, team spirit, flexibility of work are the structural keys to strategic HRM, as they are to Service-Ability. Unlike personnel management, Strategic HRM, is not just another way of managing people. Instead it becomes a major management tool in the fight for competitive advantage and profit. Like TQM, with which it is linked, it is a broad, visionary, all pervading way of life that permeates the organization and is bound up with its culture, structure and mission. To understand it in action, it is useful to look at organizations that are implementing it.

Nissan and Google

Almost 30 years ago, at the height of the Total Quality surge by Japanese companies, Nissan Motor Manufacturing (UK) Limited was leading the vanguard in the UK, implementing strategic HRM. Today, Google, although appearing to be breaking the mould in many ways, is a company that is putting into practice many of the fundamental elements of Strategic HRM, albeit in a very 'Googly'[17] way. Let us take a detailed look at both.

At Nissan, HR director Peter Wickens[18] says that, for HRM to work, it is necessary to state an objective '. . . to establish an atmosphere of mutual trust, cooperation and commitment in which all employees can identify with the aims and objectives of the company and which encourages the individual contribution of all.'

Communication in all directions and at all levels is also cultivated within NMUK Ltd. So too is the involvement of all staff, who are consciously developed and trained on a continuing basis. This is comprehensively summed up in a management philosophy statement which is made prominent in the building:

[17] From the author's notes taken at a seminar entitled 'Google and the Cloud' given by Rob Gray of Google's UK Operation. Durham Convention, University of Durham Business School, 16 April 2010.
[18] Wickens, P. (1987) *The Road to Nissan: Flexibility, Quality, Teamwork.* London: Macmillan, p. 182.

'We will develop and expand the contribution of all staff by strongly emphasizing training and the expansion of everyone's capabilities. We seek to delegate and involve staff in discussion and decision-making, particularly in those areas in which they can effectively contribute so that all may participate in the efficient running of NMUK. Within the bounds of commercial confidentiality we would like everyone to know what is happening in our company, how we are performing and what we plan. We want information and views to flow freely upward, downward and across our company.'

Recruitment at Nissan is totally focused on getting the type of people who will fit in with the culture and be of the right quality. There are no compromises. The company will delay appointment rather than hire someone who does not fit the required characteristics of team working, quality consciousness and flexibility.

Nissan's version of strategic HRM has involved the devolution of many of the responsibilities conventionally assigned to indirect departments, such as 'Personnel', back to line managers. Production supervisors, for example, take part in the employee selection process and take responsibility for selecting the people who will work for them by personally giving them the job when the decision is made. This creates a bond between the individuals concerned which is the first element in team building. These supervisors also communicate all matters of management concern on a face-to-face basis to the team, they carry overall responsibility for building-in quality to the product and they ensure continuous improvement (*kaizen*) of both quality and productivity. Attendance and timekeeping are also the responsibility of the supervisor, as is coordination of on-the-job training to ensure a matrix of skills in the team, the responsibility for cost control at the point of production and doing minor fixes to production line equipment to keep the process flowing.

A sense of 'oneness' is engendered through the adoption of common terms and conditions of employment that apply to all employees including directors. The argument goes, why should a cleaner get less holiday entitlement than a production worker or the managing director? Common terms and conditions covers not only annual leave, but it also extends to pension arrangements and a salary structure in which everyone is fairly placed. Salary ranges and progression on merit apply both to manual and white-collar workers, and advancement in each is based on objective assessments of performance applied uniformly to all.

A single integrated bargaining body exists on which all groups of employees are represented, thus supporting the 'one company' ethos, and this is reinforced in practical ways by, for example, the company having only one dining room in which everyone, including the managing director, takes his or her meals. Nissan has a formal relationship with a single trade union in a deal that recognizes the union's support of the overall company policy and aims. Although the agreement embodies a referral to ACAS, the British Government's Advisory Conciliation and Arbitration Service, if there is a failure to agree, both the company and the union are fully committed to resolving disputes 'in-house'. By July 1987, some three years after commencement of operations, Wickens says that no-one had invoked the grievance procedure, citing as the reason the powerful effect of empowering line supervisors to resolve disputes at shop floor level.

There are no job descriptions at Nissan, just generic titles within grades. Management grades are Engineers, Supervisors and Controllers and manual workers have the titles Technician and Manufacturing Staff. This avoids demarcation disputes and encourages flexibility on the job as well as between generic titles and grades. If, for example, there is a temporary shortage of a manufacturing grade on the production line, indirect workers such as material handlers would be expected to help. Similarly, a properly trained white-collar worker would be expected to do the material handler's job. The idea of flexibility is also extended to the numbers of people employed by the company at any one time. Nissan carries a core of employees in numbers sufficient to deliver functional flexibility but hires-in temporary workers to meet exceptional production demands such as seasonal fluctuations in sales. These employees are hired a month earlier than needed to ensure that they reach the required quality skill levels and attitude[19] in good time. They also form a pool of potential candidates in the event that permanent jobs are on offer. As Wickens puts it, 'Once you start on the path to flexibility, there is no logical limit'.

Nissan is a classic example in an industrial environment of the application of modern strategic human resource management practice. Even today, its north-east England plant consistently ranks amongst the most productive car plant in the world. On the other hand, Google appears to be a different animal altogether. It appears untypical but when we analyze its practices and policies, although distinctly 'Googly', we can see the same elements at play which strongly suggests the conscious use of Strategic HRM best practice.

Google is one of the most modern organizations we have, and although it appears oblivious to convention, seemingly going out of its way to reinvent the organizational paradigm, it is nevertheless using some well-known, tried and tested HRM practices, developed more than 30 years ago. Google's approach fits well with the views of Jeffrey Pfeffer,[20] who suggests seven human resource principles that seem to characterize those organizations that produce exceptional profits through people: employment security; selective hiring of new personnel; comparatively high compensations contingent on organizational performance; extensive training; reduced barriers and status distinctions (including dress, language, office arrangements and salary differences across levels); extensive sharing of financial and performance information throughout the organization; and 'self-managed teams with decentralization of decision-making as the

---

[19]Temporary workers, contrary to popular belief, can be happier than their full-time counterparts. This was revealed by a survey carried out by Catriona Russell Gardner and Paul Jackson of the University of Sheffield's Institute of Work Psychology (reported by Barrie Clement in the *Independent*, Saturday 6 January 1996). Most wanted secure full-time employment with their company but they felt less threatened and vulnerable than their full-time colleagues who felt at risk from the increasing trend by companies toward flexibility of manpower. The researchers also found that '. . . short-term contracts undoubtedly suit some people'.

[20]Pfeffer, J. (1998) Seven practices of successful organizations. *California Management Review* **40** (2).

basic principle of organizational design'. All of these can be found in Google.

Take, for example, the openly declared 'Rule of Seven' whereby a maximum of seven levels only are allowed between the CEO and the lowest grade of worker. Devolution of management is a positive policy in the intriguingly titled 'Bureaucracy Buster', a policy whereby approval of certain projects can happen much lower down the management chain.

Recruiting to the culture is a significant feature of Google's strategic HR practice. From the outset, Larry Page and Sergey Brin, Google's founders, surrounded themselves with people who were clever, focused, hardworking, passionate, challenging, discovering, and who liked to have fun, then they released them into a relatively unstructured environment to create new things, just like in the university environment out of which Google was born. When choosing employees, admittedly the organization places high value on both the level of degree awarded to the candidate and the quality and reputation of the awarding institution; but crucially it introduces the intriguing idea of 'Googliness'[21] when making the final decision about whether to employ someone.

Googliness explores elements of outside interests in candidates, such as sportiness (presumably because it provides a physical release after heavy intellectual work) and online activity such as blogging, etc., that will support the candidate's technical credibility in the job. In Google's product development function, around half of its workforce operates in small teams of 3–6 people that are self-managed, autonomous and highly focused on projects with limited objectives and short timescales, thus allowing large numbers of projects to be completed in short timescales. Even as long ago as the 1980s, organizations such as Nissan (and there are many others since) pioneered these policies in order to move from a position of 'us and them' to just 'us' in a joint spirit of common purpose as well as to increase productivity.

Above all, Googliness means being passionate about something.

---

[21]This is a term in actual use within the company.

We have already seen how extrinsic reward, such as money, coercion, threat of punishment or sanction, has a limited ability to engender better performance and secure engagement in employees, and that intrinsic motivators, such as job enrichment, socialization, recognition for effort, etc., provide more scope. Herzberg's higher motivation factors are clearly being paid attention to by Google. The provision of quiet rooms, for example, where taking a half-hour break at any time is not only allowed but encouraged, and free food laid on in Google's workplaces after 6 pm each day for those who are working late on a project, or who just want to get an evening meal after work. Policies such as 'work 15 minutes then play', 'you can be serious without a suit', funky dress days, and TGIF ('Thank Google it's Friday') where beer and pizza is delivered at 4 pm are pure 'Theory Y', that says work is as natural as play.

Maslow's socialization needs are actively facilitated by exhortations like 'don't be an email slave', encouraging people to talk to each other personally. Then there is the 'Peer Bonus', a system whereby an employee can award another employee $100 for good service to them, thus building cooperation and esteem; and culture-sustaining measures such as staff being supported not to take on too many tasks by making it all right to say 'no' and be respected; and 'Meet Grinder', an online meeting schedule monitor that issues advisories on how to minimize too much formality.

Pay is not linked to hours worked and, interestingly, although home working without supervision is encouraged, experience is showing that employees don't use it. It seems they would rather be at a place of work with colleagues and this points very strongly to the degree to which intrinsic motivation of employees through socialization is a major factor in Google's success.

Summarizing modernized management

In Nissan and Google, we see two examples from entirely different perspectives of how to manage for maximum benefit of all and yet, in the face of this, in our modern world, we see so much narrow-minded, unprofessional management that is stuck in the old industrial management paradigm. The managements of too many of our organizations are defaulting to the carrot-and-stick approach so characteristic of 19th-century thinking – selecting people just because they fit in with cold, objective criteria; over-emphasizing extrinsic reward; increasing the financial and psychological distance between those who manage and those who are the means of production – are inimical to securing the commitment, involvement and spirit of teamwork in employees in that crucial area where attention to customer needs is paramount.

This will do nothing to release the spirit of the people that is so necessary to enable them to engage and offer meaningful service to the customer. Julian Birkinshaw[22] (ibid.) says this:

> '. . . there is still relatively speaking an emphasis on the provision of extrinsic rewards, i.e. salary and bonus, in most large companies. This is one reason why the overall levels of employee disengagement in most companies are so poor . . . extrinsic motivation emerged as the de facto norm within large, industrial companies in the early years of the 20th century, and intrinsic motivation is increasing viewed as a desirable alternative as we move in into the 21st century. Of course, the concept of intrinsic motivation has been around for decades, and its benefits are well documented. But most observers would acknowledge that few large companies are actually managed according to its principles.'

After all, who is going to be intrinsically motivated and superengaged with customers whilst working in the highly pressurized environment of a call centre, servicing a hundred calls a day, needing to ask to go for a comfort break, and with incessant scrolling signs showing the average waiting time of calls waiting on the system; or sitting at a check-out till for hours on end on pittance wages, issuing the same 'service mantras' parrot fashion for fear of being mystery shopped and subjected to 're-training' in the event of failure?

This type of management may lead to compliance, but it will not result in either engagement, involvement, initiative or professionalism

---

[22]Birkinshaw, J. (2010) *Reinventing Management*. Chichester: John Wiley & Sons.

through pride in the job; those essential elements of Service-Ability. Of course, extrinsic reward has a place, but what about intrinsic motivation too, like pride in the job? Motivation, in all its forms and with its delicate balance between material drivers, social drivers and personal ones, has to be given significance if organizations are going to be able to serve their customers well in the future.

We now need to rethink our assumptions about the recruitment, control, motivation, managing performance and reward of people if our organizations are to be responsive to the new service environment in which we now live.

The model of Service-Ability shows that professionalism and pride in the job in employees is essential to increase and secure their engagement with the customer; with belief in the cause stimulated by understanding and absorbing the values, mission and vision of the company; and all in a spirit of initiative and involvement through trust in leaders and managers, as well as colleagues, throughout the length and breadth of the organization. Pay and productivity bonuses have a place, skills recruitment has a place, discipline has a place, but job enrichment for better motivation and engagement of the people must be an over-riding consideration if the culture of distance and detachment from the customer in our organizations is to be challenged and changed. These are tensions that need to be balanced. The question is, where and to what extent is the balance to be struck to get the people right?

8

In 1991, I visited East Germany on a business trip. It was the period immediately after the fall of the Berlin Wall which signalled the demise of the USSR and its socialist satellite régimes; in this case, the German Democratic Republic. In Dresden, I had a conversation with a civil engineer whose job under the former communist state was to build large public buildings. This engineer recounted how he would be given some plans one day and ordered to attend a certain site on a certain date and begin a construction project. When he attended the site and set up his offices, materials would start arriving from various suppliers. However, they would not necessarily be in the right order because they were being requisitioned by a civil servant, working in a central buying department hundreds of miles away who didn't know the project or the people building it. This caused enormous difficulties, but the engineer said he just had to accept it and get on as best he could. In one notable instance, he said, there had been a countrywide shortage of copper wire and he had had to construct a building, finish it and hand it over without any cabling behind the light switches and power sockets. When I asked him why he didn't stop the job until the materials arrived so they could be incorporated in the proper order, he replied 'I would have disappeared and my family would never have heard of me again!'

Power of the office desk

There is no doubt that most organizations of whatever kind today can trace the origin of their design to rational/legal bureaucracy and the idea that work should be split up into component parts carried out by specialists in silos of specialism where people are limited to specific tasks, repetitively, in the interests of mechanistic efficiency for greater output. However, mechanistic efficiency does not necessarily translate into overall organizational efficiency, as we saw in the German engineer's experience.

Bureaucracies are designed specifically to remove initiative from the individuals who work within them because that would militate against the uniformity of regulation-for-efficiency which is the *raison d'être* of the system, but it is the latent sense of being unable to influence the outcome of what bureaucracies do and how that affects us, that makes us uncomfortable with them. Cold and impartial bureaucracies tend to be a law unto themselves, uninterested in the individual, his or her personal needs, wants, views, circumstances, and in some cases, rights (as in the case of Dave Carroll and 'United Breaks Guitars'). This is because they are based essentially on rules and procedures intended to ensure conformity and consistency of output.

The term 'bureaucracy' literally means: 'The power (force, might) of the desk'[1] (probably better thought of as the power of the office, as in the meaning of one who holds office), and most of us at some time or other in our lives have probably encountered this to our dislike.

This feeling is not new:

> 'That vast network of administrative tyranny . . . that system of bureaucracy, which leaves no free agent in all France, except for the man at Paris who pulls the wires.'
>
> **(J.S. Mill 'Westminster Review' XXVIII, 1837.**
> *Online Etymology Dictionary)*

Put simply, bureaucracies are not intended to be responsive to customers, and if we stop and reflect on this for a moment, we realize that here

---

[1]Bureaucracy: 1818, from Fr. *bureaucratie*, from bureau 'office', lit. 'desk' (see bureau) + Gk. suffix -kratia denoting 'power of'; [as in might] coined by Fr. economist Jean Claude Marie Vincent de Gournay (1712 1759) on model of democratie, aristocratie. Source: *Online Etymology Dictionary*, http://etymonline.com/?term=bureaucracy

we are at the beginning of a new millennium, in a world that is getting smaller through social networks and technology (and as its population grows almost exponentially); a world which, as Konosuke Matsushita said as far back as 1979, '. . . is now so complex and difficult, the survival of firms so hazardous in an environment increasingly unpredictable, competitive, and fraught with danger that their continued existence depends on the day-to-day mobilization of every ounce of intelligence', a world in which the individual is asserting himself within the collective, and yet, for the most part, we are still structuring our organizations using the Weber's ideas as a model: one that actively militates against effectiveness in the very situation we need to deal with.

> We live in the most dynamic times ever experienced, where responsiveness, flexibility and engagement are most needed by organizations in our complex society, and yet time and again, we see them being run on an early 20th-century idea of organization, primarily intended for public administration through command and control, with a heavy emphasis on division of work, authority, discipline, superiority of bosses, discipline, subordination, centralization and scalar chains of command from top to bottom in military fashion.

This is not to say that bureaucracy has no place in today's society. In theory, this form of organizations is well suited to control and planning situations, and it still has its uses. Organizations concerned with the processing and status of money, or who have command over monetary funds either in an administrative sense or for remuneration purposes, need a system of rational/legal authority for their administration, because the segregation of roles inherent in bureaucracy ensures no one has complete control over the purse. The UK National Health Service, notwithstanding successive attempts by various governments down the decades since it was set up to introduce market forces, is a massive bureaucracy that works (more or less), even though it seems for much of the time to deliver its patient care despite the system, not as a result of it. Our British Civil Service is considered an exemplary bureaucracy that is running on lines set up over 100 years ago and is still working extremely effectively.

The British Broadcasting Corporation (The BBC) is a very good example of a bureaucracy that can still support innovation (albeit with enormous ongoing tensions). Sir John Tusa, former managing director of the BBC World Service, says this:[2]

> 'The BBC has always been a bit bureaucratic, pretty hierarchical, but has also fooled many by being very adaptable. . . . Within the apparently traditional practices of BBC radio, change could happen if an individual programme decided to seize it. The BBC may sometimes be sluggish in initiating radical change, but it is very open to condoning it once it occurs . . . [The BBC] is constantly changing, constantly evolving, and its capacity to seize opportunity should not be underestimated. There will always be, rightly and inevitably, a degree of centralized direction in the BBC, but it wouldn't be the organization that it is, if independent innovation wasn't delivered from within the programme-making studios . . . Change comes from the programme-making level. That is the good news. The bad news is that centrally-driven change is less successful, less effective, less creative, but that has never prevented successive BBC senior management teams from trying to impose it. They are usually obstructed because effective change will always require local consent.'

There are also some modern business organizations that display all the characteristics of bureaucracies and are successful. Take Toyota, for example: the world's biggest, most productive and arguably highest-quality car manufacturer in the world has a structure that looks highly bureaucratic judging by the quantity of formality, rules and procedures it has, and yet it manages its operations very well and it is very profitable.

Bureaucracies are at their best when applied either to administration where scale is necessary or where scarce resources are being administered

[2]Sir John Tusa, 'Fifty years in the BBC – taking stock of the future'. Newcastle University public lecture, 4 October 2011.

against possibly infinite demand; or in organizations whose inherent rationale demands security and separation of powers, or they cannot be run on any other lines. They are at their worst when speed of response, adaptiveness to rapidly changing environments and market forces, is needed. We must not demonize bureaucracy out of existence, but we must be on guard against the 'spirit of rational bureaucracy', its 'formalistic spirit', (both terms used by Weber himself). Above all, we need to be aware of the danger of too much '. . . carrying out imperative control over human beings.'

Many modern organizations, need to see the light about how they organize, because it strikes deep at the issues of employee motivation, engagement, purpose and productivity which directly impact on the ability of the organization to serve its customer.

Coercive bureaucracy

Earlier, we mentioned the work of Professor Stanley Milgram and his ideas on 'six degrees of separation', but he is perhaps more famous for another piece of groundbreaking work. Milgram was much exercised by the Holocaust, perpetrated against the Jews and others by the Third Reich of Germany under Adolf Hitler, and he sought to examine the relationship between obedience and authority, especially when it came to the commission of immoral or illegal acts carried out under authority by otherwise perfectly moral, law-abiding individuals.

In some highly controversial experiments in the early 1970s, under the direction of his researchers who wore white coats and carried clipboards, he got people to administer apparently lethal pseudo electric shocks to actors posing as human guinea pigs thus demonstrating that human beings were easily able to dissociate themselves from the consequences of their actions whilst acting under authority. One of the most staggering of his conclusions was that bureaucracies were the most effective means of delivering brutality, because the individuals working in them become not only isolated, but insulated from the moral consequences of their actions.

Those baggage handlers, working in an organizational culture that was completely detached from its customers, who so wilfully mistreated Dave Carroll's valuable musical instrument, the means of his own living, would go home to their families and friends at the end of the working day completely normal people but completely oblivious to the ramifications of their fundamentally, morally unacceptable, ethically incorrect behaviour at work.

Commenting on the work of Paul Adler and Brian Borys, Birkinshaw[3] says this:

'. . . some bureaucracies are coercive (they force people to conform to a set of procedures) while others are enabling (they provide the tools and methodologies for continuous improvement). It is not so much the formal procedures that define how things work, it is the way those procedures are interpreted and used by the company's managers.'

Today, we see the use of 'mystery shoppers' in the large supermarket chains whose sole purpose is to ensure that the checkout staff repeat the precise 'service mantra', a formula of words ('Do you want any help with your packing?', 'Do you have a Club Card?' etc.), to each customer for what must be several hundred times a shift in an attempt to enforce uniformity to a pattern of behaviour that has been decided by management, rather than management equipping them with the freedom that would allow them to deliver better interactions with customers using their own personalities.

Mystery shoppers are effectively corporate police officers used to ensure conformity to a pattern of behaviour imposed by management.

The staff know that these people pass clandestinely through their checkout lanes, and they equally know they will be made subject to 'retraining' (aka chastised/disciplined) if they are caught failing to follow

[3]Birkinshaw, J. (2010) *Reinventing Management*. Chichester: John Wiley & Sons.

the rules. This is naked coercion, and it has some very deep moral issues buried within the practice. It negates the inbuilt (and natural) desire of the employee to shape and influence the output of his or her work.

Any observation of organizations structured on bureaucratic principles will reveal the signs: setting apart separate dining facilities whilst leaving the workers to eat in their canteens; reserved parking spaces at the front door for the CEO and other executives who, presumably, are not expected to get wet when walking from their car to their office, whilst the workers have to do just that when going to the factory or office. In many bureaucratically structured organizations, the average worker would not recognize the CEO if he or she passed in the corridor, such is the degree of rank distance between them. Because these types of organizations can become so large, they often spread onto different sites, with the very senior management often locating themselves far away from where the work of production is being done and then information flows become another casualty of the bureaucratic mindset. More often than not, communication can only happen through channels that pass through department heads to other department heads for downward transmission to where the information is needed.

This form of communication is slow and cumbersome. It is highly inefficient when fast decision making is needed, and often results in the decision arriving long after events have overtaken the situation, thus rendering it useless.[4] All this engenders psychological distance, separation and lack of communication, and a sense of 'us and them' instead of just 'us' that leaves the employees feeling just part of a large, unfeeling machine which, of course, is exactly what bureaucratically organizations are meant to be.

Understanding this helps inform us how organizations need to be structured. The verticality, departmentalization, layering and distance from senior management of the bureaucratic organization leads to the

---

[4]Contrast this with Nissan whose corporate policy is explicitly stated as, '… Within the bounds of commercial confidentiality we would like everyone to know what is happening in our company, how we are performing and what we plan. We want information and views to flow freely upward, downward and across our company.'

disengagement that Milgram explored, because people become detached from the directing mind of the organization, as well as from the customer. The sole use of extrinsic motivators by management, such as bonuses and targets, sticks and carrots, which are often accompanied by coercion or threat of sanction if they are not met, is no longer the way. Neither is the pure command-and-control approach to getting things done.

A real-life example

I was once lead consultant in a firm that was suffering badly from all this. It was in a very fast-moving market that demanded fast response and focus from the firm, and it was losing business right, left and centre because its silo mentality had become so entrenched. The organization was fighting itself over turf and power, and losing sight of the customer. No amount of consulting and encouraging from the new managing director or costly training made any difference so, at one crucial session, all 150 or so employees, their managers and directors were gathered into the works canteen one Saturday morning and told to line up in order of rank in front of their department heads. There was much jostling and pushing and vying for position, but ultimately things settled down. Once each row was in place, I positioned myself at the side of the room and sounded an air horn which, in the enclosed space was extremely loud, and shouted 'Hello, I'm the customer!'

The shock of the noise caused everyone to turn sideways toward its source. Only then did the people see how departmentally focused they had become, and how much they had collectively taken their eyes off the customer at the end of a process, the chain of supply into which each department contributed. It took this dramatic act to turn the face of the organization toward the customer, and make it realize that that the customer was not just a name to be checked for credit and invoiced by the finance department; that he or she was not just the recipient of a mechanical service delivered by production, or only spoken to by the sales department The exercise reminded the organization that customers were real live people to be served by the whole organization as a team that cut across departmental boundaries and silo thinking.

In particular the senior managers and departmental heads realized that, although they were in control of their own departments, they had no ownership of the whole process, and things changed for that firm from that day on.

People kept remembering the air horn and this began a steady breakdown of the fragmented processes and turf-defending departmental cultures with their inappropriate internal competition with other departments that saw a turn round in the company's fortunes.

The underlying problem had been a bureaucratic mentality and so much division of labour, that the company had completely lost its way. It needed dramatic action but, when process clarity was achieved, people were released into a new way of thinking, and business picked up dramatically because customers were able to see that the firm had re-engaged with their needs.

Inappropriate technology

Almost 20 years ago, the warning bells were being rung about the inappropriate incorporation of ICT into the business process, and yet we see that they were not heeded. In 1993, a time when widespread use of microcomputer technology was just emerging, Hammer and Champy,[5] in expounding their ideas on business process reengineering, made these remarkably far-sighted comments:

> 'Modern state of the art information technology is part of any reengineering effort, and essential enabler . . . since it permits companies to reengineer business processes. But, to paraphrase what is often said about money and government, merely throwing computers at an existing business problem does not cause it to be reengineered. In fact, the misuse of technology can block reengineering altogether by reinforcing old ways of thinking and old behaviour patterns.'

[5]Hammer, M. and Champy, J. (1993) *Reengineering the Corporation: A Manifesto for Business Revolution*. London: Nicholas Brealey.

The Industrial Revolution brought a massive change in the nature of work and organization, all informed, no doubt usefully, by the important work of Adam Smith, Frederick Winslow Taylor and Max Weber, who were undoubtedly pioneers in their respective fields. However, things have changed. Breaking work down into small slices was the way to achieve efficiency, measuring disaggregated work units for optimization, separating the functions of organizations into separate silos of specialization, maintaining control through power and denying initiative to the worker used to be the way to manage the sprawling 19th- and 20th-century organizations, but we now live in a world where traditional patterns of work have changed.

We live in a knowledge-intensive society dominated by services. One where there is increasing free-agency and looser bonds between employer and employee.

After a century of mass production, where workers served the means of production, operating specialized machinery in a relatively unskilled way, in a very real sense we are witnessing the beginnings of a return to a form of craft system in which skilled people operate general-purpose tools (e.g. laptop computers) and offer highly specialized individual skills on a different basis: one where the psychological contract between employer and employee has changed; where individualism is re-emerging; where employees want personal engagement and autonomy, rather than corporate structure and policy; and where people no longer have jobs for life, but often make their living in portfolio careers, working for different employers on different days of the week.

The latter part of the 20th century saw a sharp change from relative economic stability to massive uncertainty and complexity. Gone are the days of long product life-cycles, mass production, and jobs for life in organizations that lasted down generations. In manufacturing for example, mass production has virtually disappeared. Today manufacturers have to produce a wide range of small batches of product, effectively trying to differentiate each on the principle of the 'market of one', where the level of customization and customer service makes the customer feel that he or she is exclusive or highly preferred.

Range, not volume, is what is needed today and that means a different way of operating.

With complexity comes ambiguity and highly structured organizations are poor at responding to ambiguity. In a slow-changing world, where ambiguity is low and the future reasonably predictable, defining roles and allocating tasks is relatively easy. There is time to plan, learn and act in a routine way. However, when complexity rules, all of these things go out of the window and organizations need to find another way to respond in the new paradigm. Flexible specialization is needed, especially in service industries, where self-organized teams of highly skilled people can come together, combining their skills in ways that meet the contingency they are facing - now!

Today, people in organizations are often faced with task ambiguity, operating in a process that is continually being defined and redesigned, whether in manufacturing or service industries, and it makes no sense to constrain them with rigid structure. No one person's role can ever be that clearly defined or specified in advance, and often there is precious little time for long training periods, and yet 'the power of the office desk' remains in the beating heart of our organizations which, all too often, become turned-in on themselves, not out to the customer.

All too often organizations become more concerned with process than with outcome: how things are done, rather than why.

Form follows function

Bureaucracy is not the only way to organize. People may need to share common resources, like a building or technology, but putting people into functional silos is not the only way to do it; there are other metaphors we can use for organizations.

The chain, for example, is a connected way of organizing. Manufacturers often align this way. Materials enter the factory to be transformed into parts that become subassemblies, combined into final assemblies and then shipped to customers. Chains are well embedded in our business philosophy to the extent that we often describe this whole process as a 'value chain'. Chains characterize much of what manufacturing business is all about today. It would be difficult to imagine a factory without 'chains', but it would be equally difficult to imagine a busy editorial office in a newspaper operating in this way with all the buzzing confusion and interaction, or the trading floor of a stock exchange, or the zig-zag processes of a new-product development department.

In these cases, we often see organization around hubs. A building can be a hub, like in a school or the trading desk on a stock exchange floor where one person or group of people is at the centre of the activity, coordinating it, but such hubs can also be created virtually through sophisticated ICT, so the people can still operate as a team even though situated in different locations. Then there are clusters which are networks without a centre. As we saw in our introduction, modern mathematics is showing us the extent to which networks are behind our social organization and one of their main characteristics is they allow open communication and continuous movement of information.

If you are in a market with short product life-cycles requiring constant innovation, a demand for speed of response and delivery, for adaptability and personalization (the 'market of one' principle where the customer needs a level of customization and service that makes a him or her feel exclusive or preferred), or a pure service industry which usually demands all of these, then you need to find a different way to organize. In the many forms an organization can take, what we need to consider is the effect its form has on how employees function within it so that we might maximize Service-Ability and successfully meet the increasing demands of customers for total satisfaction. Put another way (and mixing metaphors somewhat), 'form follows function' is 'horses for courses.'

'Form follows function' is 'horses for courses.'

The performance of organizations, their ability to allocate resources, to innovate, to adapt and to solve problems is undoubtedly related to how they are structured. In other words, it is a matter of architecture, and the field of organizational design borrows an architectural term: form must follow function. Appropriate organization is more than just technical efficiency. Kilman[6] et al.:

> 'Architects have long worried about both function and aesthetics. Until the past few years, organization designers seem to have concentrated primarily on functionality. The emphasis has been on designs that might improve the effectiveness of an organization, defined as the ability both to produce goods and services and to induce employees to contribute their energies and creativity to the production of these goods and services. Aesthetics as used here refers to the quality of working life in an organization. A high quality working life is one in which the purposes and needs of human beings are met.'

An organization needs to be designed not only to satisfy the needs of its customers, but also to satisfy the needs of its employees for quality in their working life. Bureaucracies tend to create inappropriate internal competition between departments; a team structure, because of the inbuilt culture of interdependence and cooperation, minimizes this risk.

As we have seen good social relationships at work in a spirit of teamwork is a powerful intrinsic motivator that leads to focus and involvement, and an organization seeking Service-Ability needs to structure itself to develop this essential element as part of the 'appropriate organization' element of the Service-Ability model. Focus and involvement are initiated by strategic management with thought-through core values, facilitated by middle management and implemented by line managers, team leaders, all operating in a team spirit, within a culture comprising business process clarity, systems integration and quality processes. It is a conscious process, consciously undertaken.

[6]Kilman, R.H., Pondy, L.R. and Slevin, D.P. (1976) The management of organization design: strategies and implementation. Paper presented at a conference on organization design at the University of Pittsburgh, October 1974, Elsevier North-Holland Inc.

Small is beautiful

Today, the words of Schumacher,[7] 'Small is beautiful', need to echo around us. In his seminal essay of the same title, which came to symbolize a revolt against large, impersonal organizations which started in the 1970s, Schumacher castigated the 'idolatry of giantism' and railed against multinational business corporations, megalopolitan public organizations such as the UK National Coal Board (of which he was an employee) and even nations whose internal markets were largely self-sufficient. He pointed to the achievement of Alfred Sloan at General Motors who had restructured that gigantic firm into a federation of more reasonably sized firms, each with their own drive and sense of identity, whilst still retaining the utility advantage of size, and said this:

> 'While many theoreticians – who may not be too closely in touch with real life – are still engaging in the idolatry of large size, with practical people in the actual world, there is a tremendous longing and striving to profit, if at all possible, from the convenience, humanity and manageability of smallness.'

These are remarkably prescient words in the light of Professor Robin Dunbar's work some 30 years later, which points us to 150 being the maximum number of people we can manageably relate to in any given unit of society because of the size of our brain's neocortex, and the level at which businesses start to acquire formal management structures, hierarchies and rules.

For trust in colleagues, that element of morale upon which Service-Ability is built, internal cross-function barriers need to be made transparent, or eliminated. Individual employees need to be able to exchange information freely with others across the organization at any level where that information is needed.

Problem solving is no longer the prerogative of managers. People need to be freed to interact, not only vertically, but also horizon-

[7]Schumacher, E.F. (1973) *Small is Beautiful*. London: Blond & Briggs.

tally, engaging in information searches and engaging in problem-solving activity at low level, unrestricted by artificial organizational boundaries.

This as important as the task of production itself; indeed it may be seen as the key task in Service-Ability. People must be able to connect to distant parts of the organization to obtain what they need to solve problems and do their job of service customer effectively if they are to be effective in what is now a complex, ambiguous environment in which speed of reaction is necessary to meet these changed conditions.

Rather than rigidity, organizations need shortcuts for information flows. A group of people from many different disciplines – managers, engineers, sales people, marketers (and even customers in those enlightened organizations who are customer centric in all they do) – need the freedom to talk to one another in circuitous ways, sharing views, bouncing ideas off each other, voicing their theories on continuous improvement, bumping and scraping with each other to produce unexpected creative outcomes, operating without overly strict rules and procedures.

Shortcuts eliminate the inefficiencies of silo structures. They are like bypass channels around the dam, and never has this been more needed than in the customer-serving context where the whole capability of the organization is necessary to solve customer problems. For true Service-Ability, we need to reopen the organization to the employee as well as the customer, and at all points and all levels.

Organismic vs. mechanistic

In 1961, Burns and Stalker[8] identified two types of organizational response to the environment, and they observed that each response was dependent on whether the circumstances of operation are stable or changing. They said that organizations could either follow a 'mechanistic' model, or an 'organismic' one.

[8]Burns, T. and Stalker, G.M. (1961) *The Management of Innovation*. London: Tavistock.

Mechanistic organizations act like machines, where tasks are broken down into specialisms within which individuals carry out their assigned duties under a system of hierarchical control, at the top of which rests the overall responsibility and knowledge of the organization and from which emanates orders, instructions and control in a downward cascade. The organization chart of the mechanistic organization very accurately describes what happens within it. It is, of course, the classic bureaucratic model.

On the other hand, the organismic organization is one that is more able to function in changing conditions such as we have today, where new and unfamiliar problems that must be dealt with quickly and holistically continually arise, and in which the response cannot be broken down into component parts. Organismic organizations continually adjust and redefine themselves to different situations, and the tasks they carry out are adaptive and contributive to the situation in which they function, rather than being restrictive and specialized.

Organismic organizations act like living things.

Information flows in these types of organizations take on an advisory form, rather than being orders from above, and this happens at as many levels in the organization as the situation demands. Furthermore, power resides closer to the point at which decisions need to be made. The descriptive charts of this type of organization rarely reflect the true reporting and decision-making processes that are happening within them.

These differences have been likened to the principles derived from the second law of thermodynamics, a metaphor extensively used in open systems theory. The entropic process is a universal law of nature that says all things tend to move from structure to chaos: from closed systems that have a tendency toward a levelling of differences, have form and structure, to continuous interaction with the environment.

Entropy means that systems become more elaborate by the differentiation of their internal structures and processes, and this results in greater complexity. Open systems align their internal components and processes to improve their linkages with the external environment. They acquire information and feedback, and are able to recognize opportunities as a result. In other words, organizations that are highly entropic continuously realign with emerging conditions around them: they seek a state of dynamic equilibrium with their environment and that results in spontaneous interactions between components inside the system as well as those in the external environment.

In organizations that grow bigger, the most natural reaction of management is to counteract entropy by increasing management control. Thus negative entropy becomes a counteracting force to the potential for breakdown and dissipation of organization. The problem is that this tends to turn the organization inwards rather than outwards to its environment, and the unmeasured imposition of negentropy as it is called, leads to a closed system where management and control becomes the daily focus, not serving customers. We see this in a pronounced form in public sector organizations such as the UK National Health Service.

Of course, management needs control, but it is how this is achieved that counts.

If the mindset is that managers want their hands in the wastepaper bins, they will lose sight of the broad picture, which is where true control lies. They key to gaining control is to give away power to decide things to the people who are closest to the customer. This leads not only to better employee collaboration, but also better cooperation with external parties, like customers, through the process of continuously importing, transforming and exporting information. The argument is that organizations must strive constantly to discover and invent ways of allowing a healthy degree of entropy, whilst having in place sufficient systems that allow control, and this is done through thoughtful, informed organizational design.

Teamwork

We saw elsewhere that the experiments conducted by Elton Mayo and his team in the Hawthorne plant of the General Electric Company in Chicago laid the foundations of what became a significant understanding of the importance of teamwork in an organization. He showed that the simple act of forming people into groups made them feel special and resulted in steadily increasing productivity, despite artificial variation of the conditions of their working environment. It was the standing of a group and its members in the wider context that affected their morale which gave a spur to productivity; nowadays enlightened organizations are structuring to leverage that effect.

Organizations are not just collections of people with a collective name.

Groups do not always function well, however. Relationships in groups are often much more stressful than individual relationships, and the larger the group, the greater the potential for stress there is. Individual motivations can sabotage groups. People can have hidden agendas which, whilst some may be positive and maintenance orientated, i.e. aimed at maintaining harmony, or keeping the group on track, others can be self orientated and destructive: aimed at satisfying personal needs[9]. The key issue is how the group deals with these behaviours because it is not the responsibility of one individual; all members need to have insight into these dynamics and take collective responsibility for the group's output to keep it unaffected by these entirely normal human behavioural traits. Groups can suffer collective emotions too.

In the early 1960s, the Kennedy administration in the White House, made a series of disastrous decisions on foreign policy. The invasion of North Korea was one of them, but its response to the Bay of Pigs crisis in April 1961, three months after John F. Kennedy was elected President of the USA, was particularly instructive. This was an unsuccessful attempt, using a CIA trained force of Cuban exiles, to invade the Cuban mainland and overthrow the government led by Fidel Castro, who is said to have

---

[9]Kakabadse *et al.* (1998) describe these as: attacking/defending, blocking/stating difficulties, diverting, seeking sympathy/recognition, withdrawing/point scoring, over-contributing, trivializing/diluting.

sent a note to Kennedy afterwards saying 'Thanks for Playa Girón. Before the invasion, the revolution was weak. Now it's stronger than ever.'[10] The invasion was decisively defeated after only three days and it had serious international repercussions.

In 1972, Irving Janis, a research psychologist at Yale University and Professor Emeritus at the University of California, Berkeley, coined the term 'Groupthink',[11] which describes the systematic errors groups can make when taking collective decisions. Janis had studied a number of American foreign policy errors including the Bay of Pigs incident and concluded that, under certain conditions, commitment to the group and the sense that because everyone is in agreement means that the group must be right, can override the ability to assess situations realistically. It is the cohesiveness of the group that leads to groupthink and it can be dangerous, because people who are too cohesive tend to adopt a common approach that is characterized by a failure to question a task or problem, and ignore evidence suggesting that what it is planning is ill advised. (This is another reason why barriers in organizations must be made much more transparent.)

People working in groups is one thing, but it is teamwork that is the pumping heart of the organization which encourages purpose, direction, a shared understanding of corporate mission, policies, goals and how to achieve them. The team is the environment that provides structure, where resources necessary to support corporate purpose can be utilized and it ensures the development of everyone in the organization.

Teams are a special type of group because they produce more than the sum of their component parts through teamwork: the coordination of activity and degree of collaboration necessary to tackle a discrete project or task when members know the joint objective, share responsibility and support one another in their individual tasks as well as the overall group endeavour. When members of a group become interdependent and each

---

[10] Playa Girón and Playa Larga were the landing sites for seaborne forces of armed Cuban exiles in the Bay of Pigs invasion.
[11] Janis, Irving (1972). *Victims of Groupthink: A Psychological Study of Foreign-policy Decisions and Fiascoes.* Boston: Houghton Mifflin.

member has to rely on the others in a task environment whose outcome is jointly owned by the group, when the members of the group are set to work towards a clearly defined common goal or policy, the outcome is greater than the sum of the component parts.

When groups start to act like teams their output becomes greater.

Team spirit is vital for trust in one's colleagues. When members of a team trust each other, each can get on with the job in an uncomplicated, natural way. Trust in colleagues leads to flexibility of working, where members of a team willingly switch tasks to get the job done in a spirit of understanding that minimizes conflict, maximizes performance, and produces a sense of purposefulness. Team spirit is especially important at the point where the organization and the customer meet because it results in focus, not only on task in hand, but on the ideals and aims of the organization and, most importantly, on the customer. Above all, involvement through team spirit and trust is what eradicates inappropriate internal competition, allowing people to get on with the job in hand without wasting energy and time on internal politics.

Tuckman and Jensen[12] showed us very clearly the stages teams go through before becoming effective. They described forming, storming, norming and performing. (Katzenbach and Smith[13] used different terminology to describe what are broadly the same characteristics. They used the terms 'working group', 'pseudo team', 'potential team', 'real team' and 'high-performing team' instead.)

When teams first form, the members have to examine internal differences and assumptions before they can truly come together. They engage in what someone rather disparagingly called 'ritual sniffing': the members are all polite toward one another and spend some time trying to get to know more about the others. Once the task is underway, however, differ-

---

[12]Tuckman, B. and Jensen, M. (1977) Stages of small group development revisited. *Groups and Organizational Studies* **2**.
[13]Katzenbach, J. and Smith, D. (1993) *The Wisdom of Teams.* Boston, MA: Harvard Business School Press.

ences in outlook, ways of working and values come to the fore, and this often results in rows and disagreements. If these can be surmounted, (and in many cases they are not, causing the team to fail early on, or at least never become productive), then a norming phase ensues when the members become adjusted to one another, each accepting the other and at least respecting different outlooks, if not actually coming into alignment on many things. This process is often uncomfortable and risky but it is the only way, often, that the team can hammer out its own norms and gain trusting cohesion and a sense of common purpose. Only then does team spirit emerge, the team gels and starts to perform productively. It is important to understand how this process that helps achieve team spirit and involvement, which is one of the underpinning principles of Service-Ability.

Specific customer service skills are important, but these need to be augmented with a meta skill: Service-Ability; refined by refocusing on the customer, and developed in interactions with colleagues; all in a culture of team spirit that sees the customer as the sole reason why we open the doors on a Monday morning.

Service-Ability needs a different organizational idea: a different approach of the organization to its meta environment, and that is achieved through autonomous, self-managing teams.

Autonomous, self-managing teams

If they are to be able to operate for the maximum benefit to the organization, teams need to be housed in a structure that is suitable for them and that brings us back to the need for appropriate organization. Effective self-organizing, self-managing teams can't emerge unless there is an environment in which they can happen, and the creation of such an environment is a managerial responsibility. Organizational design needs to be able to allow the formation of cross-functional, autonomous (self-managing) teams to spontaneously form at all levels, even at senior sectoral levels such as finance, marketing, operations and production.

Autonomy is self-determination as opposed to determination from outside influences. A living organism, such as a cell, an ant, or a human being, behaves as a coherent, self-determining entity in its interactions with those around it and its environment. It does not go through input–processing–output sequences, it just exists and interacts. (Contrast this with a bank ATM, which is controlled by outside influences, not least its designers and programmers.) Autonomy means self-governed, whereas its antithesis, heteronomy, means other-governed. The autonomous, self-managed team, therefore, becomes self-organizing, self-controlling, does not exist to process inputs and outputs per se and it determines the cognitive domain in which it operates.[14]

Autonomous teams find their expression through individuals who depend on each other and act *interdependently*. Such teams are a unified entity within the system (the organization) in which they exist, and determine the area, the sphere, the province in which they engage with their environment. In a sense, just like a living cell in a body, autonomous, self-managing teams determine their boundary within the organization, albeit a boundary that is relatively transparent and allows interaction with the environment (just as the semi-permeable membrane of the living cell does). The boundary is socially territorial, not a physical membrane. The entity that the team represents, is said by biologists to have organizational or operational closure, whereby its members have self circular reference to one another as a network that defines them as a unit.

Autonomous teams however, are always structurally coupled to their environment.[15] They are not rogue units. The have congruence, meaning and a part to play in the whole, it is just that they have internal, self-constructing mechanisms that regulate and control their behaviour, and the processes of exchange with their environment. They do not have these things artificially imposed from above by 'management' as super-regulated behavioural patterns. In the case of customer-facing teams, this means that they are flexible in how they interact, based on their sensitivity to the feedback gained continuously from the customers with whom they

---

[14]Thompson, E. (2010) *Mind in Life*. Boston, MA: Harvard University Press.
[15]Thompson, E., ibid.

interact on a daily basis. This is to be contrasted with the rigid strictures placed on many customer service teams through monitoring (e.g. recording) what they say, allowing them to do only what they can do by forcing so-called expert systems of customer service designed by senior managers as being the one best way to do things.

Autonomous, self-organizing customer-serving teams drive the process from the bottom up through energy and creativity, rather than it being controlled from the top down by management that concentrates on the relationship of the team and its members to the organization and its (the management's) policies. However, it is not just customer-serving employees who need this approach. It is applicable to the rest of the organization, even the managers and those who have overall directional control. All can act as self-managing, autonomous teams, cross-functionally. So too can those such as production, administrative employees, whose work it is to manage on a day-to-day basis at each level within these various disciplines.

Appropriate team organization results in high performance and, ultimately, total customer satisfaction.

Focus on the customer can only come from an organization that is united in acting with purpose that derives from trust in one's colleagues, which in turn comes from working as a team that has control over how it operates and, in the context of the larger organization, autonomy: with learning, understanding each other and flexibility of job roles as key facilitators. To do this, there has to be a move away from bureaucratically administered management steeped in the 'directing mind' control paradigm, to a team-delivered structure that is able to meet what amounts these days to a demand for a bespoke service-product.

Complexity theory

There is another area of modern science 'complexity theory' that has some amazing insights from which we can benefit in our consideration of how to organize appropriately for Service-Ability. Johnson[16] defines complexity theory as:

'The study of the phenomena which emerge from a collection of interacting objects – and a crowd is a perfect example of such an emergent phenomenon which emerges from a collection of interacting people.'

In the chapter on getting the people right, we saw that one of the most interesting aspects of Google's operation, one that tends to differentiate it from other more conventional organizations, is its encouragement of emergence, an idea that has developed steadily in the last 15 years or so. Referring to Steven Johnson[17], author of a major book on emergence in nature, Birkinshaw[18] says this:

'. . . where the imperative is for innovation, adaptability, or personal engagement in an issue, the alternative principle of emergence offers greater potential . . . The concept of emergence, as used here, refers to spontaneous coordination through self-interested behaviours of independent actors . . . when we see a community of freelance programmers coming together to build a new open-source software product; and when we see an army of termites building a 20-foot high tower, we are witnessing the principle of emergence at work.'

Emergent behaviour is large-scale, collective patterns of behaviour in complex systems and it is closely related to self-organization.[19] It is collective self-organizing at the organizational level where related elements

---

[16] Johnson, N.F. (2007) *Simple Complexity: A Clear Guide to Complexity Theory*. Oxford: Oneworld.

[17] Johnson, S.B. (2001). *Emergence: The Connected Lives of Ants, Brains, Cities, and Software*. New York: Scribner.

[18] Birkinshaw, J. (2010) *Reinventing Management*. Chichester : John Wiley & Sons

[19] Thompson, E., ibid.

such as self-managing, autonomous teams, related and identifiable, standing out from the background as it were, become a system. The collection of network elements identifying and representing locally defined needs (as perceived by those elements) feed into the collective organization, whilst being globally constrained by the logic, the rationale of the organization and its aims and purpose.

Emergent behaviour happens when the individual, the team and the whole organization merge in a dynamic interaction that produces energy, adaptability and creativity.

When interacting people engage in the 'spontaneous coordination through self-interested behaviours of independent actors' it stands at the opposite end of the spectrum from bureaucracy. In many ways, it can be seen as an antidote to the seemingly inbuilt tendency to negentropic bureaucracy. At the very least, it is a tension (an adaptive tension), which, if applied, can pull an organization back from the excesses of negentropy of which bureaucracy is undoubtedly capable.

As Maquire and McKelvey[20] say:

> 'The "gradient" driving events in firms can be usefully conceptualized as adaptive tension (McKelvey 1999). If we define the firm as an open system importing energy-matter and information (in the form of labour, capital, raw materials etc.) then in successive time slices a large collection of synchronous idiosyncratic micro state events can be seen to occur that cause the system to transition to a new state: they are put to use in creating the kind of activities, accomplishments, and competitive positioning that move the firm towards its goals and hence reduce adaptive tension. In a firm, this tension represents the difference between its current state and activities and what it needs to accomplish so as to optimize its

[20]Maquire, S. and McKelvey, W. (1999) Complexity and Management: Moving From Fad to Firm Foundations. *Emergence* 1(2), 19–61.

performance, which for many analyses can be assumed to be obtaining a competitive advantage – hence adaptive tension.'

Adaptive tension allows organizations to change and mould themselves, but it is not chaos. Fundamental to understanding it is the analogy of the Bénard cell: two plates with fluid between them. If one of the plates is heated, a temperature differential is created in the fluid and this causes the hotter molecules to start to move toward the colder plate. Below a certain level of heating, the molecules tend to remain in place, conducting energy by colliding with each other. Above this first level of heating, the molecular movement takes the form of currents of convection, which circle round from the hot to the cold areas and back again; the molecules 'wandering, bumping, responding' as it has been described. The application of too much heat causes the molecular movement to become chaotic and the system breaks down.

It is the middle state, known as the 'region of complexity', where purposeful movement activity takes place in the system, and this 'complexity field', as it is known, is said to exist 'at the edge of chaos', a place where 'adaptive tension' is created. If you think of the bureaucracy as the low heat or cold state where nothing much happens and the system is static and unchanging, and then think of the extreme situation where chaos reigns and there is no organization, then the region of complexity in the middle is where emergent behaviour can occur in an organizations; where barriers between departments can break down, and where adaptation can happen. People can flow 'wandering, bumping, responding' to one another, and be more creative and productive, in an environment where they can engage with the organization, their colleagues and their customers in a more serving way.

The clever bit is to energize the organization enough to make it come alive, but not so much that it breaks down into chaos.

This internal customer-serving culture is what translates into the total customer service that is the hallmark of Service-Ability. This is undoubtedly a much more challenging and uncomfortable environment for managers and CEOs who have to 'walk the floor' and become involved in the day-to-day activity of the organization rather than staying in their office (both literally and metaphorically) in the comfortable, predicable framework of a bureaucracy where the rule-bound rational/legalism prevails, but it is where emergent behaviour happens. With thoughtful and appropriate structuring, organizations can provide an environment in which employees are freed up to act in an engaged way in a culture of empowerment, professionalism and involvement with the organization's aims, and thus cause a realignment with the needs of the customer.

As we saw earlier in this chapter, too much bureaucracy, too much command and control, and you suck the life out of the organization, and depersonalize its employees who pass that culture on at the customer interface. However, too much energy and change, can very easily slip into chaos, causing people to lose focus and the organization to become chaotic and haphazard in its overall delivery. It is all about creating a healthy balance between a degree of sensible organization sufficient to keep things on track, and sufficient energization that provides the climate in which verticality becomes flattened, power decentralized, empowerment enabled, and in which Service-Ability can function and flourish.

However, as we saw when dealing with the concept of bureaucracies, we must not get carried away with one idea. It is all a matter of degree: of balancing the tensions between the benefits of one approach and the benefits of the other. The balance is ably struck by Birkinshaw,[21] who says:

> 'I agree with Brown[22] and Eisenhardt[23] that, as a management principle, emergence means putting in place the guiding structures that will stimulate individuals to coordinate their activities, in a focused way, of their own volition.'

[21] Birkinshaw, J. (2010) *Reinventing Management*. Chichester : John Wiley & Sons
[22] Shona Brown, a doctoral graduate of Stanford University and former consultant at management consultants McKinsey & Co., subsequently joined Google and helped put these ideas into practice.
[23] Brown S. L. and Eisenhardt (1998) *Competing on the Edge*. Boston, MA: Harvard Business School Press. (Quoted in Birkinshaw, ibid.)

The key is to get the structure right for the purpose whilst guarding against overweening, inefficient, cold management and the seemingly inbuilt tendency to the exercise of control, rationality and detachment from the outside environment which prevents the organization being adaptive, flexible and responsive to customers' needs.

Summing up appropriate organization

There can be no doubt that our organizational instincts default to the bureaucratic model. It is traditional and widespread, and there is a sound historical reason for it.

Bureaucracy is the default because we suffer from an overrun of the zeitgeist, the spirit of the age of modernism. Modernism is all we have known since industrialization began, since capitalism was invented and since scientific rationalism became the primary source of societal values and explanations. For all of the 19th and much of the 20th centuries, we knew what organizations looked like. They were vertically integrated, top-down managed through command and control, they either had or sought to have full control over their supply chain (Henry Ford even insisted on the company owning the iron ore and the sand that went into making the steel for his cars), and they were highly centralized. However, we are now in the period known as the postmodern.

Postmodernism is less a new era and more a reaction to modernism. We are leaving behind us the belief in the power of rational explanation for everything in favour of a subjective rationality where all things are held to be relative, not absolute. It displays an abandonment of pure rationality in favour of an explanation in which the complex individual rather than the rational collective is becoming the focus. Gone are the times when people believed there was 'one best way' to do things in management and organization, as F.W. Taylor and Max Weber did.

Today, we live in a different world when increasing competition and rapid external change are all around us: a world in which we see an assertion of power by the customer/consumer who is stronger and better informed than ever before; a time where the inflexible nature of the bureaucratic mindset in the workplace is becoming increasingly unacceptable. That is why those organizations that are implementing ICT so extensively to gain scale without people, and are using it as a form of coercive control over their staff and customers, are an anachronistic reflection of 19th-century thinking and practice. Their technology is cutting edge but their organizational models are behind the times: they must catch up.

Not all organizations exist to serve a customer, but most have a consumer of their output. Not all are driven by the profit motive, but all are subject to financial pressures that demand every ounce of efficiency, the most 'bang for the buck' as they say, and that means consistently delivering what they set out to deliver in the most efficient way, with the minimum of costly kick-back from the recipient of their output.

In this respect, all organizations are alike and, whatever the sector, whatever the purpose, whatever the logic behind an organization, we desperately need to embrace modern organizational theory if our organizations are to gain that focus, adaptability and general involvement with their staff and their customers. We must find a way to balance the efficiency of the bureaucracy with the flexibility needed to adapt and meet constantly changing demands. We must find a way to release emergent behaviour in our people to gain Service-Ability.

9

This reprint from an article that appeared in the *Daily Mail*,[1] London, on Thursday 29 July 2010 reminds us of the infamous war crime of the Vietnam War: the 'My Lai Massacre', which was followed by the torching of the village by young American troops under the command of 25 year old Lt. William Calley. Over 500 innocent civilians were murdered, the youngest just one year old and the oldest 82 years:

'It was with . . . dubious preparation that 2nd Lt Calley was airlifted into South Vietnam. By early 1968, soon after his arrival, the country was in the grip of the Tet Offensive: a massive push for victory which brought 80,000 North Vietnamese troops driving southwards, striking with unprecedented ferocity. Calley was deployed to the scene of the fiercest fighting, in Quang Ngai Province, and placed in charge of a platoon of some 50 infantrymen in Charlie Company, part of the proud 23rd Infantry (American) Division. While most of his charges despised the country and its people, Calley found he loved his new life in Vietnam. Rarely able to get a date with women in Miami, where he was regarded as a nonentity and a drifter, he found he had the pick of the prettiest "boom-boom girls" – cheap local prostitutes who touted for business around the US camps. He also relished having the power to dish out orders without rebuke

[1]Read more: http://www.dailymail.co.uk/news/article-485983/Found-The-monster-My-Lai-massacre.html#ixzz0v5ZqUCEL

– even though they were frequently ill-advised. More than once his crass misjudgments endangered his men, and when a subordinate was shot dead because Calley marched them into danger, they secretly discussed "fragging" – or assassinating – the bungling officer universally known as Lieutenant S***head. Meanwhile, the officers above Calley were demanding results. Charged with the mission of wiping out as many "Commies" as possible, his bosses set up "free fire zones", where anyone could be shot on the merest suspicion of collusion, and demanded daily "kill ratios"'.

According to Wikipedia, fragging is a US military term that originated during the Vietnam War and was a means by which an unpopular officer could be assassinated in the heat of battle by a fragmentation grenade thrown by one of his own men. Unlike a bullet, a hand grenade destroys itself and all the evidence, so it cannot be traced to a specific piece of ordnance, or to a specific soldier. Thus it can plausibly be claimed that the grenade landed too close to the person 'accidentally' killed, or that another member of the unit threw the grenade, or even that a member of the other side threw it. According to Guenter Lewy[2], in 1969 70 officers or non-commissioned officers were the intended victims of such attacks, and this number went up to 154 in 1970, and 158 in 1971 at the height of the Vietnam War.

In the hard world of the military in battle, bad leadership can have the most extreme consequences. Harsh, inept, overzealous leadership, undertaking dangerous or suicidal missions for self glorification of the leader, or even just being a leader without possessing any of the skills for the job is a dangerous game for the individual. As Williams[3] puts it:

[2]US House, Committee on Appropriations, Subcommittee on Department of Defense, DOD Appropriations for 1972. Hearings. 92nd Congress, 1st sess. Part 9. 17 May–23 September 1971. P 585 (updated later). OASD (Comptroller), Selected Manpower Statistics. May 1975, p.63. Quoted in Lewy, G. (1978) *America in Vietnam*. New York: Oxford University Press.
[3]Williams, R.W. (1998) *Mastering Leadership: Key Techniques for Managing and Leading a Winning Team*. London: Thorogood.

'There is all the difference in the world between real toughness, based upon personal courage, a well-informed, intelligent-reading of situations and a high sense of moral responsibility for outcomes, on the one hand – and boorish blame-ridden aggression, on the other. Generally, those unable to wear their epaulettes easily, appropriately and competently, are insecure, unsure of themselves, afraid, or, inexperienced and untutored as leaders.'

Leadership is about setting direction, stimulating change, encouraging people to adapt, innovate, improve, and it is about setting an ethical and moral framework for the community being led, whether that is in the armed forces, in society, or in an organizational setting. Above all, it is about being influential amongst people who are themselves purposeful creatures and who, if they are to be coordinated in a certain direction, need particularly purposeful people to lead them.

Some say leaders are born, others say they can be made but whatever the reality, one thing is sure: leadership is not about gung-ho activity leading the troops into battle as it were.

Professor John Adair[4], who had a colourful career including service in a Bedouin regiment, working as a deckhand on an Arctic trawler, and lecturing at the Royal Military Academy, Sandhurst, is a pioneering British thinker on the theory and practice of leadership and he says this:

'You can be appointed as a manager, but you're not a leader until your appointment is "ratified" in the hearts and minds of those who work for you. There's got to be a degree of acceptance of you by followers that is not necessary if you're just holding an appointment.'

The young man, Lt. Calley, relatively untrained, inexperienced in leadership and lacking in moral fibre, had not achieved this ratified

---

[4] Adair J., in an interview in *Director* magazine, November 1988.

acceptance. He had legitimate authority (and in the armed forces, that truly is legitimate because it carries the weight of law behind it), but he wasn't able to be an effective leader because he had neither the moral authority, nor the attributes and character for leadership. For Calley, authority didn't make him a leader even though it was formally conferred on him. Authority on its own does not make a leader; it is the power to influence that does. It is the capacity or the potential in the individual to influence people and their direction, not the raw power derived from sheer authority acquired through office, law and rationalism.

In an organizational setting, authority only gives the leader the legitimacy to structure work, decide priorities, coordinate activities and make certain things clear about what is right and wrong according to the rules and morals of that particular organization and of society, but authority doesn't make you a leader.

Leadership concepts

The subject and practice of leadership has been the source of much debate over many years but one thing is sure: the idea of what a leader is, is highly conditioned by stereotypes. Testosterone leadership is one of those stereotypes and it is widespread in the business world, as witness our reference to the management styles of the financial services industry in the chapter, Getting the People Right. This approach to leadership is found in just about all types of organization, but particularly in those that have a strong character at their head, or in those with a predominance of younger, highly upwardly mobile managers, whose personal power or leadership clout is insufficient to get people to follow them in any other way.

Leaders of this type are those, for example, who unreasonably demand reports or complex decisions on their desk, in writing, by first thing the next day, and then leave the work, the result of a midnight labour by their subordinate, in their in-tray without attention for several days, before even looking at it. The corporate world is permeated with testosterone leadership. It is also permeated with the cult of personality. Peter

Senge (1990),[5] one of the leading writers on leadership of our time, says this:

> 'Our prevailing leadership myths are still captured by the image of the captain of the cavalry leading the charge to rescue the settlers from the attacking Indians. So long as such myths prevail, they reinforce a focus on short-term events and charismatic heroes rather than on systemic forces and collective learning.'

This 'saviour' approach to leadership became prevalent in the 1990s and still persists to this day. Before that time, most people would never have known the names of the people at the head of our major corporations; today they are often household names. Even institutional investors credit CEOs of big companies with superhuman, exclusive ability to create shareholder wealth. Surowiecki[6] quotes a Burston Marsteller poll carried out in the 1990s that found that 95 percent of investors sampled said they would buy a stock based on what they thought of the company's CEO but, crucially, he says this:

> 'At any moment, of course, there are always CEOs with exceptional track records, executives who just seem better able to outthink their competitors, anticipate their customer market, and motivate their employees. But the business landscape of the last decade is littered with CEOs who went from being acclaimed as geniuses to being dismissed as fools because of strategic mistakes.'

He refers to the work of the economist Armen Alchian who, in 1950, pointed out that in the economy of America, success by striving to get ahead is not necessarily an indicator of skill in foresight, but may be '. . . the result of fortuitous circumstances'. In other words, this kind of success may be down to simple luck. Certainly there are many examples

[5]Senge, P. (1990) *The Fifth Discipline*. New York: Doubleday.
[6]Surowiecki, J. (2005) *The Wisdom of Crowds: Why the Many are Smarter than the Few*. London: Abacus.

of the loss of leadership from a failure to foresee what could reasonably have been seen. Politics is strewn with them.

Foresight (or prescience) is undoubtedly a leadership attribute. Robert Greenleaf,[7] who died in 1990, and who was a powerful voice in the dialogue to reshape management and leadership, defined foresight as '. . . a better than average guess about what is going to happen when' and argues that foresight is a significant component of the 'lead' that a leader has over others. He further argues that foresight is the 'Central ethic' of leadership and that the prescient man possesses a sort of 'moving average' mentality (to borrow a statistical term) in which past, present and future are one, and in which he or she has a sense of trends. Quoting Machiavelli he puts it this way:

> 'Thus it happens in matter of state; for knowing afar off (which it is only given a prudent man to do) the evils that are brewing, they are easily cured. But when, for want of such knowledge, they are allowed to grow so that everyone can recognize them, there is not longer any remedy to be found.'

Greenleaf goes on to list another ten attributes that characterize the leader: initiative, taking the chance of success in the face of the risk of failure; pointing direction, having a goal and being able to articulate it; listening and understanding in order to gain the insights needed to set the right course; the imaginative use of language, not simply forcing all experience into a single verbal scheme but conveying meaning through the use of triggers to the hearer's imagination, and making the connection between the verbal concept and the hearer's own experience; withdrawal, the ability to step back from the heat of pressurized situations rather than charging in in order to sense the right course of action; the acceptance of people and empathy with them, always being able to accept the person whilst sometimes rejecting the behaviour; intuition, that ability to 'know

[7]Greenleaf, R.K. (1977) *Servant Leadership: A Journey Into the Nature of Legitimate Power and Greatness*. Mahwah, NJ: Paulist Press.

the unknowable' about people and situations; awareness and perception, the ability to keep a sustained wide span of awareness that allows one to 'See it as it is'; patient persuasion (sometimes one person at a time); and conceptualizing which Greenleaf argues is the prime leadership talent in which the leader can 'see' or envision the finished scenario when the work is complete.

Very much echoing this, Warren Bennis,[8] Professor of Management at the University of Southern California, sees the leader as 'social architect' of the organization or group, and identifies four key abilities of leaders: the management of attention through having a vision that everyone can believe in and which provides a bridge to the future; the management of meaning by communicating that vision and translating it into successful results; the management of trust, 'the emotional glue that binds followers to leaders', by being consistent, constant, focused and coherent ('all of a piece' is how he described Margaret Thatcher, the U.K Prime Minister from 1979 to 1990); and the management of self, which means persistence and resilience in the face of failure, self-knowledge, a willingness to go on learning, commitment to a cause, a willingness to take risks, and the acceptance of challenge.

> Bennis argues that 'Managers do things right. Leaders do the right thing.'

At the heart of leadership, therefore, is the interplay of attitudes, skills and attributes in the individual. Effective leadership has very little to do with power and authority.

Corridors of power poem

To illustrate the point, here is a humorous little ditty I have used many times when teaching managers:

[8]Bennis, W., Nanus, B. (1985) *Leaders: the Strategies for Taking Charge*, New York: Harper and Collins.

What is it that becomes a man when put in charge of others?
What makes him change his attitude towards his former brothers?
Did God in his great wisdom upon this man bestow
Some kind of magic quality he never had before?
Is there a secret fountain where this knowledge can be gained?
Where normal men go up to drink, and come back fully changed?
And why must every candidate to this exclusive band
Decide to exercise on me, his powers of command?
How often in the still of night when thoughts keep sleep at bay,
I've thought about this breed of men: am I not just like they?
For I could strut around the deck, white helmet on my head,
And demonstrate to all that I'm the leader, not the led.
In coffer dams and engine rooms I'd proudly do my stuff.
The monarch of the shipyard scene: Swan Hunter's Brian Clough!
And while I dream my dreams away (like Flanagan and Allen),
I'm treated like a half-pint when I know I am a gallon.
But dreams are only empty. No substance, more's the pity.
Perhaps not Brian Clough at all; perhaps just Walter Mitty?
Yet through these jumbled thoughts of mine still that one question
bothers,
What is it that becomes a man when put in charge of others . . . ?

'The Corridors of Power' (Anon.)

Sources of power

In 1870, the then Pope, Pius IX declared Papal Infallibility, the dogma that says that by action of the Holy Spirit, the Pope is preserved even from the possibility of error in his teaching on faith and morals in the Roman Catholic Church. Lord Acton, an English historian and prominent member of the Catholic laity, was passionately against this. Despite his and others' best endeavours, however, the dogma was accepted and, in April 1887 in his famous dictum, he said this:

'I cannot accept your canon that we are to judge Pope and King unlike other men with a favourable presumption that they did no wrong. If there is any presumption, it is the other way, against the holders of power, increasing as the power increases. Historic responsibility has to make up for the want of legal responsibility. Power tends to corrupt, and absolute power corrupts absolutely. Great men are almost always bad men, even when they exercise influence and not authority: still more when you superadd the tendency or certainty of corruption by full authority. There is no worse heresy than the fact that the office sanctifies the holder of it.'

Power and authority are controversial ideas. They evoke strong feelings and their use creates many difficulties in personal as well as organizational relationships because they are often used simply as a means of control through coercion. There is no doubt that power in the social context is often used in this way.

We saw in Appropriate Organization, how the power of bureaucracies can be used to coerce staff and even customers, and it is commonplace for managers to face accusations of abuse of their power, or refusing to share it, or being reluctant even to use it at times in pursuit of coercive goals (coercion doesn't have to be overt and brutal – it can be subtly manipulative, insidious and difficult to detect). The problem lies in the fact that bureaucracies lack the social glue that makes an organization act as a living organism and so they have to rely on formally defined power and authority in order to function. The nature and basis of the power of the leader is much more complex than that, however, and it is vitally important that we understand what it really means in the organizational setting.

Almost 50 years ago, French and Raven[9] defined power as '. . . a measure of an entity's ability to control the environment around itself, including the behaviour of other entities' and they listed five separate sources of power within organizations: legitimate; reward; coercive; expert; and referent. This is a taxonomy that has stood the test of time. The first three of these bases of power derive from the organization itself and the specific authority or role to which a person is assigned in that

[9]French, J.R.P. and Raven, B. (1960) The bases of social power. In: D. Cartwright (ed.) *Studies in Social Power*. Ann Arbor, MI: University of Michigan Press.

organization. As we have already discussed, legitimate power is that which is expressed within the rules and structure of the organization; it is legal and extant. It is the basis of the rational/legal thesis behind Weber's bureaucratic model discussed at length already, and it is made manifest in rules, regulations and codes of conduct, both formal and informal ('the way we do things here').

Reward power obviously derives from the ability of the organization to control pay, promotion, holidays, etc., and is also legal and rational. Coercive power is the ability to apply punishment. Managers have coercive power derived from their position in the hierarchy to reprimand, demote, and sack employees, and it is hard to imagine how else it could be. These are important decisions and the power to make them must lie within a hierarchical framework. However, to rely solely on this sort of power will never work in our modern organizations whose ability depends on harnessing the intellectual capital of the combined resources of the people who work in it.

It is the last two sources of power, those that originate from the person's own individual characteristics, from which effective leadership comes. Expert Power is where a person possesses particular knowledge or skills that are in demand by others, whether by the organization, or colleagues within that organization who need what they have to offer to get their own job done. This is a form of organizational power that is emerging with greater importance than ever before as we move from an industrial to a knowledge economy. However, the real leadership power, referent power, is what makes the difference.

Referent power is what makes the difference.

Referent power derives from the identification with the leader by those who are led. It is based on affection, affiliation and respect for the leader, not just the office. Like expert power, referent power comes from within the person, but it is not rational or learned, it is largely a function of the person's character, background, values, knowledge, ethics, attractiveness and interpersonal skills. Deep down, it is all about trust. Leaders who possess referent power are able to lead in a way that makes people able to follow, even when they can't see the big picture or when times are difficult. It is about inculcating a belief in the cause of the organization so that the people are imbued with it and see their work as furthering that cause. It is also about mutuality, a relationship, if not of equals necessarily, at least one where the people being led feel that they have power too: that their views, needs, wants, etc., are heard by the leader and factored in to leadership decisions.

Treating people as cogs in the machine will not work. Leaders need to hear, not just listen, and they need to show how they have absorbed what their people are saying even if they reject it in favour of a different balance of factors.

If 'Do as I say' is all people are left with in an organization, then it will be wracked with disagreements, conflict and inappropriate competition.

As we saw with Lord Acton's protest, authority does not confer unlimited power upon an individual. It is not a licence to rule over people, interfering in all aspects of what they do. It is not a licence to boss people around, even in an organization in which the leader is given a high degree of legitimate power. Authority must always be subject to the test of acceptability based on context (the difference, for example, between a skipper at sea in a storm and the leader of a group of charity volunteers) and leaders need to balance the difference between having 'power over' and 'power to do'. The former is the command and control approach that relies solely on legitimate authority as a means to get things done but, except perhaps in the heat of battle where men's fear and instincts for survival are in danger of confounding the objective, and draconian use of legal orders is all that is left, trying to run an organization by command and control is a futile exercise.

The use of legitimate power, authority legally possessed, must be confined to those situations where reward and discipline need to be exercised, otherwise that legitimate power, the 'power to do' must be directed so as to ensure that those who are the means of production of the product or service are fully equipped and supported by the leader to get on with the job and achieve the maximum result for their organization.

The higher someone rises in an organization, the more the need to apply the legitimate power so acquired to decide where resources are best placed, whether they be human, financial or physical. The higher one rises, the more one must become a servant to those who are the means of production, using power to direct resources to aid the people who are actually doing the business and delivering the product.

Power is about directing resources to empower and aid the people doing the business, not directing the people. It is this which should characterize high-level leadership for Service-Ability.

Distributed leadership

The main trouble we have with understanding leadership is that we always think of it in the context of individuals who occupy legitimately given positions of authority in organizations, but there is another way to think about it. In the same way that we observed emergent behaviour amongst a collection of interacting people who are freed to be more creative and productive in an environment where they can engage with the organization, with their colleagues and with the customer, the dissemination of leadership activity through empowerment can also emerge.

If we see leadership as a distributed process, not just focused on one person but dispersed, then it takes on a totally different persona and we can understand appropriate leadership in a Service-Ability context. The approach is to provide a context in which people can work productively and responsibly, and generate their own motivation to work. In turn, this leads to a situation where the workers see to it that the customer is served and that 'the ink on the bottom line is black', because the business of the organization becomes their business.

When this happens, the need for much of the elaborate structure that characterizes many of our organizations becomes unnecessary and it can become what Jack Welch, CEO of General Electric, once said, a 'boundary-less corporation' where people can communicate with each other on an interdisciplinary basis and where the reduced layers of management bring the people at the top in touch with the rest of the organization.

Allowing leadership to 'break out' through distributed leadership, puts power where it needs to be: at the point where initiative and decision-making count, and where problem-solving initiative, the sort that solves molehill problems early before they have a chance to grow into mountains of discontent in the customer, can be exercised.

Leadership in the most customer-responsive organizations, therefore, is embedded within the body of the organization, at cell level if you like, directing, motivating, encouraging, deciding and problem solving right where it matters, all in an aura of trust and mutual awareness, thus making the organization accountable to its customers and to itself for that accountability. All this means that leaders must be part of the people, where leadership can be transferred tacitly, not be distant and aloof. Bureaucratic thinking creates a 'directing mind' and a distance between the bosses and the people, which leads to an 'us and them' attitude. Grubbs-West again:

'Leaders should get to know their people. Southwest was one of the few companies where leaders could get fired by their teams. It was paramount that leaders stayed in touch with their teams to ensure teams received the support needed. The upper management of Southwest Airlines possessed one common trait . . . they did not have big egos. That wasn't to say they couldn't hold their own in a battle, but ultimately, their true passion was about helping their people be the best they could be.'

Servant leadership

Robert Greenleaf (ibid.) talks about 'servant leadership', a term that to many will sound somewhat contradictory, and he freely admits that his thesis – that servants should be leaders – is not a popular one. However, he argues that we are currently in a period of radical transition regarding power, authority and decision-making: that a cloud has settled over all leadership and management in any form; and that all organizations are affected by this, not just commercial ones. Institutional leadership as a whole, he says, is becoming quite different from what it was.

In contrast to the aloof, authoritative, high-and-mighty leaders of the past, the servant leader is close to the ground and functionally far superior because he or she sees things, hears things and knows the same things as the people being led. The servant leader is part of the whole team, not part of 'the management', and this breeds trust and dependability amongst those who are led.

Above all, the servant leader has power and authority, but neither wears it as a mantle nor uses it as a tool – as Shakespeare's sonnet says, 'They that have power to hurt and will do none . . . '. Authority backed up by power is still available to the servant leader, but leadership by persuasion and example within the body is what brings results, '. . . by convincement rather than coercion' as Greenleaf puts it.

The value of coercive power is inverse to its use.

This may cause the reader to think that servant leadership is all rather 'touchy-feely', uninspiring and effete. Nothing could be further from the truth. Servant leaders are just as determined as their counterparts, it is just that they have an inner quality about them that leads in a different way. They often have enormous presence, and there is an essential artistry to their leadership. Such leaders 'walk the floor' and they 'walk their talk'. They lead from within the body of the organization, rather than from the top down, and they spread their influence, vision and values viscerally, through contact with people and by showing an example.

Greenleaf doesn't argue for an organization where everyone is governed by an ongoing consensus – where everyone's motivations and actions are fully exposed to the community. He is in no doubt that strong, able leaders are needed to organize and manipulate people and resources, if goods and services are to be produced economically, and he is clear in his view that those organizations that have the most able people as leaders will rise above the mediocre in their field. He says 'I cannot visualize a world without leaders' and goes on to say that some people lead by serving, helping to shape people's destinies without necessarily being transparent as to the direction in which they are being led.

The key issue as a servant leader is the net effect of one's influence over others. Is it dominating, authority-ridden, manipulative or exploitative and overall does it diminish and deplete others? Or is it neutral as to power and does it enrich the people led?

The servant leader is a builder, not a puller-down: a coach, not a police officer.

Rather than relying on fear and coercion, the servant leader's motivational style plays to the pride and conscience of those being led – all framed within the provision of information that guides and informs people how they are doing individually, and in relation to their colleagues. The servant leader relies on a last-resort use of authority rather than the first, seeking to serve first before being served.

Above all, he or she is intent on growing people and encouraging them to take responsibility for what they do. Greenleaf gives this hypothetical answer from the business leader who is fully committed to this ethic, as follows:

> 'I am in the business of growing people – people who are stronger, healthier, more autonomous, more self-reliant, more competent. Incidentally, we also make and sell at a profit things that people want to buy so we can pay for all of this. We play that game hard and well and we are successful but the usual standards but that is really incidental. I recall a time when there was a complaint about

manipulation. We don't hear it anymore. We manage the business about the same way as we always did. We simply changed our aim. Strong, healthy autonomous, self-reliant and competent people don't mind being manipulated. In fact they take it as a game and do a little of it themselves. Consequently, as an institution, we are terribly strong. In fact, we are distinguished. How do I know we are distinguished? Because the best young people want to work for us. We select the best of the best and, once inside, they never want to leave. Any business that can do that is a winner.'

This is not a utopian dream, it is perfectly possible provided the leadership ethic changes from command and control and the treatment of people as cogs in the machine, to the idea that the people are the organization and that it exists to facilitate them in the overall aim, not the other way round: that the organization is not a hierarchy of authority backed by power, but a community composed of mini communities of cohesive, largely self-directing workgroups of responsible people, amongst whom are servant leaders who, in turn, lead the same way.

Primus inter pares

Historically, there have been two traditions of leadership: the hierarchical model, where a single chief is the head of a pyramid-like structure (this is the most well-known image and is, of course, the standard organizational chart with which we are all familiar); and the first among equals structure, a Roman tradition that is probably better thought of as a group of people where one person stands out from the rest, influencing from within using character, charm, skill, knowledge, etc., but above all accepted as leader by those who could otherwise also be leader.

Bound up with the ideas of servant leadership is the principle of primus inter pares – *'first among equals'*.

The *primus inter pares* leader is still someone who is 'first' but that leader is not the all-powerful chief as in the hierarchy. (Interestingly, hierarchy literally means 'The rule of the priest', from Gr. *hierus*, priest, and archon, ruler, or to rule.) The subtle difference between the two is that the *primus*, or 'first', leader cannot rely on legitimate power alone. He or she must prove credibility to lead within a group of potentially equally able peers, each of whom could do the job if asked, and from each is needed tacit acceptance of the leader.

The Prime Minister of the UK has been traditionally viewed in this role (although it has progressively taken on more executive, authoritative aspects in recent years). Nevertheless, Prime Minister means 'first minister', in other words *primus*, and traditionally this was the person in the government who informed the monarch about proposed legislation and gave advice on other matters, whilst remaining a fully functioning minister of state amongst other ministers. All of this leads to referent power being tacitly granted to the *primus* by those who are led. Whereas hierarchy is the rule of the priest, first among equals is more like the rule of priests (plural) where each has a particular area of insight, expertise or knowledge that is respected by the *primus*, who takes it into account in leading, or articulating the outcome.

Sir Ove Arup, of Anglo-Danish extraction, was born in 1895 in my own home town of Newcastle upon Tyne. In 1946, the year I was born, at the age of 51 he founded a consulting engineering business based on his skill at devising engineering solutions that were technically advanced but also economical for his clients. Arup became internationally recognized as one of the foremost engineers of his time. His firm, now simply known as Arup, shot to world recognition when it won the contract to engineer the Sydney Opera house by making innovative use of concrete and steel, and today Arup engineers are working on thousands of projects out of 90 offices in 30 countries worldwide.

He died in 1988 at the age of 92, but on 9 July 1970, in anticipation of his retirement from active duty, he gave a speech to his assembled employees. The 'Arup Key Speech' still informs the company to this day. It is required reading for everyone who joins the firm, or anyone who wants to be reminded of what the organization is all about, and it is a wonderful example of Bennis's description of leadership, and of Greenleaf's too.

A short extract will serve to give a flavour of what he said:

> 'There are two ways of looking at the work you do to earn a living. One is the way propounded by the late Henry Ford: work is a necessary evil, but modern technology will reduce it to a minimum. Your life is your leisure lived in your "free" time. The other is: to make your work interesting and rewarding. You enjoy both your work and your leisure. We opt uncompromisingly for the second way. There are also two ways of looking at the pursuit of happiness: one is to go straight for the things you fancy without restraints, that is, without considering anybody else besides yourself. The other is to recognize that no man is an island, that our lives are inextricably mixed up with those of our fellow human beings, and that there can be no real happiness in isolation. Which leads to an attitude which would accord to others the rights claimed for oneself, which would accept certain moral or humanitarian restraints. We, again, opt for the second way.'[10]

Ove Arup was the quintessential social architect, servant leader: conveying vision, meaning, values, trust and, above all, revealing himself, his values and his guiding principles 'all of a piece'.

The Key Speech, with its exposition of the underpinning principles and ethos of the firm's founder, may be somewhat rambling at times, but it is quintessentially human in the way it lays down the values of the organization Arup started all those years ago. You can almost hear the man's heart in his words, and that is what provides the solid foundation for his successors.

As well as matters technical and peculiar to the business itself, the speech goes on to outline issues of sustainability, humanitarianism and, significantly, quality in service delivery, in all of which Arup stresses the

[10] Arup Key Speech.

need for the organization to act honourably in all its dealings, both with its own people and with others. Arup acknowledges the basic right of everyone in the organization to have a high degree of self-determination, albeit one that is tempered by self-regulation, and it is an excellent example of the principle of *primus inter pares* in action. Overall, it is a classic example of a bridge to the future, clearly articulated, passionately argued and honestly offered.

To this day, what Arup says is still regarded as valid by those now charged with leadership of the firm, who turn to it regularly to reaffirm their commitment to the founding principles upon which the business was built. Crucially, Arup is structured around largely self-managed teams, where people can exercise their specialist skills in a way that precisely fits the job in hand, knowing that the others will support him or her while they are doing what they are uniquely equipped to do. Birkinshaw[11] says this:

> 'Highly skilled teams of anywhere from half a dozen to 100 people come together on a project basis, with team leaders shifting according to particular expertise and need. "That's something that amazed me when I was younger in Arup's, how one week I'd be working for somebody and the next week he'd be working for me," former chairman Terry Hill commented in an interview.[12] Local leaders have a great deal of freedom in determining ways of working, and this makes for an adaptable and innovative environment responsive to the particular market needs.'

Empowerment

Concomitant with servant leadership is the idea of empowerment. Empowerment is not delegation; the two are separate ideas. Managers

[11]Birkinshaw, J. (2010) *Reinventing Management*. Chichester : John Wiley & Sons
[12]Henson, Colin (2007) Case study: Arup. *Inside Knowledge* **10**(7). http://www.ikmagazine.com/xq/asp/sid.0/articleid.3C219ACD-8D7E-462B-A136-98F17A73397C/eTitle.Case_study_Arup/qx/display.htm

often delegate parts of their job to others to relieve workload. They may say things like, 'Go and do some work on this and come back to me so I can make a decision'. They may even say, 'Go and do some work on this and come back with your recommendations and we'll make the decision together'. In extreme cases, they may even say, 'Go and do some work on this, do what needs to be done, and just run it past me when you're finished'. None of this is empowerment because the power as well as the responsibility remains with the person doing the delegating.

With empowerment, the power is given to the subordinate, and the responsibility remains with the leader: power-to-do passes to the other person, conferring on them autonomy of decision-making and action, and freeing them to do what they see fit in the circumstances, but the responsible leader still regards him- or herself as responsible for the outcome of the subordinate's decision, thus freeing the subordinate to exercise initiative. This is often one of the most difficult things for a leader to do, especially one who is steeped in the traditional paradigm.

Empowerment is perceived as dangerous because it is utterly counterintuitive.

Anyone who has ever tried to ski will understand this. Skiing can be one of the most difficult things to learn: if you want to turn left, you lean (i.e. put your weight) to the right; if you want to turn right, you lean to the left; if you want to remain stable on a steep slope and not slide down it, you lean out from the slope instead of hugging into it which is what your instinct tells you to do. Leaning in the opposite direction allows your ski's edge to carve a turn and leaning out from the slope means your skis' edges grip and prevent slipping and sliding. It is all about doing the opposite to your natural reactions. It's all counterintuitive, but it's the only way to do it and, once those innate instincts are overcome and relearned, it all 'clicks' and you wonder what all the fuss was about. Empowerment is the same.

The natural instinct of the leader is to hold power close. Somehow it's too scary to give other people the authority to make decisions whilst still being ultimately responsible for the outcome. So you cling to power: you hug into the slope – it feels safer there – but this attitude leads to a relentless desire to organize and systematize, and then you lose sight of what you are about. Organising, systems and processes become what you do, rather than leading and managing for maximum effectiveness in your people. Leadership that is empowering, hard as it sometimes is to do, is vitally important in Service-Ability because it is stimulant to adaptability, flexibility and initiative. Lorraine Grubbs-West, president of Lessons in Loyalty and a senior executive at Southwest Airlines for 15 years, to whom we referred extensively says this:[13]

> 'Employees at Southwest were empowered to "do the right thing" (versus doing what was right). Empowerment can be one of the most powerful tools a company can utilize to ensure that Customers [sic] are taken care of when things don't go as planned . . . With empowerment, however, comes the risk that your Employee [sic] may make a mistake.'

There is a story, probably apocryphal but apposite nonetheless, of an international hotel chain in the USA that implemented a policy whereby employees were authorized to spend up to $200 of company money in pursuit of customer satisfaction should a critical customer service situation arise.

One day a guest, who had checked out only ten minutes earlier, came storming back up to the concierge's desk stating that a portable radio left in his car the previous day when he had checked in was not in his car now and obviously had been stolen overnight whilst the car was parked in the hotel's car park. He went on to allege that it was probably the car park attendant, who had parked the car as he arrived and returned it to the front door the next day as he left, who was responsible. Remembering his newly granted empowerment to deal with such a situation, the concierge took the customer straight to the reception desk and ordered the receptionist to give the client the full $200 dollars that had been allowed

[13]Grubbs-West, E. (2005) *Lessons in Loyalty*. Dallas, TX: Cornerstone Leadership Institute.

to him to award, by way of compensation. The client accepted the money and left.

Five days later, the manager of the hotel received a letter. It was from the angry guest, who explained he had later found the radio in the trunk of the car where he had put it for safe keeping and forgotten that he had done so. He enclosed a cheque drawn on his company's account returning the $200 and apologized profusely for what had happened. He then went on to explain that he was president of a major international corporation whose executives used hotels around the world on a daily basis and, because of the response of this hotel to his 'problem', he had issued a companywide instruction that, from now on, all staff were to use this hotel chain whenever and wherever they travelled on company business.

That is the result of empowerment in a customer-service context. Employees need to be given leeway to do whatever is necessary on the spot to take care of a customer. It's the old principle that if the customer doesn't win, the organization loses – it is just as simple as that.

In an organization where the customer is king, empowerment is about giving employees the keys to the kingdom.

Of course, there is a risk that the customer might take advantage, and so might the employee, but if the customer is delighted, and the employee is fully engaged with and involved in the aims of the organization, operating with a high sense of professionalism, exercising initiative in the interests of customer satisfaction according to the model of Service-Ability, the risk of abuse of empowerment is put into context.

Of course, empowerment is open to abuse, but what is the worst that could happen? $200, or £100, or even £1000 lost? Or taking the 'risk' of having an unnecessarily pleased customer who comes back time and time again! How much would it have cost United Airlines to compensate Dave Carroll for his beloved Taylor guitar? $3500 for the whole instrument, or indeed only a third of that for the cost of repair if they had grasped the situation immediately, because that is all he was asking for. How much did it cost them in the long run? United's share price plunged 10% wiping

$180 million off its value in the immediate aftermath, but the true amount may never be known.

The fundamental truth is, you can never win an argument with a customer: you might win the argument, but you will lose the customer.

People don't come back for another dose of bad treatment, so you must empower people to do the right thing when it matters, rather than bind them with rules that make them do things right according to the rules but not the right thing and lose the chance of a customer-delighting moment of truth.

Giving away power-to-do whilst still shouldering the responsibility for the outcome of a subordinate's decision is a hard thing, but that is what good leadership is about. It is all a matter of character, instinct and training. Above all, it is a matter of trust by the leader in those whom he or she empowers, and that comes from knowing the people to whom the decision-making empowerment is being given.

One of the principal elements of getting to this level of trust is the realization by the leader that people are able to make decisions even though they don't carry official authority: that they want to do their best for the organization and its customers, and that they are capable of making the right decision because they are close to the circumstances. Indeed, it could be argued that the capacity to make decisions may be improved because they don't have the burden of authority upon them; the leader always has to be aware of his or her position in relation to a set of constraints that go farther than the limited sphere of one decision. It is really just common sense to say that the best knowledge and the most information about a situation is frequently to be found at the point where it is happening. That is where the power to make decisions should be, if the decision is to have maximum effect.

As we saw in the example of the hotel, more often than not that point is low down in the organization, often at the point of sale, or in some other transaction at the interface between the organization and the outside world. Effective leaders recognize this and, especially in matters of customer service, empower their people to make decisions based on the principle that doing what is best for the customer is usually in the best overall interests of the organization as a whole.

Practical wisdom

If leaders need any innate talent, it is wisdom. Psychologist Dr Barry Schwartz[14] refers to Aristotle, who coined the term 'practical wisdom', and concluded that it was the result of a combination of moral will and moral skill. The former is the desire to do what is right and the latter is knowing what to do, and when, to do the right thing.

Lt. Calley was a young, inexperienced, under-trained and badly led junior officer who neither had the moral fibre (the military term for that combination of moral will and moral skill) nor the proper leadership skills to instil into his men sufficient values to allow them to understand what 'doing right' really meant in a war-time situation. To all intents and purposes, the brutality of war and the demotivating leadership of the US Army of the time had literally 'de-moralized' him.

Schwartz says that we need to create organizations that nurture and encourage practical wisdom, and that takes leadership of a very special kind. It takes leaders who neither demoralize people, taking away their enjoyment of work as a fulfilling, purposeful activity, nor 'de-moralize' them and deprive them of their practical wisdom. (The hotel concierge in our earlier example exercised practical wisdom.)

Practical wisdom in the leader as well as in the led is essential for Service-Ability. Schwartz aptly sums this up:

> '[Wisdom] is made, not born. Wisdom depends on experience, and not just any experience. You need the time to get to know the people you are serving. You need permission to be allowed to improvise, to try new things, to occasionally fail, and to learn from your fail-

[14]http://www.ted.com/talks/lang/eng/barry_schwartz_using_our_practical_wisdom.html

ures. And you need to be mentored by wise teachers. It takes lots of experience, to learn how to care for people.'

Winterbourne View

In May 2011, we saw an example of how people can become de-moralized in their work. A BBC undercover reporter filmed a pattern of serious abuse of people with learning disabilities and autism in Winterbourne View, a residential hospital in Bristol. The mistreatment being carried out there was described as 'torture' by Andrew McDonnell, a leading expert in working with adults with mental disability, interviewed by the reporter. The parents of an 18-year-old patient named Simone told the programme that she had told them she was being abused at the hospital, but they had assured her that it would not be allowed to happen. The report[15] goes on to quote Simone's mother saying:

> 'She told us that she had been hit, her hair had been pulled and she'd been kicked and I said no, this wouldn't happen, they're not allowed.'

Allowed or not (and there is every reason to believe the company concerned would not have condoned or allowed such behaviour in their staff), it is clear that the perpetrators of this horrific activity did not possess any practical wisdom: they clearly neither had the moral will that would prevent them doing this sort of thing and neither did they display the moral skill to make an appropriate judgement of their own or colleagues' behaviour.

Eleven people were charged over these activities and all pleaded guilty at trial. At the time of going to press with this book, sentencing has yet to take place. The case has stimulated much debate about how social services did not pick up on what was happening and why the regulatory body, the Quality Care Commission, did not identify it and stop it. However, it raises several questions: Where was the leadership in that

[15]http://www.bbc.co.uk/news/uk-13548222

organization? Where were the guardians, exemplars and guides with practical wisdom to keep it on moral track? Who was leading the culture of care (or the lack of it)?

Re-moralizing work – Schwartz

Schwartz says we should try to re-moralize work itself. Using the job description of a hospital janitor, he observes:

> 'This is the job description of a hospital janitor . . . and all of the items on it are unremarkable. They are the things you would expect: mop the floors, sweep them, empty the trash, restock the cabinets. It may be surprising how many things there are, but it's not surprising what they are. But the one thing I want you to notice about them is this: even though this is a very long list, there isn't a single thing on it that involves other human beings . . . not one. The janitor's job could just as well be done in a mortuary as in a hospital. And yet, when some psychologists interviewed some hospital janitors to get a sense of what they thought their jobs were like, they encountered Mike, who told them about how he stopped mopping the floor because "Mr Jones" was out of his bed, getting a little exercise, trying to build up his strength, walking slowly down the hall. And Charlene told them how she ignored her supervisor's admonition, and didn't vacuum the visitors' lounge because there were some family members who were there all day, every day. Behaviour like this doesn't just make people feel a little better, it actually improves the quality of patient care and enables hospitals to run well. Now, not every janitor acts like this, but those who do, think that these sorts of human actions, involving kindness, care, and empathy, are an essential part of the job, and yet their job description contains not one word about other human beings. These janitors have the moral will to do right by other people, and beyond this, they have the moral skill to figure out what "doing right" means.'

Hierarchy

At this stage, it seems appropriate to make the point that, eventually, someone has to make decisions if things are to move forward and there can be no doubt that, as an organization grows, it needs some scalar chain of command, otherwise it simply can't function.

> *Organizations are not democracies because they answer to agencies other than the people they comprise.*

The Arup Key Speech, for example, refers to the need for: 'Some sort of hierarchy which should as far as possible be based on function' and that 'There will always be a need for a strong coordinating body' in the organization. Even in those large organizations that have severely delayered in recent years, there is still some form of hierarchy-like structure, albeit one which recognizes that knowledge is a distributed, shared property, not the prerogative of the individual to be dispensed as a sacrament.

Birkinshaw (2010, ibid.) points out that hierarchy gives direct accountability for decisions made and it provides legitimate authority to leaders, as well as being broadly and soundly based on the presumption that there is usually greater experience, wisdom and knowledge in those who have become leaders. Quite often, he says, several different hierarchical constructs can operate in tandem – a 'hierarchy of position', a 'hierarchy of knowledge' and a 'hierarchy of action' – and this comes to define the actions and conduct of the people lower down the pecking order. However, he also summarizes the limitations of hierarchy.

First, the assumption that the boss always knows best fails to take account of those in the organization who might be more in possession of the facts needed to make the right decision, and who under this regime would be ignored. Second, people are reticent to say too much to their bosses and the bosses are cautious about revealing too much to employees, thus resulting in poor information flows and a general air of distrust; third, those higher up the hierarchy often fail to add any real value to the work of their subordinates and frequently steal their decisions, passing them off as their own, which produces further distrust as well as disenchantment and disengagement among subordinates.

Over time, hierarchy will emerge simply because of the increasing complexity of size, but the danger is that 'the rule of the priest' comes to be the only way of leading, and older, longer-established organizations, especially those that have lost their original conceptualizing leader, are particularly susceptible to this condition. (Ove Arup, of course, foresaw this danger and left a lasting legacy in his Key Speech.) The key is to get the balance right between efficient decision making and appropriate application of power, whilst not dumbing down the staff and causing disaffection and disengagement.

Collective wisdom

Appropriate leadership will always seek to avoid the pitfalls of hierarchy, and one of the ways of doing this is to embrace 'collective wisdom': the principle that suggests that the combined expertise of a larger number of people can produce better forecasts of possible outcomes and, therefore, better decisions than those of a small number of experts who possess legitimate power to make those decisions and impose them on the rest.

At his court marshal, Second Lt. William Calley was found guilty on 22 counts of premeditated murder and two days later, 31 March 1971, he was sentenced to life imprisonment. The court's verdict unleashed a storm of protest across the USA. In a survey, conducted on 1 April for President Nixon, 78% of respondents disagreed with the sentence. A Gallup poll of 522 adults commissioned by Newsweek later that month revealed 79% believed the sentence too harsh, 56% disapproved of the sentence because they believed 'many others' beyond Lt. Calley shared the responsibility for the crime, and 70% believed he had been made a scapegoat. Also in that month, Louis Harris and Associates polled 1600 adults across the country and found that 77% of the respondents thought that Calley was simply carrying out orders from those higher up the chain of command and 77% also thought he had been made a scapegoat for his commanding[16] officers. In a country already torn over the Vietnam War, with human rights struggles causing significant tension, this widespread social unrest caused President Richard Nixon to use his absolute authority as Commander-in-Chief to order that Calley be released from the military stockade and be placed under house arrest pending presidential review of the case. Ultimately, Calley's sentence was reduced to five years of house arrest, of which he served three and a half years before being released.

We could discuss endlessly the leadership qualities of President Nixon (whose ultimate impeachment and removal from office over his complicity in burglary and lying to cover it up in the infamous Watergate scandal is a matter of historical record), or the issues of an army leadership that talked of 'free fire zones' and demanded daily 'kill ratios', but that is not the point of exploring what happened in the aftermath of the Calley conviction and sentence.

The point is that the American public were expressing their collective 'take' on the whole situation. They clearly resented him being made the scapegoat for the serious and obvious shortcomings of those who led him, in what was also widely believed to be an unjust war. In a very real sense the crowd sensed the truth. It was as though the American people as a whole was able to hold a complete picture in its collective consciousness and make a balanced judgement on these deep issues.

The wisdom of the crowd had found a widely accepted level in an extremely complex set of moral and ethical issues.

Earlier we referred to the work of James Surowiecki, whose work (along with others) helps us understand the mechanisms behind collective wisdom. He speculates that human beings, through evolution, may have been equipped to make sense of the world around them. Under the right circumstances, he says, groups are remarkably intelligent and are often

[16]University of Missouri-Kansas City School of Law. http://www.law.umkc.edu/faculty/projects/ftrials/mylai/SurveyResults.html

cleverer than the cleverest people in them. In fact, they do not need to be dominated by intelligent people to be collectively clever. He says this:

> 'Most of us, whether as voters or investors or consumers or managers, believe that valuable knowledge is concentrated in a very few hands (or rather a very few heads). We assume that the key to solving problems or making good decisions is finding that one right person who will have the answer. Even when we see a large crown of people, many of them not especially informed, do something amazing like, say, predict the outcomes of horse races, we are more likely to attribute that success to a few smart people in the crowd than to the crowd itself. As sociologists Jack B. Soll and Richard Larrick put it, we feel the need to "chase the expert." . . . chasing the expert is a mistake, and a costly one at that. We should stop hunting and ask the crowd (which, of course includes geniuses as well as everyone else) instead. Chances are it knows.'

The wisdom of the crowd in an organizational context is an enormous resource into which appropriate leadership needs to be able to tap. It is the source and the repository of the tacit knowledge, the 'know-how', of any organization. Leaders may have a power base in their own expert knowledge, but the only person who knows best how to do a job is the person whose job it is – if for no better reason than he or she does it every day.

The boss may know how to do the job, but the person who owns the job is the most expert at it.

That is why leadership that is always interfering, always trying to tinker at the edges, always trying to redesign or redefine the job, always imposing ever more rules, regulations and orders from above, will suck the life out of the person doing the job. This form of leadership has its hands in the wastepaper bins and has lost sight of the broad picture.

Here is a salutary tale taken from *The Reinventor's Fieldbook*, by David Osborne and Peter Plastrik,[17] to illustrate the point:

'Virgil Lee Bolden had been laying water pipes for the city of Fort Lauderdale for about 30 years when he heard he would be transferred and retrained for a different job in city government. The city commission wanted to outsource his work to private contractors. "They said the pipe-laying crew wasn't productive," Bolden recalls. "After all these years, I had to move. I felt everybody was kicking me around." A few days later, the president of Bolden's union, Cathy Dunn, convinced management to listen to the crew's ideas for improving the unit's efficiency. The employees delivered a simple message: the problem isn't us, it's the system. They described the way management's design of their work prevented them from working full-time, and they suggested some changes. "The managers added on to our list," says Bolden. "The department director said he was with us, the city manager – they seemed to listen to us." The meeting persuaded Mike Bailey, manager of distribution and collection, to re-examine the decision to contract out pipe-laying. He checked what it cost the city crew to lay a foot of water pipe, on average, and compared it with prices charged by private contractors. What he found shocked him. "It was costing us \$68–\$74 a foot; contracting was \$82," says Bailey. Earlier estimates had understated the contractor's costs. "We looked at that and said, it's a bad idea to let good pipers go." At that point the guys said "Wait a minute, we still have a lot of good ideas about how to make it cheaper for you." The employees said they weren't spending enough of the work week actually laying pipe. They lost time at the beginning of the day because they had to report to the administration building before going to the job site. So the rule was changed to allow them to report directly to work sites. To further increase time on task, they

[17]Osborne, D. and Plastrik, P. (2000) *The Reinventor's Field book: Tools for Transforming Your Government*, Part V, Chapter 18: *Employee Empowerment*. Hoboken, NJ: Jossey-Bass.

suggested longer days; a four-day, 40–hour work week became the norm. They began storing equipment on site, having the police keep an eye on it, rather than hauling it back to the city's equipment facilities. "So many of these changes were no-brainers" says Bailey, that he asked the crew foreman why they hadn't been made long ago. The foreman said "That's the way your predecessor said to do it. That's the way we've always done it." Once the changes were made, says Bailey, productivity soared. The cost of laying pipe dropped to about $38 a foot, more than a 50 percent reduction. In the first six months after the changes, the crew laid 15,000 feet of pipe, more than double the amount laid in any previous year. They weren't working harder, just smarter. "They didn't work any overtime," says Bailey "But there was a certain amount of motivation. They were saying, These are our ideas and we don't want them to flop." '

Being able to listen to the voice of the crowd reduces boundaries and highly defined roles, and frees up the flow of information vital to the overall decision-making process. If employees, especially customer-facing ones, constantly have to rely on leaders to provide their 'wisdom' in priest-like fashion, this process will lead to, at least inefficiency and, at worst disaster. Chasing the expert prevents the upward flow of information back to the centres of legitimate decision-making where the power-to-do can be exercised to make sure the organization keeps moving forward in its declared aims.

In just the same way that having decision-making power through empowerment close to where decisions need to be made for proactive, responsive customer service is essential for Service-Ability, it is also important to have the voice of collective wisdom being expressed there too. Listening to the wisdom of the crowd, letting staff freely articulate what they can see are the problems as they occur in the dynamically changing environment because they interact with it on a daily basis (far more than the leaders could possibly be able to do as individuals), and letting them have a hand in introducing innovations in response, helps in the process of staying open to that environment.

Properly harnessed, collective wisdom is a valuable boundary scanning mechanism and yet another counterbalance to the inevitable tendency of organizations toward entropy.

Harnessing the wisdom of the crowd, however, requires leadership that is fundamentally different from the: 'Do as I say' style. Harnessing the collective wisdom of an organization demands a leadership style that allows:

- diversity of opinion in the people based on the individual possession of knowledge or information gained personally;
- individual independence (rather than being part of a herd or subjected to a powerful corporate propaganda that instils its own opinion into the individual);
- a degree of decentralization (as opposed to the centralized bureaucratic idea) sufficient that the people within their own sphere of operation, drawing on knowledge gained locally about how to do things, can be specialists (rather than the specialist knowledge for which, perhaps, they were originally hired); and
- aggregation, a mechanism in which their privately formed knowledge and judgements can be factored into the collective decision.

Surowiecki (ibid.) says this:

> 'The idea of the wisdom of crowds . . . takes decentralization as a given and a good, since it implies that if you set a crowd of self-interested, independent people to work in a decentralized way on the same problem, instead of trying to direct their efforts from the top down, their collective solution is likely to be better than any other solution you could come up with.'

He goes on to explain that decentralization is found in nature: in flocks of birds, shoals of fish, or colonies of ants building an ant hill; and in human social activity such as cities, free markets, computer networks; and in some modern organizations (Google, for example). The common factor is that power does not rest in one central location. Instead, he says, decisions need to be made by individuals, based on their own localized, specific knowledge, not by an omniscient or far-seeing planner. The underlying principle being, the closer a person is to a problem the more likely he or she is likely to have a good solution to it (Remember the German civil engineer and his problems with central purchasing?).

However, decentralization presupposes that everyone is playing on the same team. If it is mismanaged, it can very easily slip into disorganization. This is the danger we identified in Appropriate Organization, when we likened the organization to the Bénard cell. If we allow an organization to become too energetic it will fall apart into chaos.

Decentralization has to be harnessed in such a way that it stays within the zone of adaptive tension described by complexity theory, in which the 'spontaneous coordination through self-interested behaviours of independent actors' can take place. All this demands appropriate leadership: one where the leader is able to create an appropriate environment in which there is only honesty, not fear.

Honesty without fear

While attending a garage sale a few years back, Gerry McBean[18] of National Technical Systems, Detroit, MI, came across a coffee mug that had a company logo printed on its side and the following three words etched next to it: 'Honesty Without Fear'; and he reflected that this one three-word phrase perfectly captures the leadership environment that we are trying to create in our contemporary companies.

In a paper of the same title published jointly with Theodore Lowe, he points out that what we mainly have in many of our organizations is the opposite: fear without honesty. Fear of providing information, fear of not knowing and fear of change that are pervasive in the workplace and can lead to negative behaviours in the people. These fears are described as 'monsters' that destroy teamwork and prevent an organization achieving

[18]Lowe, T.A. and McBean, G.M. (1989) Honesty without fear. *Quality Progress*, **22**(11), 30–34.

the collective capability of its people, and they are principally due to the fear of giving up control by those who lead organizations.

Lowe and McBean identify six principle culprits:

1. Fear of reprisal, of being disciplined, fired, receiving poor appraisals, transferred to less desirable work, being ridiculed or cast out from one's peer group and subjected to witch hunts, or being picked out as an example, all to ensure a please-the-boss mentality;
2. Fear of failure, of being wrong, of making a mistake or making a career-limiting move, thus ensuring a workforce that is reluctant to accept risk, to contribute new ideas, to get involved, and to be willing to accept responsibility;
3. Fear of providing information; in other words the 'shoot the messenger' syndrome where people are labelled as complainers or troublemakers if they speak out about things that are wrong, all leading to an 'Emperor's New Clothes' syndrome where no one dares tell the king he is naked;
4. Fear of not knowing, and being ridiculed because of it by leaders who are more knowledgeable but too weak to see that inappropriate use of their knowledge does not make them powerful, it only renders their followers defenceless;
5. Fear of giving up control where the leaders seek not only to control people but processes, where they confuse fear with discipline and treat people like a herd of sheep, making sure nobody deviates from the set path, rather than providing the vision and direction, and trusting that the faithful will follow; and finally
6. Fear of change.

Summing all this up, Lowe and McBean say this:[19]

> 'The beliefs of management create the environment for the organization. If management believes that people won't contribute and

---

[19] It is accepted that management and leadership, whilst each containing elements of the other, are not the same thing. For the purposes of this discussion, however, what Lowe and McBean say applies to management as well as to leadership.

can't be trusted (a fear in itself), then management will see their role as to control the people. If the objective is to keep the current order in control, then change and new knowledge are not welcomed, and management does not want to hear about problems. The beliefs of management are reinforced by their practices. Control results in intimidation, confrontation and subtractive management. When new ideas are presented, intimidation takes place through a form of executive neurosis: The boss withholds his evaluation criteria to the very end so that he can wait for all the options and find a reason to reject the change. He trumps your ace before you even find out what suit trump is. Subtractive management is management by finding things wrong and is a useful device in showing your subordinates why you're the boss. Management practices that reinforce a fear-driven culture include adversarial relationships, a win–lose struggle for power, and narrow functional interests. Adversarial relationships can occur within a company through internal competition as well as between unions and management, and buyers and suppliers. Micro-managing for narrow individual and functional objectives leads to management by confrontation instead of collaboration. While these management practices could be seen as winning through intimidation and the path to power, they have a legacy of a culture of fear without honesty. Management systems reinforce the beliefs and practices through rewards, communication and training. If not used properly, management by objectives can become an adversarial management reward system that pits the subordinate against his boss in the negotiating of objectives. Appraisal processes that focus on finding things wrong with employee performance to justify the ratings are another reward system that can reinforce subtractive management. If promotions and other rewards go first to individual achievements, than competing for the "gold stars" will foster internal competition. When it comes to communication and training, the old line "If your boss wants your opinion, he'll give it to you" describes the one-way communication that so effectively keeps management sheltered from the problems. Unfortunately, many managers believe that the essence of good communication is to be able to sell their ideas and beliefs to their workers. If management believes that people are just pawns to execute their decisions, then little emphasis will be given to training and development beyond the necessary skills to perform the job assignments.'

This is fear without honesty, the inverse of what is needed for an organization that needs to be responsive, flexible and customer-satisfying. Therefore, leaders who seek Service-Ability need to become actively involved in addressing those attitudes in themselves that prevent their people from contributing to the overall aims of the organization. Their leadership must be based on moral authority and truth.

If the leadership ethos in an organization fosters the belief that it is the job of the leader to plan, organize, direct and control and that the workers' job is just to wield the screwdrivers, then Service-Ability will not emerge.

Appropriate leadership involves collaboration and teamwork, servant-hood, empathy and humility, not fear, confrontation or adversarial relationships. Only by promoting teamwork, helping, teaching, listening, and leading in a serving way those who are the means of production – by being willing to let go of raw power and distribute it, trusting people to do the right thing as well as do things right – will the transition to a Service-Ability culture be able to take place.

10

An encounter, just a few years ago, with that world-famous carrier, Amtrak, serves perfectly to set the scene for this chapter. There could be few better examples of organizations losing their way – losing sight of their *raison d'être* – and it prompts us to reflect on the attitude to customer service many large organizations have. Here is the exchange of correspondence to set the scene:

> ' – – Original Message – –
> From: Kevin Robson
> Sent: 21 November 2007 16:22
> To: Quality
> Subject: Complaint of poor service
> I should be grateful if someone could contact me urgently by phone with a view to resolving a problem I have with delivery of a consignment.
> Kevin Robson"

And the reply (file this, frame it, dwell on it, inwardly digest it, hang it on your office wall; above all, please learn from it as to how not to deal with a customer):

> 'Amtrak: Registered Office: Netfold Ltd, Northgate Way, Aldridge, West Midlands, WS9 8ST. Company Registration Number: 6051125
> Dear Consignee

Thank you for your recent email. Your comments have been duly noted and, if deemed necessary, will be acted upon accordingly.

May we take this opportunity to request that, as a recipient of an Amtrak delivery, you direct any further questions or queries to your supplier. They will then deal with any issues through their direct contact within Amtrak.

Yours sincerely'

'Dear Consignee.' (So do I not have a name then?) 'If deemed necessary' (… Err?) In other words 'Get lost, we don't see you as a customer, we get paid by the sender of your parcel'. Would I ever use a carrier such as this again? Never! Furthermore, what about the supplier who uses such a carrier as part of their order fulfilment to me? Will their choice of carrier be a significant buying decision for me in future? You bet! No way am I going to do business with any firm who directly or indirectly sees me as only a 'Consignee'! I recommend all who read this to do the same.

It is almost beyond rational understanding how an employee of an organization can feel at ease sending such a communication to someone who is not just a beneficiary of their service, but paying for it too. How can a company get itself into such a knot as to lose site of the reality that their 'consignees' are actually their consumers and their customers: that it is they who have paid for the carriage and that the sender of the parcel is only passing that payment on to them?

The answer to this is simple: the employee was disengaged both from the customer and the organization that had failed to ensure that its employees understand who the customer really is, and had failed to put in place a meaningful understanding that customer service is its purpose not carrying parcels.

Mission, vision

In almost two decades of advising organizations how to answer that simple question 'Quo vadis?' ('Where are you going?'), I have encountered many that had a mission/vision statement and many more that didn't. Rarely have I found those that did, following those statements in any meaningful way, nor have I observed the results on the ground equal to the exhortations and high rhetoric. What is more, rarely have I found any significant difference in the success between those who had articulated their mission/vision and those who had not.

The act of articulating a strategy of some kind in the belief that somehow it will all come true is not going to work. Head-office exhortations on their own, rarely reach the rank and file and they can never change hearts and minds. That has to come from within and it is a cultural issue.

The theory is, of course, that thinking about strategic direction as a whole and writing it down helps keep the organization on course, and the hope is to get people motivated and pulling together by instilling a shared understanding of the overall corporate mission, its broad goals and its strategic plan, and that is fine as far as it goes. However, rarely, do these statements, published on placards at head-office receptions and in corporate annual reports seem to penetrate to the people and achieve the hoped-for result. Much of it is faddism. Mostly it is done because that's what organizations do, and a lot of it is little more than wishful thinking or empty rhetoric.

Steve Shirley, president of the FI Group, which was a pioneer in home working using technology, says this:

'The management books that I read were talking about being loose on strategy and tight on control so that you told people exactly what you wanted them to do. You know, McDonald's works like this: very, very tight control but I think . . . I've always espoused the reverse. You need to be very tight on strategy so that everybody in the organization, small or large, understands what the strategy is and knows where the organization is trying to get to and then very, very loose on implementation because if you have that empowered work force, everyone that's facing customers (and management is far too far away from customers to really advise), the really important decisions are made on the spot by the person doing the work, because they understand the strategy and their responses are much more positive than when you've got this sort of cookbook that certainly FI used to have in the early days. So I believe it's much more tied up with communications and using the innate power, it is enormous power, of the individual to create, develop and exploit . . . There have been some studies that organizations that are co-owned consistently out perform others in their sector and I believe the sharing of wealth, and also the sharing of risk (it goes both ways) with the workforce is of vital importance in actually driving it forward . . . everybody understands the strategy, there is no "them and us", they know where the organization is going. They know how they fit in to it; they know how they will benefit.'

Mission/vision statements are all about securing employee engagement in the pursuit of customers and satisfying their needs – profitably. When it comes to serving customers' needs, management may declare their strategy, but it is the people who will see it through and they need to know why, if they are to drive forward and produce the return on investment shareholders are seeking.

The people (who, after all, are the organization), need to know the reasons for the organization's existence, why it opens its doors on a Monday morning. They need a reason why they should give their enthusiastic support to its aims; in other words, they need a 'belief in the cause'.

Obliquity vs. narrow strategy

As organizations grow, they often lose sight of their original meaning and purpose. They find themselves becoming increasingly accountable to more stakeholders, and they often try to adapt to the strongest demand. The most obvious example of this is the demand of shareholders for dividends on their investment, although political demands on public sector organizations can become just as clearly articulated and powerful.

Too often this leads to choices being made that serve these interests and not those of the customer or consumer of their output. They default to more structure, more rules, more narrow definitions of what the organization is about, and this introduces a challenge to management.

Too much focus on narrow goals, too much specialization can easily lead to a mechanistic, cold, uncommunicative, unresponsive result.

John Kay,[1] one of Britain's leading economists and first director of Oxford University's Said Business School argues for 'obliquity' in our corporate intent.

He describes obliquity thus. If you were in a ship in the Atlantic Ocean off the east coast of Panama and you wanted to get to the Pacific, which direction would you take? The obvious and immediate answer of course, is westward through the Panama Canal. However, if you use the Panama Canal, you end up by travelling eastward. Kay explains it thus:

> 'The American continent separates the Atlantic Ocean in the east from the Pacific Ocean in the west. But the shortest crossing of America follows the route of the Panama Canal, and you arrive at Balboa Port on the Pacific Coast some 30 miles to the east of the Atlantic entrance at Colon. If you want to go in one direction, the best route may involve going in the other. Many times, goals are more likely to be achieved when pursued indirectly. The happiest people are not those who make happiness their main aim; the most profitable companies are not the most profit-oriented.'

Kay first introduced the idea of obliquity in his lecture 'The Role of Business in Society'[2] at Said Business School on 3 February 1998, where he explored the paradox that an oblique approach to achieving aims and objectives often has success over a narrowly defined strategy.

Kay defines obliquity as being 'When a characteristic is selected for in an uncertain and imperfectly known environment, deliberate

[1] Kay, J. (2010) Think oblique: How our goals are best reached indirectly. *Independent*, 8 March.
[2] http://www.johnkay.com/1998/02/03/the-role-of-business-in-society/

action to promote that characteristic is often self-defeating, and the
highest values of the characteristic will often be achieved by chance'.

In support of this contention, he quotes George Merck, founder of
Merck & Co., Inc. one of the largest pharmaceutical companies in the
world (known outside the US and Canada as Merck Sharp & Dohme or
MSD): 'We try never to forget that medicine is for the people. It is not for
the profits. The profits follow, and if we have remembered that, they have
never failed to appear. The better we have remembered it, the larger they
have been.'

An extract from an article in the *Observer*[3] completes the picture:

'Obliquity is the notion that complex goals are often best achieved
indirectly. For example, happiness is the product of fulfilment in
work and private life, not the repetition of pleasurable actions, so
happiness is not achieved by pursuing it. The most profitable companies are not the most dedicated to profit. (Few companies in the
history of the world were as profit-oriented as Bear Stearns and
Lehman – so profit-oriented, in fact, they were ultimately destroyed
by the greed of their own employees.) Buildings designed as
"machines for living in" proved to be machines their occupants did
not like living in. The planned cities of the world, such as Canberra
and Brasilia, are dull and lifeless; the great cities of the world, such
as Paris and London, grew over centuries with little assistance from
any designer. But surely we will be more successful in achieving
something if we adopt it as our goal? That would be true if we were
clear about the nature of that goal, and knew not just all there is to
know, but all we might hope to know, about the means of achieving
it. We find out about the real nature of our goals in the process of
accomplishing them, and our understanding of the complex structures of personal relationships or business organizations is necessarily incomplete. We not only do not know what the future will
hold but cannot anticipate even the range of possible events. The

[3]Kay, J. (2010) Ideas for modern living: Obliquity. *Observer*, 11 April.

world in which we operate changes, partly as a result of our actions. The great utilitarian John Stuart Mill recognized in his autobiography that happiness was best achieved indirectly: "aiming thus at something else [happy people] arrive at happiness along the way." Donald Trump expressed a similar sentiment: "I don't do it for the money. I do it to do it. Deals are my art form." The paradox of obliquity is all around us.'

There is an inherent tension between the rational logic of clear focused, narrow strategic alignment intended to maintain overall focus and direction, and broader, oblique approaches implemented on the basis of values, in the belief that profits will accrue.

Kay, again:

'The simple but fundamental reason we do not maximize shareholder value or the length of our lives, our happiness or the gross national product, is that we do not know how to and never will. No one will ever be buried with the epitaph "He maximized shareholder value". Not just because it is a less than inspiring objective, but because even with hindsight there is no way of recognizing whether the objective has been achieved. Obliquity is characteristic of systems that are complex, imperfectly understood, and change their nature as we engage with them.'

This is why obliquity, in the pursuit of values, is such a powerful means of engaging people in a common cause.

Engagement

Employee engagement has long been considered the 'holy grail' of management. An organization full of committed, enthusiastic, engaged employees is every CEO's dream. According to research carried out by The Institute for Employment Studies, the independent and highly respected British centre for research and evidence-based consultancy in employment, labour market and human resource policy and practice, engaged employees deliver improved customer satisfaction, higher customer loyalty and better financial returns for their organizations[4] as well as an inverse correlation with employee turnover. In other words, employees who are engaged with their organizations remain more loyal which, as we have seen has significant impact on customer retention and satisfaction levels.

In their report 'The Drivers of Employee Engagement', Robinson, Perryman and Hayday say that the strongest driver of engagement in the employee is a sense of feeling valued and involved. Bruce Temkin, Managing Partner of The Temkin Group,[5] in his model of four customer experience core competencies, echoes this by saying that employee engagement derives from employees being aligned with the organization, and that customer connectedness comes from infusing customer insight across the organization.

In another report in 2011, BlessingWhite Research[6] says that employees who work in departments close to strategy decisions and customer relationships tend to be more engaged and, by way of reverse illustration, the most disconnected workers are those who are looking for greater clarity in organizational priorities. BlessingWhite emphasizes the point that individuals in organizations need clear direction on what the organization is trying to achieve by saying this:

> 'Engaged employees are not just committed. They are not just passionate or proud. They have a line-of-sight on their own future and on the organization's mission and goals. They are enthused and in gear, using their talents and discretionary effort to make a difference in their employer's quest for sustainable business success.'

Robinson *et al.* at the IES confirm the idea of closeness to the strategic centre when they say that engagement operates at a different level from

[4]Robinson, D., Perryman, S., and Hayday, S. (2004) *The Drivers of Employee Engagement*. Brighton: Institute for Employment Studies.
[5]Temkin B (2010) 'The Four Customer Experience Core Competencies: Assess Your Strengths and Gaps.' www.temkingroup.com
[6]'Beyond the Numbers: A practical approach for individuals, managers, and executives'. Employee Engagement Report, BlessingWhite, Inc., Princeton, NJ.

the job itself. They say that employees need to understand the context in which the organization operates and that they need an element of business appreciation and to see how their work and their job has business benefits thus perfectly echoing Nissan's practice of open communication up, down and across the organisation, bounded only by commercial confidentially.

The idea of engagement embraces a need for employees to be able to be connected with the whole organization, and what it stands for.

Engagement is one step beyond just commitment in the employee. Committed employees may stay with an employer simply because they feel that they get a fair economic exchange in return for their labour, or they may stay because there is no good reason to leave. Maybe there are barriers to them leaving, such as good working conditions, pensions, or generous pay rates. This is called 'structural commitment', and it can be transactional. Another form of commitment is 'affective commitment'. This is a step toward engagement in that it involves satisfaction in the employee with the work and colleague relationships, and it often manifests in employees going beyond the call of duty at times, for the good of the organization as a whole.

One thing that is absent from both of these aspects of commitment is the idea that distinguishes it from true engagement, and that is its two-way nature. Certainly engagement involves the commitment of employees in terms of their right attitude toward the organization, but it also demands actions on the part of the organization in return. The organization must be able to create the right conditions for engagement to happen. It is the interactions with the organization that distinguish engagement from commitment and that dictate the degree of engagement its employees have. Engagement goes far beyond job satisfaction and personal state of involvement and contribution, therefore, and it embodies elements of the emotional, the intellectual and the behavioural.

The IES offers a useful definition of engagement, which captures these elements:

'Engagement is a positive attitude held by the employee towards the organization and its values. An engaged employee is aware of business context, and works with colleagues to improve performance within the job for the benefit of the organization. The organization must work to nurture, maintain and grow engagement, which requires a two-way relationship between employer and employee.'

Note that this definition introduces the idea of the employee's identification with the organization's values, it is an issue we shall come to later in this chapter. For the time being, however, let us reinforce the definition of engagement with another finding from the BlessingWhite research, which says:

'We believe that aligning employees' values, goals, and aspirations with those of the organization is the best method for achieving the sustainable employee engagement required for an organization to thrive. Full engagement represents an alignment of maximum job satisfaction ("I like my work and do it well") with maximum job contribution ("I help achieve the goals of my organization").'

In their paper entitled 'Towards a model of work engagement',[7] Arnold Bakker and Evangelia Demerouti cite research carried out in 2006 amongst Danish midwives by Engelbrecht[8] that shows how engagement translates into behaviour. Participants in the research were asked to describe a highly engaged colleague and the interview data revealed that an engaged midwife is '. . . a person who radiates energy and keeps up the spirit at [sic] the ward, especially in situations where work morale is low and frustration spreads. An engaged midwife is willing to do whatever needs to be done, and is viewed as a source of inspiration for herself and her colleagues.'

[7]Bakker, A.B. and Evangelia, D. (2008) Towards a model of work engagement. *Career Development International* **13**(3), 209–23.
[8]Engelbrecht, S. (2006), "Motivation and burnout in human service work: the case of midwifery in Denmark", unpublished doctoral dissertation, Roskilde University, Roskilde.

Bakker *et al.* go on to observe that engagement is contagious. They say that engaged employees often experience positive emotions, including happiness, joy and enthusiasm (and, incidentally also better health), and that they transfer these emotions to others. They describe this as 'emotional contagion'. Engagement can cross over between members of the same workforce increasing performance by creating a positive team climate that is independent of demands placed upon them or resources available and which serves to break down interdepartmental barriers.

In attempting to articulate a framework for measuring engagement within an organization, Robinson of the IES gives a list of 12 statements that engaged employees are likely to say about their organization and their work. These are as follows:

- 'I speak highly of this organization to my friends.'
- 'I would be happy for my friends and family to use this organization's products/services.'
- 'This organization is known as a good employer.'
- 'This organization has a good reputation generally. I am proud to tell others I am part of this organization.'
- 'This organization really inspires the very best in me in the way of job performance.'
- 'I find that my values and the organization's are very similar.'
- 'I always do more than is actually required.'
- 'I try to help others in this organization whenever I can.'
- 'I try to keep abreast of current developments in my area.'
- 'I volunteer to do things outside my job that contribute to the organization's objectives.'
- 'I frequently make suggestions to improve the work of my team/department/service.'

In these statements, we can see the nature of engagement and how it expresses itself in the individual. However, Robinson *et al* repeat the point that organizations wanting to foster greater commitment from their employees must first provide evidence of their commitment to them, and they cite trust and a just attitude by the organization to its employees as key themes in this regard. Effective leadership puts these characteristics into practice, day by day.

Engagement is not just an attitude in the individual, it is really a measure of the degree to which that individual is absorbed into the organization and attentive to its aims and success. It is to do with how individuals apply themselves to the performance of their job and it contains within it a clear emotional element as well as rational, cognitive and behavioural aspects.

Purpose

All human beings need to engage in activities and projects that allow them to realize their highest potential (even if the outcomes are not always successful). This is what gives dignity, and meaning to our daily lives. Work is a social experience, a way of living, as much as a means of making a living. Indeed, work often becomes our identity, as witness the question most people ask when meeting someone for the first time: 'What do you do?'; for many people, what they do is who they actually are, and that identity needs to have purpose.

Having a purpose is one of the most powerful intrinsic motivators there is. Studies[9] have been carried out that demonstrate students who have a sense of purpose are most likely to succeed in higher education, and the absence of purposeful activity, for example where people are induced to work making products that they don't consider worthwhile purely to earn money to live, or where they are coerced into working under the threat of punishment (as in a prison camp, for instance), lose interest and do as little as possible to get by. People who spend time in activity that they do not value inevitably ask themselves the questions 'What is this for?' or 'Why am I doing this?'

Purpose for work has an important role to play in the individual's life. We all need congruence in each aspect of our lives. For example, people

[9]Talbot, G.L. (1990) Personality correlates and personal investment of college students who persist and achieve. *Journal of Research and Development in Education* **24**(1), 53–7.

may want to be part of something that is a leader in its field. In another, it may be that the organization does what nobody else can do, or helps people, or solves problems cleverly, or is protecting the environment, or delivering health and quality of life etc. The list is endless.

Purpose-striving and the ability to carry out meaningful tasks successfully has been correlated with human health and well-being. It is a deep biological urge connected with the striving for existence of all biological organisms and it is what gives humans self-worth. The human brain cannot sustain purposeless living – millennia of evolutionary programming has seen to that. Our whole system is programmed for purposeful action and if we are prevented from fulfilling this basic human need, it induces extreme discomfort, loss of productivity and, in extreme cases, ill health.

We all need to have a sense that what we do has purpose. People in an organization need to be engaged in what they do, and that is a motivation beyond simply earning money.

Of course, not all organizations have the same purpose. Commercial organizations are based on the logic of profit and that implies competitiveness, measurable targets (not least financial ones) and reward systems aimed at achieving those aims, e.g. performance-related pay. On the other hand, public sector organizations are based on the logic of accountability, which means impartiality, strict control of resources and universal values that treat each consumer of their output the same, irrespective of need. Then there is the third sector, or social economy. Here we find the logic of commitment, where people are strongly influenced by shared values and do what needs to be done to fulfil those values. Each of these types of organization demonstrates different approaches to purpose, but clarity of purpose is what is needed in all of them.

Purposefulness

Organizations are not random clusters of individuals; their *raison d'être* is common purpose. They are a combination of objectives, people and structure in pursuit of an aim. Any strategic plan needs enthusiastic, committed, confident people, dedicated to seeing it through if it is to have any chance of success, and the lack of purpose (better thought of as the absence of clarity of purpose) is an issue frequently neglected in strategy implementation programmes.

When an organization's purpose is clear to its employees they are much more likely to identify with it and become actively engaged and committed to making their very best contribution to its overall success. They become ambassadors and apostles for the organization, on stage as it were for the organization, 24 hours a day, and you can only achieve that by imbuing them with a sense of purpose.

Organizations need to create clarity of purpose because it underpins strategy: it is the foundation without which no amount of rational planning will be secure.

No matter how well thought-through the strategy is, if the organization is full of different agendas, with ambiguous or conflicting ideas about its purpose, it will be incapable of effective implementation.

The most significant factor to be found in those organizations whose employees are obviously engaged and achieving what the organization sets out to achieve, is a sense of *purposefulness*: that subtle sense of travelling towards a clear goal that galvanizes people each day, giving them a reason for their work.

Beckhard and Harris[10] list ten characteristics of effective organizations. The first is that they need to be 'purposeful and goal orientated'. They say that day-to-day goals and some relatively explicit long-term objectives that are known by the people comprising the individual units of the organization, not just kept in the minds or offices of the leadership and heads of functions, are top priority.

Purposefulness leads to better employee retention, and it aids in the attraction of prospective employees with talent, who will want to work

[10]Beckhard, R. and Harris, R.T. (1987) *Organizational Transitions*, 2nd edn. Reading, MA: Addison Wesley.

in such an organization. It also ensures that cohesive groups and teams can be developed and sustained, and that all adds to the power and resilience of the organization in facing its environment and making it able to sustain a stronger presence.

Purposeful systems

McKelvey and Kilmann[11] expand our thinking about purposefulness. They define organizations as '. . . purposeful systems containing one or more conditionally autonomous purposeful subsystems' and purposefulness as '. . . the ability to exercise will or conscious choice'. More crucially, they say this:

'The foregoing definition of organizations offers a synthesis of the natural system and rational models of organization. The rational model focuses attention on how and why top managers should condition the autonomy of their subordinate groups and individuals so as to orient them toward the overall objectives of the organization. Since purposeful subunits can exercise their will, they are able to deviate from the overall objectives of the organization, so their autonomy does need to be conditioned to some extent to avoid anarchy and loss of organization effectiveness resulting from unrestrained autonomy . . . The natural system model recognizes the forces and energies in organizations that flow from the natural tendencies of individuals and groups to meet their needs for social relations, influence, and psychological growth by seeking autonomy to exercise their own purposefulness. In addition to being more motivated, purposeful subunits are important in organizational effectiveness when the organization faces frequently changing and uncertain task environments (Burns and Stalker, 1961; Likert, 1967; Bennis, 1974), since they can more quickly and

[11]McKelvey, W. and Kilmann, R.H. (1975) Organizational design: a participative multivariate approach. *Administrative Science Quarterly* **20**(1), 24–36.

accurately respond to environmental changes. Changes involv-
ing the subunits are not delayed or misinformed because of the
filtering affecting information flows up and down the managerial
hierarchy . . .'

They suggest a possible design approach, which is to find ways of
developing purposeful subunits whose purposefulness in some way provides a link between the purposefulness of the individual employee and
that of the organization as a whole, and they go on to point out that this
subunit purposefulness can, through appropriate structures and procedures, be made to function within a rational system of organization rather
than in opposition to it. Even in bureaucracies, therefore, purposefulness
can still be achieved, although only by breaking the large organization
down into smaller subunits where the inherent tension between the
rational/legal mindset, predicated on rules and standardized procedures,
and the need for cross functional team working, with that essential
element of spontaneous behaviour, can function. This is the 'small is
beautiful' idea we explored in the chapter on Appropriate Organisation.

Whatever the logical driver of organizational purpose and design, one
thing is common and that is the need to allow sufficient autonomy to
orient the sub-unit (the team and, within it, the individual) to the overall
purpose of responsiveness to the customer. Integration of these sub-unit
systems together with the other business systems which are the driving
technology of the organization and the core strategy, combine to create
purposefulness, something that PowerPoint presentations or glossy
mission/vision statements on head office walls can never do.

Values – The fuel tank that never runs dry

The organization's values are as crucial to the development of purpose as
they are to engendering engagement in the people. Specific performance-
related goals will never excite the human heart. Crucial to the whole issue
of employee engagement is identification with (and the espousing of)
the organization's values. When people can embrace these, when they can
express what their organizations stands for, when they have a narrative

about why they do what they do, they take on a sense of purpose that drives the whole organization forward.

An organization's values are 'a fuel tank that never runs dry'.

Sir John Tusa (to whom we have referred elsewhere in this book), former managing director of the BBC World Service, argues that an organization can run and succeed on its values even in the face of adverse external pressures: that organizational values are 'a fuel tank that never runs dry'.

As he puts it:[12]

> 'Broadcasting from Bush House had at least two other distinguishing characteristics. The first was our closeness to the audience. . . . It was immeasurably enriching to be able to think so specifically about whom you were broadcasting to, when, why and possibly with what effect. The second set of characteristics was the external services' set of values. These were very strongly held and deeply internalized, not because they were formally implanted or imposed through training or induction. They were certainly part of the folklore of the canteen culture. Bush ran on the existence and the diverse mingling of 37 language services in one subterranean canteen (there was incidentally, never an executive canteen). I suspect too that people chose to work at Bush House because they already recognized, respected and held those beliefs (I certainly did), and the existence of this deep core of shared values allowed the external services to resist opposition from governments abroad, attempts at pressure from governments at home, indifference or downright patronage from third broadcasters, and to endure underfunding and general under resourcing, even neglect, for decades. An organization can run and succeed on its values; that fuel tank never runs dry.'

[12]Sir John Tusa: 'Fifty years in the BBC – taking stock of the future'. Newcastle University public lecture, 4 October 2011.

Referring to the BBC specifically, but with a message that applies universally, especially in the core message of this book, Tusa argues that organizations need to rediscover and celebrate their long-held values and articulate those values in vocabulary that expresses them effectively. They need to re-express what they stand for:

> 'If what I believe to be the true, human, rich vocabulary of trust, standards, programmes, ideas, curiosity, originality, audiences, publicity, belief, ambitions, purpose, responsibility, judgement and quality was allowed to elbow out the dead, mechanical, reductive vocabulary of accountability, systems, process, genres, formulae, consumers, marketing, targets, objectives, distinctiveness, compliance, benchmarking and risk analysis, what a great organization the BBC would be. I believe that such a shift of thinking and vocabulary, would lead to a huge uprush of energy, originality and creativity that the staff would welcome and audiences would notice, respond to and love.'

Matshushita on purpose

Konosuke Matsushita was perhaps the most striking example of leader-entrepreneurs to enunciate the idea of purpose and to show how deep it goes into the nature of corporate purposefulness.

John P. Kotter is the Konosuke Matsushita Professor of Leadership at Harvard Business School and recognized as one of the world's leading experts on leadership. In his book on the life and lessons of Konosuke Matsushita, he recounts the story of how, in 1932, and in similar fashion to many great leaders, Matsushita stood before his entire workforce and spoke about his vision for the company.

Anecdote has it that Matsushita opened his speech by saying: 'I have been thinking about purpose . . .'

Matsushita was very clear on the nature of his company's purpose. He didn't focus on maximizing shareholder wealth or short-term profits, nor market share, the number of patents, or the return on equity. Instead, he talked of higher ideals, far above lowly corporate goals.

After reminding his people of their achievements thus far, Matsushita progressively built to a bold proposition. 'The mission of a manufacturer' he said, 'should be to overcome poverty, to relieve society as a whole from misery, and bring it wealth'.[13]

Reminding his people that things only improve because far-sighted people are willing to tackle ambitious things, Matsushita was clear that his vision would take many years to achieve, but he went on to stress that this apparently daunting proposition should not deter those present from making a start. Kotter reports him more fully as saying this:

> 'Beginning today, this far reaching dream, this sacred calling, will be our ideal and our mission, and its fulfilment the responsibility of each one of us. Inasmuch as fate has brought you to work at Matsushita Electric, I trust you will share the joy and responsibilities of pursuing the mission that lies before us . . . I am determined to lead and guide all of you in this endeavour with fresh energy and enthusiasm . . . The most important thing is that we enjoy happiness to the fullest in our own lives and at the same time strive for the benefit of the generations that are to follow.'

On that day, Matsushita set within his company a spark of purpose based on five principles – values that became the driving force behind its phenomenal success, and a major factor in the recovery of Japan after defeat in the Second World War.

Matsushita's five principles are as follows:

- *Service to the public*: to provide high-quality goods and services at reasonable prices, thereby contributing to the well-being and happiness of people throughout the world.

[13]Kotter, J. P. (1997) *Matsushita Leadership: Lessons from the 20th Century's Most Remarkable Entrepreneur*. New York: The Free Press.

- *Fairness and honesty*: to be fair and honest in all business dealings and personal conduct, always making balanced judgements free of preconceptions.
- *Teamwork for the common cause*: to pool abilities and strength of resolution to accomplish shared objectives, in mutual trust and full recognition of individual autonomy.
- *Untiring effort for improvement*: to strive constantly for improvement of corporate and personal performances, even in the worst of adversity, so as to fulfil the firm's mission to realize lasting peace and prosperity.
- *Courtesy and humility*: to always be cordial and modest and respect the rights and needs of others, thereby helping enrich the environment and maintain social order.[14]

Clarity of purpose based on the articulation of values, therefore, goes far beyond maximizing shareholder value, or meeting public sector legislative obligations, or satisfying the *raison d'être* of a charitable cause. When it comes to serving customers' needs, management may declare it's strategy, but it is the people who will see it through and they need to know why if they are to drive forward and produce the return on investment.

Kotter again:[15]

> 'When he [Matsushita] died in the spring of 1989, his funeral services were swamped with a crowd of over 20,000. In a telegram of condolences to the family the president of the USA called him "an inspiration to people around the world." His legacy is daunting. After World War II, Matsushita was one of the central figures who helped lead the Japanese economic miracle. Through Panasonic,

[14] In 1937, two years after these five principles were enunciated, Matsushita added two more: 'Accord with natural laws' and 'Gratitude for blessings'; and these seven principles became the published management philosophy and company creed of Matsushita Electric that remains, in various modifications, in place to this day.

[15] Kotter, ibid.

and other brands, the firm he founded supplied billions of people with household appliances and consumer electronics. By the time of his death, few organizations on earth had more customers. Revenues hit a phenomenal $42 billion that year, more than the combined sales of Bethlehem Steel, Colgate-Palmolive, Gillette, Goodrich, Kellogg, Olivetti, Scott Paper, and Whirlpool.'

Such is the power of purpose espoused to values.

Systems integration and process clarity

Two additional guiding structures that assist clarity of purpose by stimulating the coordination of organizations are systems integration and business process clarity. Let us briefly examine them in that order.

Systems integration is an engineering term, borrowed by management science. Here is a definition from Wikipedia:

> 'In engineering, system integration is the bringing together of the component subsystems into one system and ensuring that the subsystems function together as a system. In information technology, systems integration is the process of linking together different computing systems and software applications physically or functionally.'

In organizations, systems consist of people, structures and processes that should methodically work together to make the organization achieve its goals, and only by integrating them can we achieve a coherent delivery mechanism for providing customer service through Service-Ability.

Systems integration has two aspects to it: bringing together the component subsystems; and ensuring they function together – and we mention both for specific reasons. First, because of the importance in understanding the use of ICT in our organizations, and second, in an organizational sense, because of the importance in ensuring that all the component parts of the Service-Ability model can work together in an integrated, holistic way, because any one of the elements without the others will not ensure the intended result.

The inappropriate application of ICT subsystems in our organizations has been made a number of times already. It is sufficient to repeat that we have put the technology in the wrong place. Instead of putting it behind our customer-facing employees as an aid and support, we have managed to put it between our employees and management and between our employees and the customer, mediating the relationship in each case.

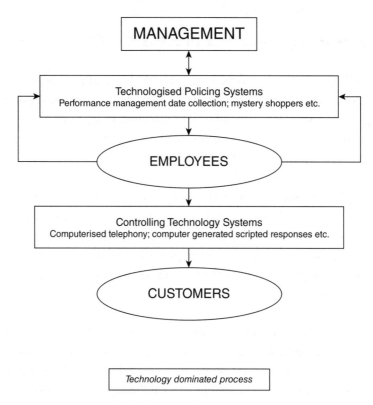

Technology-dominated process

It is essential to reintegrate people, structure, management, leadership and technology in a better way, producing processes that support and facilitate employees to relate appropriately to the customer. This is the entire object of Service-Ability.

The technology has become our master, not our slave, and in the process we have lost sight of the reality that people do business with people.

Achieving excellence in processes throughout the many complex activities of a business can only be achieved when: the processes themselves are well defined and understood; the measures of their success are understood, actively monitored and measured; people understand their roles and responsibilities within the processes; organizational design facilitates the process; leadership and management is also committed; and the entire process delivery system is directed toward the customer for improved customer service levels, placing the technology in its appropriate place.

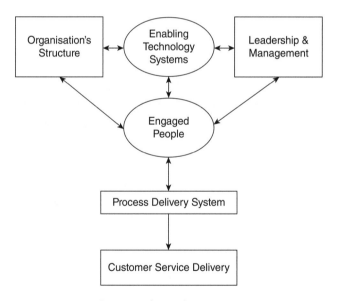

Customer-focused process

All these elements fall within the emerging discipline of 'Service Design' (I would prefer to call it 'Service-Process Design' because strictly speaking, that is what it really is), which deals with the way in which services are delivered: the customer touch points (the service interfaces with the customer), the usability, the efficiency and effectiveness of the service being offered. In a very real sense, service-process design is the equivalent of product design and it takes into account performance, reliability, safety, aesthetics and ergonomics etc. Today, process is one of the additional 'P's' of the extended marketing mix. It cuts across the boundaries created by division of labour that compartmentalize an organization and instead creates a value-adding chain of service delivery that the customer perceives, in which he or she participates, and from which customer-satisfying value results (just as we saw in my consultancy example given earlier). Customer-focused process destroys the silo mentality where people see themselves as separate from their colleagues in different departments and not engaged with the customer.

In 1993, Hammer and Champy (ibid.) said this:

> 'We define business process as a collection of activities that is of value to the customer . . . In other words, the delivery of the ordered goods to the customer's hands is the value that the process creates . . . [Business Process] Reengineering is about beginning again with a clean sheet of paper. It is about rejecting the conventional wisdom and received assumptions of the past. Reengineering is about inventing new approaches to process structure that bear little or no resemblance to those of previous eras. Fundamentally, reengineering is about reversing the Industrial Revolution. Reengineering rejects the assumptions inherent in Adam Smith's industrial paradigm – the division of labour, economies of scale, hierarchical control, and all the other appurtenances of an early-stage developing economy. Reengineering is the search for new models of organizing work. Tradition counts for nothing. Reengineering is a new beginning.'

This was a radical shift from the thinking of the past and it was groundbreaking stuff. No one had seen it like this before. Hammer and Champy were advocating a new way of thinking about the organization. Not as divided into vertical functional silos, but as one horizontal process for value creation – a chain. To do this, they advocated business process reengineering, or BPR as it became known, as the way forward, but as we have seen, process is incapable of being established unless the organization in which it takes place is appropriately structured, and above all, process is incapable of harnessing the hearts and minds of the people in the production of the product or service-product. That needs a different approach.

Total service quality

Britain has always been good at making tangible products: we still are; but now we need to be good at delivering intangible services. Service quality is the direct equivalent of manufacturing quality, and we can learn much from the developments in that field in the post-Second World War period. In that period of over 60 years, we have seen a developing idea of quality in management thinking and the idea has come to be seen as a powerful tool, not only in production operations, but also in the toolbox of organizations of all types, and in all sectors.

Quality is not 'quality' as we normally understand it; it is 'fitness for purpose'. A Rolls Royce car with walnut dashboard and deep-pile carpet is instantly recognizable as out-and-out quality, but a small town car can be fit-for-purpose as long as it does what it is designed to do, and does it consistently well in line with customer expectations. A quality car, a quality education, a quality prison service, or a quality holiday will mean something completely different to different people according to their needs, wants, demands and expectations. Nowadays, many organizations think seriously about how to ensure that their product or service is fit for purpose and satisfies their measured criteria for product or service quality.

Quality is both an objective term and a subjective one, and in a service context it depends on the perceptions people have of their whole experience. If we accept the idea that the purpose of an organization is to deliver services and products that satisfy customer expectations of them, consistently and fit for purpose, then we see that service quality is central to the work of all employees in that organization.

Throughout the 1980s and into the 1990s, product quality transformed our manufacturing industry and was rightly seen as the factor that would make a company stand out in the market place. The concept started in a big way in Japan in the 1960s but had its roots in the work of Deming and Juran in the USA in the 1950s. Deming's message was one of the creation of constancy of purpose to improve product and service to the customer through a culture of building-in quality achieved by training, continuous development and employee involvement. Juran's intrinsic message was that quality does not just happen, it must be planned, controlled and continuously improved and that the process starts with identifying the customer and his needs, developing products to satisfy those needs and ensuring delivery to the customer 'right first time'. In other words 'Total Quality' which became Total Quality Management (TQM), a body of management science that, at its heart was not just the concept of quality, but the way in which the product or service delivery is carried out. Service quality can learn much from TQM.

Arnold Feigenbaum,[16] former director of US giant General Electric, who devised the idea of total quality control (later to be known as TQM), sees the customer as king and the whole process as starting '. . . with customer requirements and end[ing] only when the customer is satisfied with the way the product or service of the enterprise meets those requirements'. Kaoru Ishikawa,[17] Japanese quality expert and university professor observes that quality leading to customer satisfaction must be the domain of all members of the organization and '. . . the sub-contractors, distribution systems and affiliated companies' associated with it, and Masaaki Imae,[18] founder of the Kaizen Institute, stresses the need for corporate systems and goals to be aligned to support quality, and this includes not only organization structures and manufacturing systems, but also issues such as personnel practices, training and compensation. Finally,

[16]Feigenbaum, A.V. (1983) *Total Quality Control*. New York: McGraw Hill.
[17]Ishikawa, K. (1983) *What is Total Quality Control? The Japanese Way*. New York: Prentice-Hall.
[18]Imae, M. (1986) *Kaizen: The Key to Japan's Competitive Success*. New York: Irwin/ McGraw-Hill.

Edwards Deming,[19] regarded by many as 'the father of TQM', says that organizations, in order constantly to decrease costs, must improve quality and productivity to '. . . improve constantly and forever, the system of production and service . . . ' It is the mention of 'service' in this context that gives us a clear signpost as to what service quality can learn from Total Quality Management and where lies the key to sustainable competitive advantage in the future.

Approaches to quality

There are two approaches to quality. The conformance approach is what we saw in the examples we examined earlier in call centres and super-markets, where telephone calls are monitored to ensure conformance to procedures (this is particularly driven by strict conformance standards imposed on companies from outside regulatory agencies such as Financial Services Authority) and mystery shoppers are used to 'police' company-imposed standards for the way their employees are expected to deal with customers.

Policing conformance to customer service standards by call-monitoring or mystery shoppers is never going to engage the ability of people in an organization to bring their own particular skills, talents and personalities to the production of quality, even though that may be the intent.

The European Foundation for Quality Management Excellence Model (EFQM) and its ISO 9000 derivatives, for example, have a strong emphasis on customer satisfaction and echo many of the principles underpinning Service-Ability, but they are very much about management and process that ensures conformance to decided definitions of what quality should be, rather than empowering people to create it as well as deliver it.

[19]Deming, W.E. (1986) *Out of the Crisis*. Cambridge, MA: Massachusetts Institute of Technology.

They are steeped in the idea of conformance and that places them outside the ethos of Service-Ability, which has at its heart the capture of the imagination as well as the hearts and minds of the people in an organization, through engagement, empowerment and freedom from too much proscription and overly restrictive organization. The spirit of Service-Ability sits much more comfortably in the ideas that underpin TQM.

The idea of quality started with inspection, i.e. checking that things were made to a repeatable standard, and rejecting them if they were not. Inspection was the responsibility of the inspection department, not the worker. It developed into quality control that employed statistical techniques and feedback loops of information from the production line into a quality management system, but still at its heart it sought to remove the operator from involvement in the quality process by putting reliance on systems. It still had within its process a reactive, fault-finding approach to quality and a strong emphasis on meeting management-decided specification. Quality assurance was the next stage and had at its heart a focus on proactively preventing defects from arising in the first place, thus removing the cost of defects. The ISO 9000 quality management systems with their manuals, procedures, processes and systems are quality assurance systems and, whilst they embrace a wider business process, starting with the purchase of materials, they pay no attention whatever to the customer and his or her needs. They are very internally focused.

ISO 9000 quality management systems have been widely accused of being perfectly capable of producing poor product but still 'quality assured' only because the product conforms to the set standards.

Total Quality

Total Quality Management represents a paradigm shift from previous ideas. It switches the emphasis from the application of tools and techniques to the changing of attitudes. Its very title is deliberate. 'Total' means that the achievement of quality is something for everyone and every process in the organization and, as we have seen, the customer is the one for whom the quality is produced. Poor design of a product or service, a clerical error in the accounts department over an invoice, or poor delivery at the point of sale may anger a customer just as much as a product failure in use.

> *Total service quality is a total focus by engaged employees intent on satisfying customer expectations and requirements, and it adopts the perspective that every employee can and should have an impact on quality, not just systems, rules and procedures.*

In a Total Quality environment the people are not only heavily involved, they become their own quality inspectors and even originators of improvements, often bombarding their managers with ideas about how things could be better. Even suppliers are involved in the never-ending quest for quality so everyone is encouraged to see the whole organization as a system of interconnected people and processes lining up before the customer, not only delivering product that is 'right first time', but also listening to the voice of the customer, and feeding that back down the chain. This leaves no place for the silo mentality of bureaucracies with their interdepartmental barriers.

Total Quality simply cannot operate in a culture of 'them and us'. It is more than the formal structure of an organization, it is the sum of the totality of all the interrelationships in it; and the sum of all its activity. The responsibility for quality becomes far more than what the organization chart says and it needs a freer organizational structure in which to operate than that which the bureaucratic mind dictates. TQM is really a philosophy that can apply to services as well as manufacturing, and to all organizations. It is manufacturing independent because its aim is to inculcate a commitment to quality through changing the beliefs and values of everyone in the organization. In a Total Quality environment, everyone seeks not only to meet the expectations of the customer, but to exceed them. It doesn't have a 'one best way' to do things, there is no measure of what success really means other than customer satisfaction (although in industry, TQM employs some hard-headed techniques such as statistical process control). Total Quality is simply based on the underpinning belief in the need for continuous improvement in everything in the organization does. This is the Japanese principle of *kaizen*: continuous improvement; a concept that sees quality as a never-ending journey rather than an arrived-at goal.

Kaizen is a strategic culture for competitive advantage through ever-increasing superior performance, and threading its way through this is another Japanese quality term: '*hoshin kanri*'. *Hoshin* means 'shining metal, compass or pointing the direction', and *kanri* means 'management or control'. Loosely translated, it is 'The glinting light of the compass needle'.

In the hurly burly of business life, in the difficult times when people lose sight of the whole picture, hoshin kanri *keeps things on course.*

Clarity of purpose is a core strategy, therefore. In a sense it is the glinting light of the compass needle that engenders an organization-wide, intrinsic acceptance of the mission, and a clear understanding of where the organization needs to be in the future. It is underpinned by quality of service-product using lessons learned from manufacturing, co-ordinated by systems integration, driven by purpose, by meaning and by engaged employees whose values align with those of the organization. Clarity of purpose gets everybody buying-in to, and engaged with, the true purpose of the organization, which is service to the customer, and it gets everything lined up to support that purpose.

11

Britain has an overwhelmingly service-orientated economy. Today, we do things rather than make things as a source of revenue, and more than ever before the way we deliver what we produce is an essential component of what customers buy. This holds true even for manufactured product, not just service-product, and is irrespective of where the product originates. Whether from the private, public or third sectors, truly customer-satisfying service always adds value.

The competitive differentiators of the past are now taken as givens. Product quality, 'right first time', or business processes reengineered for maximum efficiency, important as these things are, are no longer enough. They are no longer able to make the tangible product or the service-product offering stand out from another as they used to do. Only by enhancing these with exemplary customer service will organizations achieve better customer retention, lower costs of staff replacement and be able to build their brand value through better reputations.

There is now overwhelming evidence to suggest that profit is directly linked to customer service. That consumers form opinions and make judgements about an organization based on the employees with whom they interact is just a simple truth; the process is packed with all the basic issues that exist in human relationships and interactions. Customer service is about how the customer experience is dramatized – how it is acted out on the stage of the customer interface – and in a world dominated by technology that is creating ever more distance between the organization and the customer, getting this right is more important than ever before.

In all sectors of our economy, technology is fundamentally changing the way we do business. In the gold-rush fervour to leverage their benefits, computers and sophisticated telecommunications are increasingly being used by organizations to mediate the relationship with the customer to the extent that the old axiom, 'people do business with people', is becoming abandoned. Customer relationships are becoming impersonal, and focus on the customer is being lost. Tension is rising. Customers are becoming increasingly cynical, disaffected, aggressive and footloose, often using the same technology to trade one supplier off against another, and some are even using it to fight back using social media, as we saw in the case of 'United Breaks Guitars'.

The need for organizations to realign to deliver exemplary customer service is becoming an urgent necessity. The current paradigm must be challenged if a major opportunity is not to be missed. Only by refocusing on their customers through their people, treating both in a way that satisfies each, not the technology nor the organization, can organizations differentiate themselves. In the current technological wilderness, only the value-added of exemplary customer service allied to service/product quality will achieve sustainable competitive advantage.

Customer service is emphatically not just about training staff in service skills, important as these skills are. Neither is customer service about designing service processes for maximum efficiency. Obviously efficient processes are necessary, but products and services become sterile and depersonalized without the value-added of customer service, applied at those 'moments of truth' when customers come into contact with the people delivering the service-product.

Service skills and well-designed service processes, the combined 'service-product', can only be effective if they draw their meaning, their gearing, from overall Service-Ability. That is the true driving mechanism: the real power behind customer satisfaction.

However, you cannot just bolt-on customer service to an organization that is unfit holistically to sustain and support it. True customer service is more than skin deep. Money spent on competence training of customer-facing staff is likely to be wasted unless systems and cultures that prevent the fullest implementation of those new-found skills are radically changed, and organizations that fail to recognize this court disaster.

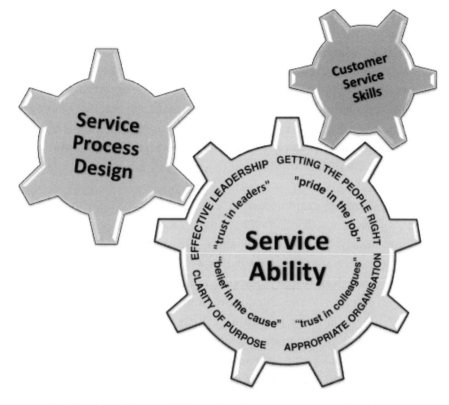

Relationship of Service-Ability to the other elements of service delivery

Customers now are demanding a meaningful experience. People now want to be treated like human beings, as well as receive a good product or service. Customer service is a culture as much as it is a function, and it is the role of every employee in the organization, not just a specialized few. Simply having a customer service department that only services customer enquiries or complaints is totally to miss the point.

Furthermore, you cannot replace people with machines in those areas of interaction that inherently demand human-ness. Increasingly we see technology being used as a surrogate for the personality of the employee, or as a mediator of the relationship with the customer. We need look no further than the plethora of multi-choice phone systems and call-centre operations to see this in action. The technology is being used to command

and control (even the customer!). It is depersonalizing the way business is being done and that is raising ethical as well as practical issues.

Just as in the Industrial Revolution, many of our modern organizations are treating their people as a commodity to be used and exploited in the machine. We seem to have forgotten that the way the organization serves its people translates into the way customers are served, and that employee satisfaction is the glue that binds the relationship between the customer and the organization, sealing the transactional value. The indiscriminate, widespread, often inappropriate use of technology is removing the ability to serve.

In call centres for example, employees are now simply machines sitting in front of machines. The *Little Britain* television sketch, 'Computer Says No!' humorously, but tellingly, illustrates this. Customer-facing employees are no longer able to act on their own initiative to satisfy the need in the customer for creative solutions, and this is leading to stress and burnout in employees, and antagonism from the customer; all induced by the very systems that are meant to facilitate customer interactions. The whole syndrome is degrading the relationship to such a degree that the satisfaction for both parties is being prevented.

Technology has an amazing potential as a facilitator of business processes. It is a wonderful thing. It is undoubtedly making organizations highly efficient, but mechanistic efficiency does not necessarily translate into overall organizational efficiency, especially in the customer interface. We see this time and again in the sorry stories that abound in our press and broadcast media about poor customer service and the lack of organizational responsiveness to their needs. TripAdvisor.com is causing near panic in some quarters of the hotel industry and, at the time of going to press, 'United Breaks Guitars', the YouTube video published by Dave Carroll in 2009, has spread that damning message of United Airways' appalling attitude to its customers to over 12 million people worldwide.

Willy nilly, organizations are being forced to have their customer service levels mediated in the social media and the issue has become so important that many are now monitoring Twitter and Facebook for negative chatter and pouncing on it so as to mitigate damage. It is now

common knowledge that a simple tweet will often bring the most solici-
tous response from a company, when a call to its customer service help
desk has miserably failed.

Technology is not the only problem in poor customer service, however.
There are other blockages too, not least the uniquely British disease: that
legacy of our history that somehow translates into the idea that service
work is inferior, demeaning, unskilled and low paid, and which leads to
resentment in customer-serving staff and arrogance in consumers who
often treat service staff as servants. It is, after all, only 100 years since to
be in service meant being a servant.

Then there is the industrial mindset, another product of the Industrial
Revolution, that sees employees as cogs in a machine and treats them in
an equally mechanical way. Industrial-era management and organization
was an evolving, ad-hoc affair: its techniques learned on the hoof; and
they were steeped in the engineering mindset. The first management
theorists, F.W. Taylor and Henri Fayol, were engineers who steadfastly
believed that people in organizations were like parts of a machine and
that there was one best way of managing them for optimum efficiency,
using them and replacing them, rather than developing them for future
value.

The early part of the 20th century saw the insights of Mary Parker
Follett and Elton Mayo (the 'Hawthorne experiments') that recognized the
social needs of people at work, but the end of the industrial management
mindset found its real momentum after the end of the Second World War
when we saw remarkable developments in management theory in the
behavioural science movement that challenged the old industrial paradigm. There was an increasing recognition of the importance of the individual: of his or her needs, aspirations and higher motivations; and of the
need to harness these attributes for higher productivity.

Yet, once again in the name of efficiency and lowest cost production,
we are witnessing a resurgence of the old paradigm of organization
based on control through the use of power. Employees are still being
managed using industrial approaches. Today's economic environment
demands involvement and engagement from employees, and yet in a
remarkable echo of the past the revolution in technology is causing a

resurgence of the mechanistic mindset. Once again, we are seeing people being managed just like their counterparts of the 18th and 19th centuries were. Call centres, for example, seen by many as the sweatshops of the modern era, are full of underpaid, under-trained people, placed under continuous pressure to deal with customers within a set period of time, and for whom the work is often only stopgap and who stay in the job less than a year. We have taken several steps forward and one rather large step back.

The problem is not just an outdated management approach. Paradoxically, many of our organizations are designed in such as way as to militate actively against customer service. Despite the fact that we are living in the most dynamic times ever experienced, in a complex, sophisticated society where flexibility and responsiveness to customer needs are paramount, we still see organizations being run on the highly inflexible model of bureaucracy: an early 20th-century idea born out of forms of industrial organization that had reached their zenith after 150 years of industrialization.

There is no doubt that most organizations today, of whatever kind, owe their basic design to the bureaucracy, which literally means: 'The power (or force) of the desk' (probably better thought of as the power of the 'office'). In advocating bureaucracy, Max Weber passionately believed it was the most efficient form of organization, and to this day his ideas remain deeply entrenched in our organizational consciousness, even though our society is now massively different. Bureaucracies were never intended to be responsive to customers. They were intended for efficient administration and stable output in a totally different society from that which we have now. Today people do not respond to rational legalism, but to supporting relationships, job enrichment, involvement, socialization and collaboration. That is the road to efficiency in the 21st century.

We must move away from the bureaucratic idea. No longer can our organizations just be armies of faceless people, heads down, inwardly focused, obediently under the control of the few; and concerned only with efficiency. Today, even in the public sector, organizations need to be accountable to the needs of their employees as well as their customers who demand total satisfaction as the price of their loyalty. We need organizations that are deliberately designed to embrace the individual employee's contribution, and allow emergent, self-organizing, self-managing behaviour to happen. The people, who are the organization after all, need the freedom to function more effectively: self-actualizing and bringing their personality and relational inventiveness to the job in hand for the overall benefit of the customer.

Organizations must create quality in their people's working lives. They must engender high morale and motivation, greater autonomy, and trust. There must be a change, from the idea that says employees serve the organization, to one that says the organization serves the employees, if those employees are going to be able to totally serve and satisfy the customer. From this new stance will flow profit, efficiency and the overall objectives of the organization.

An organization needs enthusiastic, committed, confident people imbued with the wish to see it succeed if it is to have any chance of success. Everybody in the organization must buy-in to the extant strategy if they are to have a sense of purpose. People who work in organizations need to know why they come to work on a Monday morning, why the organization exists and what is their part in its aims and objectives. They need a *reason* why they should give their enthusiastic support to organizational aims, day in, day out. And they need to agree with that reason. The purpose must be relevant to their lives.

For example, they may want to be part of something that is the leader in its field, or does what nobody else can do, or helps people, or solves problems cleverly, or is protecting the environment, or is delivering health and quality of life, etc. – the list is endless. The people in an organization need to believe in the cause. This is a fundamental pre-requisite for overall organizational success through customer service. It is the foundation without which no amount of rational planning will be secure.

Of course, not all organizations share the same logic. Commercial organizations, for example, are based on the logic of *profit*, which implies competitiveness, measurable targets (not least financial), division of labour and extrinsic reward systems, e.g. performance-related pay. On the other hand, public sector organizations are based on the logic of *accountability*, which means impartiality, strict control of resources and universal values that treat each consumer of their output the same, irrespective of need. The third sector, or social economy as it is also called, is based on the logic of *commitment*, where people 'do what needs to be done' and are strongly influenced by shared values. The public and private sector could learn much to their advantage from this idea.

Whatever their logic, however, all organizations need a different meta-idea: a different approach to how the organizational entity as a whole relates to itself and its environment. We need a different theme: that of the living organism, not the machine; one that sees organization from the bottom up, instead of the top down. And we need to instil a sense of purpose: of purposefulness. When an organization's purpose is clear to employees, it is much more likely that they will identify with it and become actively engaged and committed to making their very best contribution to its overall success.

Lack of clarity of purpose is an issue that frequently goes unnoticed by organizations. In the daily effort of 'doing the business', the emphasis can easily change from *why* things are done to *how* they are done. (The UK National Health Service is the prime example of this. The total focus is on managing budgets, waiting lists, etc., and patient care is almost a secondary output.) When process takes precedence over outcome, it results in people becoming detached, disengaged, from the organization and, worse, from the customer.

With clarity of purpose comes an intrinsic acceptance of the mission and a clear understanding of where the organization wants to go in the future. That sense of purpose needs to permeate the organization to its farthest reaches, galvanizing its people each day they come to work; giving them the reason they need for their work. This leads to a belief in the cause that in turn leads to engagement in employees who identify with the purpose. Engagement is an expression of high morale and that is what drives organizations forward in the pursuit of customer satisfaction.

All this needs a special form of leadership. Servant leadership is a term that, to many, will sound contradictory. The idea that servants can be leaders appears topsy turvy, but the paradigm of autocratic, authoritative, power-wielding leadership is becoming increasingly unacceptable; and it is proving ineffectual in ensuring the motivation of people to serve the customer.

The servant leader has power and authority, but neither wears it as a mantle nor uses it as a tool. As William Shakespeare put it in one of his sonnets, 'They that have power to hurt and will do none'. Leadership by persuasion, by influence, by example is the approach of the servant leader who, remembering that the value of coercive power is inverse to its use, brings results by 'convincement rather than coercion'.

Servant leaders are just as determined as their counterparts who use other leadership models, but they have an approach that sees leadership in a different way. They lead from *within* the body of the organization, not from in front or above, or behind, but as first among equals (*primus inter pares*); and they spread their influence, vision and values through contact with their people, by showing an example rather than by issuing orders and policy. Servant leaders are trusting, and they are trustworthy.

Servant leadership is functionally far superior to the other models of leadership for service-orientated organizations because the servant leader is part of the whole team, not 'the management'. The servant leader is close to the customer because he or she is close to the people. Servant leaders not only 'walk the floor', they 'walk their talk'. They are able to be customer focused because they have servant hearts, and they help to shape other people toward that end.

There is an essential artistry to servant leadership. Leaders who are servants, and fully embrace servant leadership as a concept, change the leadership ethic throughout the organization, from command-and-control and the treatment of people as cogs in the machine, to the idea that the people are the organization, and that the leader exists only to serve them. By their *modus operandi* they breed trust and dependability amongst those whom they influence.

Servant leaders have power, but they don't rely on it as their power base. Instead, they use the legitimate power given to them by the organization to allocate resources to their people, so that they in turn can serve the customer. The servant leader gives power away, empowering people to do things whilst still carrying the responsibility for the outcomes. This leads to a freedom to exercise initiative in the customer-facing employee and puts power-to-decide where it needs to be: at the point where decisions matter for the customer. In a very real sense, servant leaders cascade their power from the top down and get it to where it matters most.

Servant leadership is at the heart of Service-Ability, because it ensures that the organization is not a hierarchy of authority, backed by raw do-as-I-say power, but a community composed of mini communities of cohesive, largely self-directing work groups of responsible people, amongst whom are also servant leaders; and all serving the needs of the customer for total customer satisfaction.

The very essence of Service-Ability is that employees are the central theme, and the customer is the focus. It is about a depth of commitment extending from the very centre of the organization to the loyal, satisfied customer, through the loyal, satisfied employee. It is based on the principle that high employee satisfaction positively affects employee morale, which in turn secures employee loyalty and commitment. This then translates into high levels of customer service, which engenders increased customer loyalty, and that leads to growth and profitability.

The Service-Ability message focuses on the people, but it speaks to senior management. Obviously, customer-facing employees must have appropriate interpersonal skills and be equipped with service-enabling knowledge, technology and training if they are to perform customer service effectively, but training people in customer service skills does not mean they are at the centre of management concern. That is only going to be achieved by strategies, structure, policies, leadership, management, teamwork, motivation, selection, development, and the alignment of these elements effectively to produce people enabled to deliver what the customer needs, wants and expects.

For true Service-Ability, employees need to have clarity of purpose and be *engaged* with the aims and values of the organization. They need to be *involved*, through appropriate organizational design that allows the whole organization to act like a team. They must be *empowered* by effective leadership, servant leadership, to exercise initiative, and they need *professionalism* through pride in a job well done, which is achieved by getting the people right. Using this approach, organizations can rejuvenate that most important of all business relationships, the relationship with the customer through the employee, and overcome the relentless tendency of technology to de-personalize.

Today, only totally satisfying the customer will secure sustainable competitive advantage. No longer can any organization, even those in the public sector, rely simply on being efficient. They must be not only serviceable, but service-able. That is the one thing that will cause them to flourish. Those organizations that acquire Service-Ability will be noticeably different from those that continue to offer de-personalized relationships with their customers. They will be more profitable, more stable, better able to utilize their financial resources, and they will stand out in the otherwise indifferent crowd. Service-ability will be the key to competitive advantage in the early part of the 21st century: it will separate the best from the rest.

INDEX